T0006817

Praise for *One Bright Moon*

'An incredibly powerful book' Benjamin Law

'[A] moving family saga, shot through with yearning and hard-won joy' Fiona Capp, *Sydney Morning Herald*

'A few pages into this compelling memoir proves it was written by a master storyteller' Sharon Rundle, *Australian Book Review*

'A work of startling clarity ... reminiscent of *Angela's Ashes*' *South China Morning Post Magazine*

'Kwong's understated but highly effective account of a childhood in Maoist China and his eventual journey to Australia is both historically informative and moving in its description of his family's sacrifices for him' Suzanne Falkiner, Senior Judge, National Biography Award, 2021

'Deeply moving ... The unique perspective of a child ... places *One Bright Moon* in the vicinity of *Night*, Elie Wiesel's pathbreaking memoir of his early life prior to and of his time in German concentration camps' Meenakshi Bharat, *IIC Quarterly*

'An unforgettable tale told simply: one of resilience and courage, of love and hope triumphing over the most terrible of odds. This book will live on in your heart long after you've read the last page' Vicki Laveau-Harvie, author of *The Erratics*

'Heart-breaking, honest, personal, Andrew Kwong's moving journey from oppression to freedom is inspiring' Susanne Gervay OAM, award-winning author

'*One Bright Moon* is extraordinary writing that encapsulates long-term hunger as a background feature of daily life in Mao's New China. In the foreground are images of adults and children populating the world of the pre-teenage boy with a photographic memory who would later write of them. The book is rich archival material for the study of China's social history' Mabel Lee, PhD FAHA, writer and translator

'A profoundly moving and spellbinding story that perfectly illuminates the terror of the times and the irrepressible yearning for something better' Carol Major, author and writing mentor

'Reading this memoir is a healing experience' Devika Brendon, award-winning writer and editor

Andrew Kwong was born in Zhongshan in the Pearl River Delta, China, and educated in China, Hong Kong and Australia. He works as a family physician on the Central Coast of New South Wales. He has been the recipient of numerous writing awards and fellowships and his stories have appeared in a number of anthologies, including *Fear Factor: Terror Incognito* (2010) and *Alien Shores* (2012).

ONE BRIGHT MOON

Andrew Kwong

HarperCollins*Publishers*

HarperCollins*Publishers*
Australia • Brazil • Canada • France • Germany • Holland • Hungary
India • Italy • Japan • Mexico • New Zealand • Poland • Spain • Sweden
Switzerland • United Kingdom • United States of America

First published in Australia in 2020
by HarperCollins*Publishers* Australia Pty Limited
Level 13, 201 Elizabeth Street, Sydney NSW 2000
ABN 36 009 913 517
harpercollins.com.au

Copyright © Andrew Kwong 2020

The right of Andrew Kwong to be identified as the author of this work has been
asserted by him in accordance with the *Copyright Amendment (Moral Rights) Act 2000.*

This work is copyright. Apart from any use as permitted under the *Copyright Act 1968,*
no part may be reproduced, copied, scanned, stored in a retrieval system, recorded, or
transmitted, in any form or by any means, without the prior written permission of the
publisher.

A catalogue record for this book is available from the National Library of Australia.

ISBN 978 14607 5862 5 (paperback)
ISBN 978 14607 1239 9 (ebook)
ISBN 978 14607 8243 9 (audiobook)

Cover design by Hazel Lam, HarperCollins Design Studio
Front cover image of Andrew Kwong, courtesy of the author
Back cover images: author's permit to leave China, 1962; Mama, Baba, Ping, Ying and
baby Andrew; both courtesy of Andrew Kwong
Author photograph by Sheree Kwong
All other photographs courtesy of the author, except where noted
Maps by Map Illustrations, mapillustrations.com.au
Typeset in Sabon LT Std by Kirby Jones
Printed and bound in Australia by McPherson's Printing Group
The papers used by HarperCollins in the manufacture of this book are a natural,
recyclable product made from wood grown in sustainable plantation forests. The fibre
source and manufacturing processes meet recognised international environmental
standards, and carry certification.

I dedicate this book, with much gratitude and love, to the memory of my Mama Wai-syn Young, and Baba Shek-tong Kwong, who endured the utmost pain as parents watching their family being torn apart, yet who, with fortitude, perseverance and amazing grace, ensured the family's final reunion.

Also, with much appreciation, to the memory of Brother Casimir, Principal of La Salle College, Kowloon, Hong Kong, who gave me the courage I needed to navigate the world.

With all my love, to my children Serena, Harmony and Andrew-James. The love of a parent is forever.

And, last but not least, to my seven little Australians: Bruno, Louis, Clementine, Charlie, Fleur, Henry and Felix. For you are the reason I wrote this book.

Classes struggle, some classes triumph,
others are eliminated.
Mao Tse-tung

CONTENTS

HISTORICAL TIMELINE

1911   Sun Yat-sen leads overthrow of Qing dynasty

1912   Founding of the Republic of China

1921   Establishment of the Communist Party of China

1927   Beginning of Chinese Civil War between Communists and Nationalist government

1928   Chiang Kai-shek becomes leader of Nationalist government

1934   Communist forces escape Nationalist encirclement and undertake a 9000-kilometre retreat to northern China, the so-called Long March

1935   Mao Tse-tung becomes leader of the Communist Party

1937–45   Second Sino-Japanese War

1946   Resumption of Chinese Civil War

1949   Mao declares victory and founds the People's Republic of China

1951–52   The Three-anti and Five-anti campaigns urge Chinese people to rid themselves of bourgeois, capitalist elements

1953–57   First Five-Year Plan begins modernisation and industrialisation of Chinese economy

1956   Hundred Flowers Campaign encourages citizens to express their opinions of the Communist regime

1957–59   Anti-Rightist Campaign initiates a purge of 'Rightist' (i.e. anti-communist) elements from society

1958–62   Second Five-Year Plan, or Great Leap Forward, Mao's campaign to collectivise and industrialise the agrarian economy, leads to widespread famine and the deaths of millions

1958	Citizens encouraged to kill rats, mosquitoes, flies and sparrows under the Four Pests Campaign
1966	In Australia, Harold Holt's government markedly reduces restrictions on non-European immigration
1966–76	The Cultural Revolution, aimed at further eliminating bourgeois elements from society, leads to mass persecution of intellectuals in China
1967	Pro-communist activists riot and plant bombs in Hong Kong
1971	China joins the United Nations
1972	US president Richard Nixon visits China
1973	In Australia, Gough Whitlam's Labor government officially ends the White Australia policy
1976	Death of Mao Tse-tung
1978	Deng Xiaoping becomes head of Chinese government
1980	One Child Policy introduced in China
1989	Tiananmen Square Protests in Beijing lead to killing of hundreds of protestors by Chinese military; Australian prime minister Bob Hawke responds by granting asylum to 42,000 Chinese students living in Australia

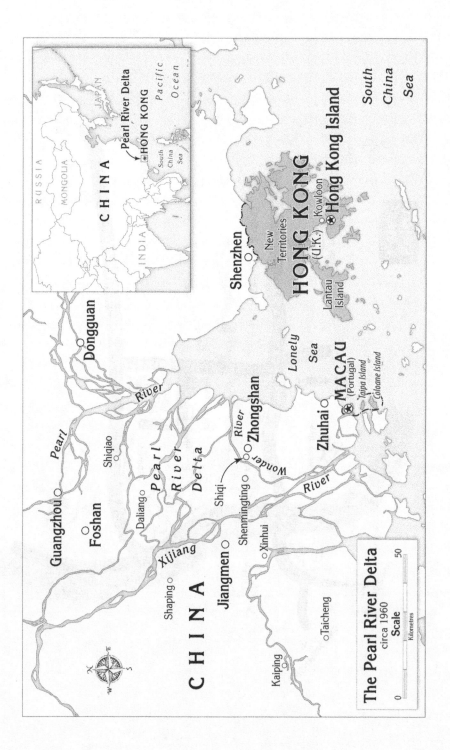

The Pearl River Delta
circa 1960
Scale
0 ──────── 50
Kilometres

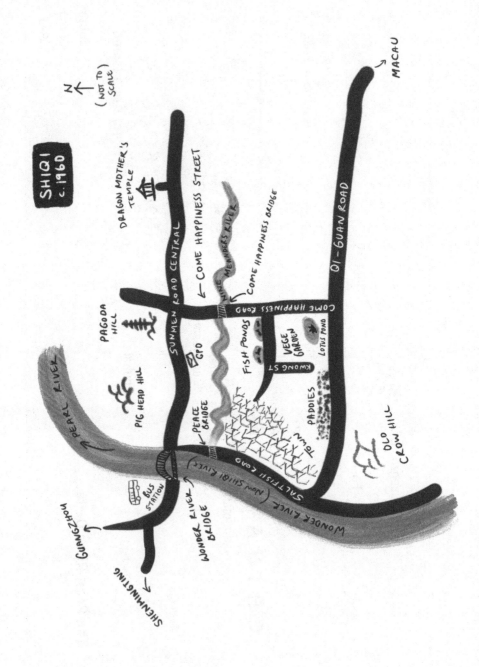

PROLOGUE

Sixteenth Day, Third Lunar Month, 1894
In Shenmingting, a small town situated in the vast estuary of the
Pearl River in Guangdong, my great-grandfather Fu-chiu awaits his
bride. He strolls around the large courtyard of his ancestral home
where more than twenty tables stand ready to seat relatives and
distinguished guests. The tables and guests spread onto his cousin's
front yard next door.

Both houses have been splashed with a good coat of whitewash
to conceal the ageing grey bricks of the otherwise handsome
homes. Days before the happy occasion, the painters had been
about to brush over the decorative panels beneath the eaves of
the two houses when Fu-chiu's father had intervened. 'Stop,' he'd
shouted at them, aghast at their ignorance. 'Leave them alone.
Those are story panels.' The panels depicted many Chinese legends
that had captured the imaginations of past generations and would
do the same for generations to come. He'd made sure they were safe
before directing other servants and helpers who were putting the
final touches to the wedding preparations.

On either side of the courtyard gates and at the back of the
houses, incense sticks burn and paper money has been left out as
offerings to the door-gods and other supernatural guardians who,
in return, it is hoped, will protect the household. The offerings are
also made to repel the ghosts that are said to wander constantly

seeking souls to take their place in the spirit world and free them to be reborn and reach enlightenment. First and foremost, the aim is to ensure the smooth execution of the important day.

Fu-chiu mingles with the guests and, to ease his nerves, takes deep breaths of the abundant smoke lingering in the sweet-scented spring air. He turns back to look at the panels and is pleased his father chose to keep them, even though their colours have faded under the subtropical sky. Much to his delight, they break the sterile monotony of white paint, and preserve the vivacity of the life he has known. The image of the exuberant General Guan Gong on the panel depicting events from the fourteenth-century historical novel *Romance of the Three Kingdoms* is his favourite. How fondly he remembers the tale told to him by his father who, in turn, had been told it by his father. Such was Guan Gong's courage and loyalty in leading the forces of Liu Ban, founder of one of the Three Kingdoms in the third century AD, that he later became not just a folk hero but a god for the Chinese people. From the panel, he seems to beam approval on the family's important day. The tension eases inside Fu-chiu.

Because he has just turned twenty, the coming of age for Chinese men, it is fitting that Fu-chiu be married. He has never met his bride-to-be; he doesn't even know her name. While he was away attending high school, the village go-between was arranging a suitable marital candidate for him under his father's instruction. The process of choosing a wife has remained much the same since his ancestors arrived from the north. People do not marry someone from the same village in case the potential spouse is a descendant of shared forebears who fled the onslaught of the mighty Mongol armies a thousand years earlier. The expertise of the go-between is important for her intimate knowledge of the many families in the surrounding area. Gossip, hearsay, facts, half-truths and, of course, family trees all help her to assess her clients' backgrounds and ensure a good fit. When the go-between enters a match-making deal, her vivid and creative imagination, coupled with a keen sense of how well partners will suit each other, is put into play to ensure success. The bride-to-be must not only be obedient, attentive and devoted, but also beautiful, virtuous and able to produce healthy children. As for the potential groom, he should, of course, be handsome, intelligent and rich, and if he is not wealthy yet, he will be one day, as predicted by her fortune-telling skills.

Fu-chiu accepts this way of finding a wife but he is also a modern young man. A few years attending a progressive high school in the big city of Guangzhou has opened his mind to the possibilities of an expanding universe and life beyond the walls that surround his ancestral home. He now sports a smart Harris Tweed waistcoat over his traditional wedding gown of fine black linen, which reaches down to his shiny black shoes. Befittingly, atop his thick dark hair, tamed by imported hair cream, is a Western-style hat: a gift from his father's cousin in San Francisco. Gone is his long pigtail, even though some young men in town still keep theirs. Instead of the traditional ball of red ribbons fashioned into a big round bouquet attached to the middle of his chest, he has a smart gold watch secured to the left pocket of his waistcoat; the matching chain trails from his top button in a gentle curve. He is a new type of groom in Shenmingting, a prosperous little town made wealthier still by money sent back by the sojourners, the many men who have left China to seek their fortunes in places such as California (known since the gold rush as the Old Gold Mountain) and Australia (the New Gold Mountain) – an exodus that has steadily increased since the defeats of the Opium Wars and the subsequent influx of traders telling tales of riches to be found overseas.

*

It is now well past the third hour after noon, the most auspicious hour for the wedding ceremony to begin. The soft sun above the courtyard has tilted to one side, losing much of its glare. Drums, gongs and trumpets that will herald the bridal procession from a thousand paces are silent. Fu-chiu glances at the long red strings of firecrackers that hang high on strong bamboo poles, ready to ignite. He takes his fob watch from his pocket, flicks open the golden cover and notes the late hour while reminding himself that patience is a virtue. Waves of murmuring begin to ebb and swirl among the guests, like the sounds of the receding tide in the nearby Qi-jiang, or Wonder River, one of the many tributaries that feeds into the Pearl River as it approaches the South China Sea. Perhaps it is best if a messenger is sent to find out what's causing the delay.

The messenger soon returns with news. One of the two poles of the bridal sedan has snapped, and the bride has tumbled out. The silk scarf covering her face has flown off, exposing a sad maiden with full lips and features as pretty as the moon. Her red-and-gold wedding gown has been stained, and her dainty feet, so carefully bound for the past sixteen springs by her parents for her big day, have pushed through her fine embroidered wedding shoes. It is a sorry scene. Passers-by are shaking their heads in disbelief. The musicians have stopped playing, and the porters are too upset by the misfortune to carry on.

It is a bad omen. The chirpy sparrows flitting to and fro around the courtyard become still. The women of the family rush forward to burn more incense sticks to appease the door-gods and other guardian spirits. Children offer more paper money to pacify the wandering ghosts.

Fu-chiu, his father, the family elders and the go-between congregate in the inner room of the house. A decision is needed, immediately.

'The wedding cannot go on,' declares the most senior relative. The glow on his face has vanished. 'It is not good for the family.' He shakes his head and wipes away pearls of sweat that are rare on a fine spring day.

'How do you feel about this?' Fu-chiu's father asks his son.

The trembling go-between lifts her head and shifts her gaze to the young man.

Fu-chiu feels the watch ticking in his pocket. Head down, he ponders his father's question for a while, but the future of the maiden weighs more heavily on his mind than the embarrassment to the family. Still burdened by many rituals, traditions and superstitions, his world doesn't seem to be changing fast enough.

'Maybe this is not meant to be, my son,' his father consoles him. 'We have underestimated the might of ghostly forces. Perhaps we have angered our ancestors this spring. Barely thirteen nights after the Qingming, when we honour our departed ancestors, is perhaps the wrong day for a wedding, even though thirteen days would be perfect, for "three" means "life".'

Fu-chiu raises his head and says quietly, 'I am not superstitious like all of you.'

The noisy room falls silent, somewhat baffled by this calm rebellion.

'It would be most unfair to the maiden if she were to be turned down now,' Fu-chiu continues, looking past everyone in the room. 'No one would ever marry a maiden who broke the bridal sedan pole, not even with her tiny, exquisite feet that the go-between has boasted about.'

The go-between stops quivering. Confidence creeps back into her face.

'But the hour we chose for the ceremony has lapsed twice,' his father points out, trying to appease the senior members of the family while feeling proud that his son has spoken.

'Masters,' says the go-between at once, touching her fingertips against her thumb in a quick calculation, 'the hour following this one is the sixth. "Six" means "officialdom". Wealth follows power.' Her face beams, and she nods like a starving sparrow feeding on spilled grain. 'It looks like this maiden is overloaded with fortune, so heavy that the pole ...' The go-between is grinning now, secure in the belief that her boundless imagination hasn't failed her and that her reputation as the best go-between in Shenmingting is intact. She jumps eagerly to her bound feet and shuffles after Fu-chiu and his father, who are returning to the front of the house.

'Bring on the firecrackers,' father and son shout in unison.

Drums boom, trumpets blast, cymbals and gongs resonate. The town of Shenmingting erupts back into life.

Fu-chiu marries Loy-chuo, whose name means 'wrong arrival'. Immediately after the wedding, the family changes her name to Loy-ho, or 'good arrival'.

She goes on to bear five sons and two daughters. With so many children arriving, the family appreciates the blessings from the gods and ancestors of Shenmingting, even though Fu-chiu has not stopped pondering the possibilities of adventure beyond the town, perhaps even far from China. However, news of his cousin's demise in the 1906 San Francisco earthquake and fire reminds him of the perils of foreign shores. Fate urges Fu-chiu to remain in Shenmingting and be content, despite the fact that a series of rebellions led by a local son, Sun Yat-sen, are beginning to shake the huge, rapidly declining Qing Empire.

My maternal grandfather, Dai-jun Young, the eldest in the growing family, is born and brought up during the turmoil of the last years of the Qing Dynasty. As a teenager, he witnesses the establishment of the Republic of China under Sun Yat-sen in 1912, ending four thousand years of Chinese imperialism. When he comes of age, he too is married with the assistance of a go-between. Working in the small family business that Fu-chiu established leaves Dai-jun little time to fathom the many social and political implications of the conflicts, upheavals and cultural confusion, brought on by new ideas both foreign and local, that are occurring all around him.

Meanwhile he watches ocean-going vessels sailing up and down the Pearl River, bringing foreigners and their strange goods and customs, and listens to the stories of the sojourners who have returned home to find a wife and settle down, and he can't help but dream of what the world is like outside Shenmingting, outside China. One day in 1920, soon after my mother is born, he tells Fu-chiu, 'I don't want to stay around fathering more babies. I'm off to the Gold Mountain.' He names my mother Wai-syn, 'safe return', after calling her older sister Wai-hung, or 'safe journey'. In 1921, following in the footsteps of many Shenmingting men, he leaves for Hawaii as an indentured labourer. My mother is six months old.

Shenmingting prospers through the efforts of its many sojourners as the years go by, but much of China remains in poverty. Like my grandfather, many people from the Pearl River Delta leave for foreign lands in search of a better future and financial security for their families. They are spared the increasing chaos and bloodshed that follow: the Japanese invasion of China in the late 1930s, during which 35 million Chinese perish, and the brutal civil war between Nationalists and Communists that costs 10 million lives and leads to the founding of the People's Republic of China (PRC) under Chairman Mao on 1 October 1949.

With the establishment of the PRC, peace finally arrives after more than fifty years of turmoil. Hopes for a normal life are high under Chairman Mao. Even though embargoes are promptly declared by the rest of the world against this latest communist state, Mao's government makes many wonderful promises: there will be ample food for all, housing for the displaced millions, gender equality, free education, full employment, freedom in marriage – and it will restore much-needed national pride to the downtrodden Chinese people.

*

Into this new era of optimism and promises, I am born. We children are the bearers of hope, harmony and prosperity. Most importantly, we're regarded as the future leaders of a stable and strong PRC, custodians of a peaceful life that has eluded past generations.

By the time the PRC is proclaimed, my parents have settled in Shiqi, a thriving administrative town in the county of Zhongshan, formerly known as Hongshan, or Fragrant Mountain, but renamed in 1925 in honour of Sun Yat-sen, who was known in Mandarin as Sun Zhongshan. The town is only a few kilometres east of Shenmingting and close to the South China Sea. Mama and Baba are proud and progressive university graduates, who trained as high-school teachers and met and fell in love while working in Hong Kong before the revolution. They're ready and eager to help rebuild China. The thought of sojourning to goldfields overseas, returning to Hong Kong or moving to Portuguese Macau doesn't enter their minds; indeed, to them, the colonies are now a national shame.

Life has never seemed more promising and exciting for Mama and Baba, and for the Chinese people as a whole.

My story begins in these auspicious times.

PART I

By the Wonder River

CHAPTER 1

'Long live Chairman Mao!'

'Long live the Chinese Communist Party!'

'Down with the capitalists!'

In Shiqi, surrounded by a sea of red flags and accompanied by a thundering roll of drums, trumpets and gongs, my classmates and I shouted at the top of our voices.

On my first day at kindergarten in September 1954, I was proud to already know the revolutionary slogans, songs and jingles. I'd been born amid the drone of them, into a noisy world filled with enthusiasm for a good life and hatred for the evildoers, both local and foreign, who had exploited China for centuries. Since infancy I'd been infused with cries of revolution, denunciation and the struggle for freedom – indeed, they were my first babbling words, and now I loved shouting them with the other children. The red stars on the flaps of our schoolbags shone in the morning sun and reflected in our happy faces. We were a sea of little soldiers in khaki, ready to conquer the bad world under Chairman Mao.

The Party Secretary of the town's First Central Primary School and Kindergarten spoke to us through the megaphone. 'Precious Ones, Little Masters of New China, welcome to the big family of Chairman Mao. Welcome to our kindergarten. You are our first pure proletariat generation. You are Chairman Mao's children. You are our future!' His face glowed, exuding passionate and progressive pride as he punched the tepid air along with all the big people around us. We clapped. Our parents and teachers clapped too. Our spirits soared even more, and we felt invincible and patriotic. The teachers then led us into our classrooms to begin our education as the first 'pure' generation of the PRC.

Reaching our classroom, we hurried to discover what our parents had packed inside our schoolbags. My neighbour Ah-dong, my old friend Sammy (nicknamed Flea from when he was a toddler), and a few new friends pulled out long green spring onions, some with roots still attached, and lettuce leaves, all neatly wrapped in string or a strip of red paper as a good omen for the first day of learning, even though it was only a half-day introduction to the kindergarten.

'The vegetables mean intelligence, and they bring you wealth,' I heard one boy tell some others while he chewed on his crunchy lettuce leaf. Then they pulled out lucky money in red packets: aluminium coins of two or five fen (cents).

I searched my schoolbag, similar to the ones my older sisters had. I had waited a long, long time for it – then suddenly, the week before kindergarten was due to start, there it was, right next to my pillow as I opened my eyes one morning, this khaki schoolbag with a belt that you could swing over your shoulder. Every day I'd put it on and march up and down the house like a little People's Liberation Army (PLA) soldier, feeling like I couldn't wait for the big day to come. I smelled its sweet raw cotton, felt the strong coarse fabric and cherished the red star.

Now I looked carefully in every pocket and corner of my schoolbag, hoping to find some lucky money. All I found was a sharp pencil, a small eraser and a thin writing pad. *How am I going to be intelligent like my father without spring onions and lettuce leaves, and wealthy without the two fen?* I must have looked inconsolable because the teacher told me to cheer up.

'Baba, why didn't I get what my schoolmates got?' I asked my father as soon as he arrived to pick me up from school at noon.

'Those things are superstitions, Ah-mun,' he said without a

pause, 'nothing but decaying traditions that we and modern China don't need anymore under Chairman Mao.'

Baba crouched down to look me in the eye, holding me close with his large hands. He kissed me, then smiled. I loved it when he called me Ah-mun – a shortened, endearing version of my full name, Yiu-man. I craved for the cuddle and warmth of Baba. His mention of Chairman Mao also made me happy.

'You've got to be progressive like the comrades. One day you can become a scholar, or a scientist, or even a leader like Chairman Mao,' he continued, reinflating my spirit even more. 'But you must be diligent in learning.' Baba pushed his PLA flat cap, khaki with a red star at the centre, away from his large eyes. His handsome face looked like those of the revolutionary figures on posters that covered every available wall in town.

Although I didn't quite understand what he meant, I was proud of Baba. I'd always felt fortunate to have a father like him. I couldn't wait to get to the kindergarten every morning to learn to read and write like he did.

*

Shiqi, a river town near the mouth of the Pearl River Delta, is not far from Hong Kong and Macau. It became an important town following the Chinese defeat in the Opium Wars of the mid-1800s against British and French forces. Many local heroes, such as Sun Yat-sen – by then known as the father of modern China – and his comrades in the struggle to defeat the Qing emperor, had made us proud. Shiqi had a relatively small population of fifty thousand but had a rich folklore of fascinating stories and legends, the most memorable of which described how the region was indebted to Buddha's magical control of an unruly tiger. I drew comfort from living in a tranquil place where a seven-storey pagoda on a hill held down the head of the once-wild tiger, while a smaller pagoda pinned its tail. The town had grown around Pagoda Hill, whose slopes descended to the surrounding flatland

and allowed people to easily escape to higher ground when summer floods came.

Our kindergarten was housed in the ancient Dragon Mother's Temple, which, when I was very young, was hidden behind thick shrubs and imposing banyan trees that made the temple seem mystical and scary. Inside were ghostly cold rooms with unfathomably high ceilings and huge round pillars, where towering statues of deities stood. The temple's big, ancient bell had long tolled on the hour, resonating across Shiqi to assure its residents of peace and equanimity. Baba said the temple had been there almost since the founding of the thousand-year-old town; people had prayed there for compassion, safety and blessings to help them endure summer floods and other disasters.

I was puzzled by the story of the Dragon Mother and her adopted sons: five little snakes that hatched from a rock she found by the Xijiang River, a big tributary of the Pearl River, far, far upstream from us. The snakes grew to become five dragons who helped their mother to protect and guard the local people from unpredictable weather and anything else that was evil or perilous. It perplexed me that the five dragons later took human form and became scholars in order to continue the good work their mother had started; but it excited me that Shiqi was close to the South China Sea, to which the dragons had returned after accomplishing their mission to help the people.

Given this folklore, it seemed logical to turn the Dragon Mother's Temple into a place of learning. And the townspeople didn't need reassurance from the temple bell anymore, because the PRC's many slogans boosted their optimism for a bright future. So the grounds were cleared and the buildings converted into our school and kindergarten.

After that, I was no longer frightened of the place. The choking smoke from incense sticks was gone, leaving only noisy sparrows and swallows that had been there for generations. They seemed to take pleasure in aiming their droppings at us as they stuck to their flight paths. My friend Ah-dong, with his big head, skinny limbs and protruding stomach, seemed to cop the most, and he often reeked of bird poo. He didn't seem to mind, chuckling each time it happened and saying it was good luck. He sat next to me in class.

The name plaques of the town's dead, once revered on the temple walls, were just the right size to make stools for us kids. Sitting on these plaques didn't worry me – I even farted on them. Some of my classmates peed on them when they couldn't hold their bladders until the bell rang.

Comrade Teacher Wong greeted us each morning with, 'Good morning, Precious Ones. You are Chairman Mao's good children.' Like many female Party comrades, she wore a PLA cap over two plaited ponytails. Baba told me Mama had taught Comrade Wong in primary school, before she'd run off with the propaganda brigade of the PLA when they'd first reached town. Mama said she'd been a good singer.

'Good morning, Comrade Teacher Wong,' we chorused with pride.

She smiled at us before leading us into 'The East Is Red', our favourite song:

> The East is red and the sun rising,
> Now our great saviour Mao Tse-tung
> For people's happiness he is fighting …

Chairman Mao was on posters at school and on walls along the streets. I loved him, and I loved my parents and my three sisters too.

I'd already decided to be like my progressive parents, so I kept up the long walk every day to the kindergarten and didn't complain about not getting the two fen to be rich. My little legs grew tired along the seemingly never-ending Come Happiness Road to Come Happiness Bridge, which ran over the Nine Meanders River, a small branch of the Wonder River that traversed the town. Come Happiness Street began there, taking me to the town square, and that was only halfway to the kindergarten. Every day one of my parents, sometimes both, walked with me all the way to make the slog easier. They had still not been assigned jobs by the Party, but I was happy they spent time caring for me and my sisters.

At kindergarten we sang revolutionary nursery rhymes and songs about the Long March, the Second Sino-Japanese War, the civil wars and the recent Korean War. We marched around with our schoolbags on our shoulders like little PLA soldiers, our heads high and our chests puffed out. Our days were devoted to exalting our great Chairman Mao while studying communism. From an early age we knew of the revolutionary pioneers, such as Stalin, Lenin, Marx and Engels, and the many heroes and martyrs who had sacrificed themselves for the founding of the PRC – and for our freedom. Comrade Teacher Wong told us every morning, 'China, together with big brother Russia and little brother North Korea, and our archenemy the United States of America and their running dogs, make up the whole wide world. We must continue our struggle against our capitalist enemies, ridding ourselves of the corruption of the past, and setting ourselves free from the tentacles of ancient customs and superstitions.'

For reasons unknown to me then, our teacher also wanted us to be vigilant: to be aware of the hidden counter-revolutionaries and bad elements who might undermine Chairman Mao's vision for a strong China. She told us that class struggle must eliminate the unwanted classes of people as designated by the Party, at any cost.

Our teacher always concluded the morning's political lesson with the message that China, together with our communist brothers, would be the triumphant proletarian power of the world. We repeated these words after her, not knowing what they meant, before moving on to other subjects.

Much to my envy, many children at school wore a red scarf or neckerchief – the symbol of revolutionary youth – to indicate that they were members of the Young Pioneers of China; when they reached high school they would begin learning Russian. You had to be selected for this coveted organisation in primary school, and now that I had my schoolbag I aspired to become a 'Red Scarf' myself one day and learn Russian so that I would be even more revolutionary. The motto of the Young Pioneers was 'To fight for the cause of communism. Be ready. Always ready.' We were all proud that our town was very much part of the revolution with so many Red Scarves and PLA soldiers, comrades and of course the khaki schoolbags flooding the streets every day, not to mention the red flags with gold stars.

Our teacher told us that many millions of ordinary people like us had lost their lives during the drawn-out wars that had led to the founding of the PRC. So when a campaign to replenish our country's population was initiated by the government, we eagerly took part. Our first task was to stir up the revolutionary spirit of young women with a new song:

> Eighteen-year-old girls go get married soon,
> Bring up your sons, and quickly will they grow
> To be men and Liberation heroes,
> Defend our Motherland bravely will they go ...

At first, the young women in town couldn't stop giggling when we sang it to them in the streets, parks and wherever else we came across them. At home I was proud to teach my younger sister Weng and cousin Yiu-hoi to sing it too. Later we saw many wedding processions, and before long there were pregnant women everywhere. My parents said the many babies that were subsequently born were the direct result of our revolutionary action.

*

My family lived at Number 1 Kwong Street, on the southern edge of Shiqi, in a larger-than-average house that my paternal grandfather Woon-duk Kwong had built for himself, his wife and their nine sons. Baba, Shek-tong, the seventh son, told me that Grandfather had intended his descendants would live there happily for generations to come. The building was one of ten single-storey houses in a neat row, all with similar façades. They had been constructed around the same time from grey bricks that it was believed would withstand the typhoons and floods that ravaged Shiqi almost every summer. The houses were also protected by a long double-brick levee wall. The compound had two entrances, one at either end, each wide enough to admit people four abreast, but too narrow for cars and large carts.

I couldn't wait to get home from kindergarten every day. The broad, concreted, level street was a safe playground for me and the other local kids – our oasis. There, facing the glorious east, we, the Precious Ones, were well protected.

I was enchanted by my family's house. Its ten main rooms were separated by two courtyards that opened to the sky, making it an airy, light-filled home. The three large lounge rooms were lined with heavy rosewood chairs inlaid with pieces of cool marble, breaking the monotony of the grey brick walls. Decorative wooden partitions sectioned off parts of the lounges as indoor playgrounds for the children. An incense stick burned all day long in the third lounge room where the ancestors were revered, creating a tranquil space filled with a sense of magic and awe.

I had three sisters. Ying was the oldest of the four of us, and Ping two years younger. I had arrived three years after Ping, then another two years later my little sister Weng had come along. Poor Weng was a limp baby for the first three years of her life and many a time she was not expected to live. I can still remember how worried and upset I was whenever she was sick; I wouldn't leave her side.

Ying was the big sister I looked up to and admired; my parents often said she was an intelligent and strong-willed child. We all knew how Baba adored her. I didn't know Ping well, because when I was a baby she moved to Shenmingting to live with my maternal grandmother, Grandmother Young, in order to lighten the burden on my unemployed parents; however, she had recently returned to Kwong Street. I was more than glad that I had an extra older sister at home. I soon learnt that Ping was gentle and pleasant, if not a quiet girl to have around.

My sisters occupied the living quarters that had formerly been used by our Third Aunt, who was married to Third Uncle, my father's third elder brother. Long before the PRC had come into being, he had moved overseas, just as other sojourners had done, to seek a living to support his young family. Around the time I started kindergarten, with Western anti-Chinese and anti-communist feeling rising, sojourners were prevented by foreign governments from transferring money directly to China. They could, however, send money to relatives in Hong Kong or Macau, from where it could be redirected to China. In response, even though it restricted the movement of its citizens in and out of the country, and even between districts, the Chinese government began to encourage relatives of Patriotic Overseas Chinese, as the sojourners were known, to move to those nearby colonies so that they could maintain the supply of foreign currency, which was desperately needed to help rebuild China. Third Aunt and Grandmother Young answered the call.

After being granted an exit visa by the local authorities in Shiqi, Third Aunt had gone to live in Macau before I started kindergarten, where she received money monthly from Third Uncle, who was by then residing in New York. More recently, Grandmother Young had moved to Hong Kong, so that she could continue to receive and transfer money monthly from our grandfather in Hawaii. I overheard my parents saying how important it was to keep foreign money coming into China to increase prosperity – something I didn't understand – and that the more money our relatives sent, the more ration vouchers we would receive from the government (there was even a special shop in town, the Overseas Chinese Friendship Store, where you could exchange these vouchers for goods not available elsewhere). The adults also talked about what a good opportunity it was to leave China, and lamented the fact they couldn't go too – only one member of each family was permitted to do so. Many from Zhongshan had already gone.

I shared my parents' room, which also served as our family room. By the time I began kindergarten, my paternal grandparents had passed away and my father's other brothers had left home. My Sixth Aunt and her daughter Yiu-wei took up one of the quarters. My father always looked out for Sixth Aunt, the widow of the brother born before him, my Sixth Uncle, who had been closest to him growing up. He and his ten-year-old son had been killed in a house fire in Hong Kong before the PRC was proclaimed. Baba often talked about him. Sixth Aunt was an office worker at a local hospital.

My Eighth Uncle, the brother born after my father, and Eighth Aunt lived in the other living quarters in the front section of the fathomless house. Standing 185 centimetres tall, Eighth Uncle was a giant in town as well as in the family. He and Eighth Aunt somehow still had jobs and they spent a lot of time away teaching in schools in different towns, and came home only one weekend a month, usually at different times. Their two boys, Yiu-hoi and Ah-ki, were cared for by their maternal grandmother, who lived in one of the other rooms. When Eighth Uncle was home for his monthly break, he filled the house with his wonderful singing, ranging from opera to revolutionary songs. Despite all these occupants, the house seemed happy and peaceful to us children.

At the time, Shiqi was divided into several administrative districts, and ours was the Wonder River District. The Party-appointed district heads had control of our daily lives, including local policing and security, training of the People's Militia (a local law-enforcement and army reserve force), political education and job allocation, as well as travel in and out of the district, and even marriages. They were also responsible for protecting their districts from any 'undesirables', such as petty criminals or spies from the colonies, and re-educating those with unfavourable family classifications, such as small landlords (those who owned less than an acre of land), capitalists (anyone who owned a business large or small), rightists, and intellectuals, including teachers like my parents. To assist them in these duties, the district heads formed local committees made up of one resident from each street whom they considered communistic, progressive and patriotic.

Our District Head was a returned PLA officer, a thin man with a voice hoarse from constant smoking. In between phlegmy coughs, his eyes glinted with revolutionary spirit. My father said this man had directed the district during many campaigns, from the bloody land reform and 'mopping up' programs in the years just after the PRC was founded – during which the landowning class and those resisting the young republic were exterminated – to the subsequent ruthless nationalisation of all industries and businesses, as well as the frequent summary executions of recalcitrant landlords and counter-revolutionaries, and the enforced exile of many others who were sent to re-education camps in remote parts of the country. Everyone was fearful of the District Head.

One day, the District Head and his committee members trooped into our house and marched past us kids as we were playing hide-and-seek in the first lounge room. They went straight to Baba, the only man of the family in the house at the time, and demanded to check out all the living quarters. He wasn't allowed to accompany them. They stomped into every room, noting down on a scrap of paper how each was occupied. Yiu-hoi, Ah-ki, Yiu-wei, Weng and I stopped playing and went over to the adults. Ying and Ping were away at school at the time. Baba was frowning, and I could see he was upset. Mama stood by him with her head down, not daring to meet the comrades' gaze.

'There are five unoccupied living quarters in this house, and you have two large kitchens,' said the District Head, who was wearing his faded PLA tunic. He had one fist pressed deeply into his waist and the other thrust close to Baba's face. His voice bounced off the grey brick walls in the third lounge room as he accused Baba of not reporting the vacant rooms to his office.

'But ... but they are my brothers' rooms, and they have their furniture in them,' Baba replied with his head bowed and his hands held together in front of him.

I clung on to his arm, staring at the District Head's PLA tunic and feeling baffled.

'Haven't you been to street meetings? Haven't you heard the rules?' the District Head shouted at my father. 'It's rich people like you who don't care about the proletariat! Who don't care about communism! People like you need more political studies and re-education.'

I was trembling, and my sister and cousins were all quiet. Because they were regarded as redundant intellectuals from the past, my parents were already attending evening political studies classes with many of our neighbours, and they were regularly sent to re-education camps, usually for a week at a time, sometimes just a weekend, though Baba had once been away for over a month. I hated the idea of him going away again.

Baba nodded and said softly, 'I'll write to my brothers and let you know as soon as they reply.'

'Not good enough!' the District Head roared. 'We need all the empty rooms now.' He turned and marched out of the house with his committee members. We were all shaking.

Within days, five families had moved in, and our house became as noisy as Come Happiness Road at lunch hour. We children were curious of the strangers in our once-peaceful home, and we didn't know what to do, so we stopped playing and quietly watched the chaos set in.

Baba explained that many people came to town to look for jobs while others were relocated there on government business. The Korean War soldiers had returned home, and war casualties needed treatment. 'There are many homeless people out there and we must help,' he said to us. 'Now go and play with your cousins.' At other times my parents said to us, 'We share the house just like we share food, so that every citizen is catered for.' We kept our spirits high, singing and dancing to celebrate our revolution. We were so proud of our parents.

Unlike placid Ping, Ying grew unhappy as the house became crowded. She avoided the new residents for weeks. No greetings. No eye contact. She was now a senior in primary school and was looking forward to learning Russian soon. So she felt she deserved a room of her own, but all the unoccupied rooms were taken up by residents assigned by the housing authority in town. She began talking back to my parents and slamming doors.

'It's only kind to let people share our large home,' I overheard Mama say to her one day. 'Besides, the Housing Control Bureau has the authority to make sure every unoccupied room in town is filled. It's not our family's choice.'

One of the people allocated to our house was a young comrade called Choi-lin, who worked in the ration-voucher store in town. She wore smart blouses and pretty floral frocks, which stood out in a sea of green, grey and blue. Ying and Ping took to her and admired her dresses.

Choi-lin immediately showed an interest in our family. Once, when Baba was out doing voluntary labour, Choi-lin asked Ying, 'Where are the other uncles? What do they do?'

Ying said she didn't know.

'What about your baba, what did he do before the revolution? Was he a teacher?'

Ying gave her a blank look.

My mother appeared from the kitchen with her cooking utensils. Choi-lin stopped the conversation and gave each of us a sweet wrapped in colourful transparent paper, at the same time telling Mama what good children we all were. You couldn't help but like her.

When the authorities allocated a small corner in one of the two kitchens for Mama to cook in, she became unhappy. She discovered that the new residents had used her pots, wok, saucepans and other utensils, and left them dirty or even taken them away. But Baba said it was hard to accuse the new residents of stealing even if we saw them with the items we had 'lost'. The District Head believed that the haves had to share with the have-nots, and that the proletariat, the chosen people, would never steal from one another. The front door, which Baba had been so particular about locking up every night, was now left unlocked under the instruction of the housing authorities. 'There are no thieves under communism,' the District

Head assured my parents. 'Everyone is equal. There is no need to steal.'

Nevertheless, Mama asked us to help her collect all the remaining utensils and store them in our room, together with our bowls and chopsticks. Later, we kept firewood there as well. With the doors to my parents' room locked, we felt more close-knit than ever. There was a cosy sense of belonging to one another as a family, despite the presence of many strangers in the house.

CHAPTER 2

I enjoyed spending more time with my family, especially Baba. At home I followed him around and helped with the chores: when he swept the floors, I gathered up the rubbish and took it to the bin. We chatted as we worked together.

Around this time, he began showing me how to fish in the waterways. 'Ah-mun, see the water in the creek? When it's clear, you won't catch any fish. If there were fish there, the water would look murky because it would have been churned up by the fish as they play.' He recommended the best times for fishing: 'Fish early in the morning or when the sun goes down for a better catch. Sometimes big fish feed in the night and you can hear them in the fishpond or the river. And always remember that patience helps.'

Passing near our house and skirting the whole of Kwong Street was a 1.5-metre-high levee wall, which, Baba explained, was meant to reduce flooding every summer. Outside the wall was the communal land, where the paddy fields and vegetable gardens were; on the embankment under the wall was our family vegetable patch. We also kept a few rabbits, chickens and ducks in a walled-off side lane of the house. The levee wall became my favourite spot to talk with my father; there were so many interesting things to learn from him.

'Why can't we eat the lychees?' I asked one day. I was thinking of the many lychee trees, laden with green fruits in large bunches, that swayed back and forth in the summer breezes along the banks of the fishponds not far from our house. My mouth began to water.

'They need nutrients and the sun to grow bigger,' Baba explained, 'and then they will turn red to tell you it's time to pick them.'

'Why don't the birds eat them now?'

'Because they are green like the leaves, making it hard for the birds to see them, and they have tough, bitter skin.'

'Oh. What about the green bok choy?'

'You have to cook them before they taste nice.'

'I like the colour red.'

'It's a revolutionary colour, my son.' Baba was always moved by the many red flags around us. Their colour, he told me, symbolised the blood spilled by the martyrs who had sacrificed themselves for us and our country so that we could have a peaceful life under Chairman Mao.

'How do you spill blood?'

'Your skin opens up when you get shot, cut or stabbed, and blood gushes out; if you lose too much blood, you can die.'

Baba scooped me up and held me close to him every time I asked unusual questions like this, and I would put my arms around his neck, savouring the cigarette scent he carried. 'My dear Ah-mun, you are too young to think of this, about death and dying. Remember, my son, you only have one life, and you must treasure it. Now go and play.' Baba always kissed me before letting me down.

Late one afternoon in early May 1955, my father and I were sitting on the levee wall in front of our house, catching the breeze from the South China Sea. We looked towards Come Happiness Road, admiring the ripening lychees that hung low near the fishponds next to the sea of jade-green rice that rippled in the gentle wind. The air was thick and humid, and the sun blazing. Baba explained to me how the sun sucked up lots of tiny water droplets and strung them together, forming a veil of moisture that floated in the warm air.

Yet, while the young rice was lush and the lychees were thriving, other vegetation was suffering in the heat. Even the resilient lotus plants in the pond looked limp, their leaves singed at the edges. (How I loved their roots, which Mama cooked, and the seeds she used in soups.) Why, I wondered, were so many plants withering when the air was so damp? It was all very confusing to me. And it seemed to mirror another puzzle: although we were promised that the revolution was bringing us great benefits, my parents had still not been allocated jobs, and their concern had begun to show on their faces. I didn't want to see them become shrivelled like some of the vegetation around us.

I began to distract myself from the heat by capturing the humidity with both hands, then watching the liquid drip from my fists to the thirsty earth. It was almost like squeezing ripe lychees.

Baba was amused. 'Ah, water, the life juice of our universe,' he said. 'Fortunately, here in the Pearl River Delta, we're blessed with an abundance of it – usually enough to maintain three good rice harvests a year, plus a vegetable crop or two in between.'

'But what's life juice?' I asked, looking up at Baba as I swung my legs against the brick wall, feeling the coolness between my toes.

'Well, my son, it's what's required for plants and other living creatures to grow properly. I suppose even for plants it's more than just water: it's water, good soil and nutrients.'

'And what do we need to grow?' I asked.

Baba looked at me, frowned and said, 'Well, for us it's a little bit more complicated. A meaningful life needs more than food, nutrients and water. You need to be free, like the sparrows and swallows that fly wherever they want to.' He gestured to the hazy blue above us and looked at me again, his heavy eyes widening. 'You also need education, nurturing and an opportunity to thrive. When you grow up, Ah-mun,' he added, 'you'll understand what I mean.' He then turned to the east, from where the sea breeze came, and frowned again as he looked towards the horizon.

That was the first time in my life that I knew my father was really worried about something – perhaps about his own predicament, the family or our future. With both parents unemployed, the money we received from Hong Kong didn't last long, even just for essentials like food, and we children often sensed our parents' anxiety towards the end of each month and the arrival of the next allowance.

*

Coming home from school a few days later, I overheard my parents in a heated discussion. 'I don't think they trust us intellectuals,' Baba said to Mama, who sat on the edge of the bed folding the laundry. 'Just look around. All our university friends have no jobs. Writers and poets and other artists have no jobs. The accountants and lawyers are all unemployed or in prison. The government is trying to get rid of us ...' Baba's voice dipped to a whisper as he saw me walk into the room. He moved closer to Mama, mumbling, 'Without the intellectuals and educated people, a nation of illiterate peasants is a lot easier to rule.'

Mama paused in her task, her eyes growing large. 'Be very careful of what you say, my dear,' she said. 'We'll be in big trouble if the tenants hear this.'

It was then my father pulled me close and said, 'Son, you didn't hear what we were talking about, did you?'

I didn't know what to say. Instead I stared at him and Mama.

'If you've heard anything at all, you must keep it secret. You don't want Mama and Baba ending up doing more political meetings or more re-education camp time, do you?' He tried to look straight into my eyes, but I avoided his gaze.

'No. No, Baba, I didn't hear what you were talking about.'

My parents had wanted to contribute to the rebuilding of China, but things hadn't worked out as they'd wished. In the beginning they were proud to be regarded as the so-called 'high intellectuals' – those with university qualifications.

'We are among the very few university graduates left,' I often heard my parents reminding each other. 'Our Motherland needs us to educate the next generations.' They had refused to relocate away from China before 1949, when the border was still open and many of their friends had left. Instead they had waited for a call from the

28

District Head, who was in charge of employment locally. But the call never came. 'Wai-hung and Beng'e work like peasants in the field when they should be teaching,' Baba said to Mama, speaking of my aunt and her husband who lived in Shenmingting, Mama's ancestral home.

'Like us, they were educated before 1949,' Mama mumbled.

'I hate relying on your mother to send us money from Hong Kong,' Baba said as he lit another cigarette while one still burned between his fingers. He shook his head. 'The re-education camps are full to the brim with so-called intellectuals. The ones not there have to do long hours of volunteer work.' He sucked hard on his cigarette before turning to Mama. 'But "volunteer"? I don't think so. It's forced labour ...'

'Keep your voice down,' she said.

I hated seeing her endearing smile disappear from her pleasant face. Her slim body hunched up and the glint in her eyes died. She seemed to grow old faster behind the shut door to our room whenever Baba was in a funny mood.

'They don't trust us – just look around,' Baba said to her on another evening. 'Denying us job opportunities is like the Qin Emperor burying scholars alive. Didn't Stalin try to stop intellectuals from working by sending them to Siberia? Now Mao is doing the same to get rid of us.'

Sometimes I heard them complaining between themselves that jobs had gone to Party members, revolutionary heroes, returned soldiers from Korea, the many martyrs' families, and peasants and proletariats, all of whom had better classifications than my parents.

But unhappy as they were, I never heard them argue with each other. Baba always apologised later for any surliness, which brought back Mama's smile. Then I loved my baba again.

*

After overhearing Baba's grievances and Mama's quiet acceptance of his complaints, I started to fear that they both weren't as progressive and communistic as I'd believed them to be. I hoped they would become more like the comrades in charge of us, including the District Head, Comrade Teacher Wong, Choi-lin and some of my classmates' parents: patriotic, solemn and totally devoted to Chairman Mao. If Baba or Mama had been directly involved in the liberation of China, I now realised, they would have jobs and we'd have received more food vouchers and wouldn't need to rely on capitalist dollars from Hawaii.

At school, we were told that high intellectuals weren't needed in the new China and advised to report any members of the community who weren't pulling their weight. I wanted to be a good communist when I grew up, but how could I ever report my parents to the authorities, even if a few of my schoolmates reported their own parents?

To make myself feel better, I'd make up patriotic stories about Baba as I sat on the levee wall, watching the birds fly freely in the hot sky. I began to fantasise that perhaps his real role was top secret. After all, despite my father's lowly classification, people in our town seemed to look up to him. Most of them had never been to school, so he helped them fill in application forms for jobs or for permission to stay overnight with relatives outside the district. He wrote letters for people who wanted to ask out fellow workers; he even prepared marriage proposals. He fetched drinking water from the river and washing water from the wells for the elderly in the street. Many of them had watched him grow up to be an educated man, and they were proud of him.

During his years of unemployment, Baba tried hard not to submit to despair and lethargy. He read and re-read his beloved Chinese classics, like *Dream of the Red Chamber*, *Journey to the West*, *Romance of the Three Kingdoms* and *Water Margin*, under the dim light of our regulation fifteen-watt globe. When I came home from school, I often found him sitting at the large rosewood table in the third lounge room, practising calligraphy with a fine bristle brush.

Mama would be busy collecting laundry from outside, mending our clothes or preparing our evening meal. Still in her mid-thirties, she was thin and seldom smiled. She planned the month's expenses carefully and would make sure there was enough rice in the big urn in our room to last the month. Before communal dining was introduced, she would bargain hard at the market, and she bought only essentials, such as kerosene (the electricity supply was very unreliable), sugar and peanut oil for cooking. She'd alter clothes to make sure they lasted as long as possible. We seldom had treats and never ate out (there were no cafés or restaurants in town anyway). She saved hard so that we could have a family photograph taken once a year to send to her father in Hawaii and mother in Hong Kong. We might go to a movie once a year, usually in the Lunar New Year, unless it was to see one of the free films shown by the government (though Baba said they were 'propaganda', whatever that meant). If for some reason the money from Grandmother was late arriving, Mama would become worried and pace up and down anxiously, waiting for the postman to arrive.

Baba's calligraphy helped us too. He'd write out good wishes for neighbours to hang on their walls or front doors during festivities such as the Moon Festival, in mid-autumn in the Eighth Lunar Month, and the Lunar New Year, and in return they might bring him a bunch of vegetables or a freshly caught fish, and usually a few cigarettes. Though he grumbled at times, doing things for people generally made him happy.

Yes, I thought, he must be working undercover on a secret mission that was extremely important for the Party and China.

'Yiu-hoi, can you keep a secret?' I asked my cousin one day.

'Whoa, Big Brother,' Yiu-hoi said, using the traditional term of endearment for close male cousins. 'I swear on all my toys that I'll tell no one.'

'My father is a secret agent for the Party.'

Since the triumph of the Party, there had been one population-cleansing campaign after another. But no matter what happened, the constant activity on the nearby Wonder River offered reassurance that our community would endure. In my infancy there had always been fishing junks and sampans dotting the idyllic waterways, quietly providing their operators with a decent living; now an increasing number of tugboats, barges and riverboats had taken over, busily transporting grains and other produce for export.

One evening, Baba was sitting in his usual place under the fifteen-watt globe when he commented, 'Our people have survived many wars and natural disasters in the past hundred years, just as their ancestors survived the many ruthless tyrants in past dynasties. I think we can make it, no matter what.'

I wasn't sure whether he was trying to restore his faith in revolutionary China, or if he'd just fallen into another funny mood.

*

One late spring afternoon in 1955, the District Head came to our house and told Baba he was a capitalist intellectual with an outdated education. The man then marched off humming his favourite revolutionary song, 'The East Is Red'.

Baba was devastated. I gathered he knew then that he would never be needed as an intellectual, despite his times in re-education camps, and that it was unlikely he would ever be offered a job.

Baba sank into depression. He sat in his cane chair in one corner of the bedroom for hours at a time, not talking to anyone, and ignoring what went on around him. He shrivelled like a garden snail shut in its shell. He smoked more and did not go to bed until late at night, but slept a lot during the day. We could hear his sighs and felt the weighty air in the room. Before long we caught his dejection and gloom, and sighed with him.

I started to have my doubts about his activities. Was he really a secret agent for the Party? I was no longer sure.

On one of those humid days towards the end of May that year, I went and sat by Baba in our room as I often did after school. He didn't respond when I gave him the news that I was the best in the class at the two- and three-times tables; nor did he respond to my plan for my summer holiday in July. So I laid my head on his lap, hugging him around his waist. I felt his gentle strokes on my hair, his warm touch on my scalp and I could smell his crude Red Flag cigarettes. I snuggled close to him and felt good. We cuddled in silence.

Then we heard muffled rumbling from the Wonder River. At first it was almost inaudible; then, one beat at a time, calm and rhythmic, the sound of drums drifted into our consciousness, like incense smoke rising in still air, and lifted the heavy weight that had descended on our room. The unhurried yet constant tempo roused us. I looked up at my father. He raised his head towards the low beats in the distance. His eyes grew bigger and glinted for the first time in many days. 'Ah.' He let out a long sigh. 'They are practising hard for the annual dragon boat race; it's not long now.' Originally initiated to honour the patriotic poet Qu Yuan (343–278 BC), southern China's annual dragon boat races took place on the fifth day of the fifth lunar month (late May to early June), and the event had been declared a public holiday by the new government, with the aim of promoting patriotism.

Baba nodded to the rhythm from the river, then rose from his chair, taking my hand in his, and we walked outside the house. Together we sat on the levee wall in silence, listening to the distant drumbeats until dark, ignoring the unfair world around us.

*

'It's futile to carry on here,' I heard Baba telling Mama in bed that night. 'There's no future for us, no future for our children. We must leave.'

'But there's nowhere to go except Macau and Hong Kong.' Mama's voice was soft and comforting, like her touch on me every day that made life so much more tolerable and pleasant. 'We need a visa to go, and I don't think the District Head would approve it. Our family's classification is too unfavourable.'

But Baba sounded determined. 'We have to make a start somewhere, my dear. We must seize every opportunity from now on, by whatever means available to us.'

I loved my father's decisiveness. It made me feel secure.

'The family won't survive here,' he continued. 'The wheel of the revolution is spinning fast towards us, and it will spare no one. I can see it coming now. We have to go.'

Mama thought sending us children to live with my grandmother in Hong Kong was the best way to move ahead. Over the next week or so I listened to their discussions in bed every night until I dropped off to sleep.

'If Ah-ying and Ah-ping apply together they'll be company for each other,' Mama whispered in the dark.

'It's hard enough for one person to be granted a visa – two would be impossible,' Baba said in a low voice.

Mama sighed. She turned over in bed, quietly sobbing, as Baba also sighed.

For a while they couldn't come up with a good enough reason for the application. They also found it hard to choose which older sister to send first, as Ping and Ying were as close as twins and already attending primary school. And Weng was definitely too young and sickly. So in the end they decided I should go to Hong Kong. At the same time, Mama worried that my sisters would never be allowed a visa if I didn't return, while Baba was still hoping things might improve enough that none of my sisters would need to go, and that I might even come back to Shiqi.

There were so many ifs and buts, ideas and dismissals of ideas, sparks of hope here and there, and then the silence of despair, often followed by my mother's quiet sobs and my father's sighs.

'Let's simply apply for Ah-mun to spend a summer holiday with his grandmother,' Baba said. 'The District Head wouldn't think we'd let our only son go, boys being so precious.'

Mama didn't reply, but I could sense how she was feeling.

The problem was, a five-year-old couldn't travel to Hong Kong alone. This put my parents in a dilemma that soon became a torment when the District Head approved my visa application with a grin.

To my parents' great relief, they found out that Mrs Ng, the aunt of my Third Aunt, who we respectfully addressed as Great-

Aunt, had just been granted an exit visa to Hong Kong with her son Sammy so that she could receive American dollars from her husband, a sojourner, and support her family in Shiqi.

Sammy and I had been buddies since infancy, often playing at each other's homes. He lived in town in a big house they called Sojourner's House – all big homes seemed to be owned by sojourners and their families. Everyone called Sammy 'Flea' because he was always running, tumbling and jumping around from dawn till dusk. In fact we were both energetic boys. Every day after kindergarten we raced along the street, climbing trees, kicking pebbles, throwing rocks and constantly jostling each other until we were flushed and soaked in sweat. Mama and Mrs Ng would walk behind us, and our laughter brought smiles to their faces, despite all their worries.

Outside our kindergarten at Mother Dragon's Temple, a huge banyan tree flourished in the subtropical weather, its thick foliage forming a giant canopy that kept the sun away. Its chunky roots were spread out like baby dragons suckling mother earth. On hot summer days, a storyteller would sit under the ancient tree surrounded by a big audience of children, parents, and grandparents minding toddlers and babies. They enjoyed his fascinating renditions of local legends and the classics of literature loved by my parents.

Flea and I would persuade our mothers to take us there after school. Keen to arrive before everyone else, we'd rush out of the classroom as fast as our little legs could carry us.

One day, Flea fell and split open his forehead. I wasn't sure if I'd pushed him or if he'd tripped. It was the first time I saw blood spill, and it covered his face, hands and clothes. For a moment, remembering what Baba had told me about spilling blood, I thought he was about to die. We were so frightened and upset that we couldn't stop crying. The thought that my best friend was dying, and that I might have caused it, shocked me so badly that more than half a century later I can still remember the event in vivid detail.

Mrs Ng stopped the bleeding and cleaned up the wound without making a fuss. On the way home she bought some fresh water-buffalo meat. The next day, with a thin slice stuck to the wound on his forehead, Flea was full of beans again. I stopped feeling guilty and started laughing with him. As if by magic, the cut healed in a few days.

After that I gave up the idea of becoming a high intellectual like my parents, who were sad, had no jobs and had needed to go away to re-education camps. Even though Baba said Mrs Ng wasn't a doctor, she clearly had special skills to be able to heal people. I decided I wanted to be like her and perhaps even become a doctor one day.

CHAPTER 3

On the night before my departure from Shiqi with Flea and Mrs Ng, Mama cried herself into a fitful sleep after holding me tight in her arms and covering my face with kisses and caresses. Baba sighed more and shook his head the next morning when Mama still didn't stop her tears. I couldn't tell whether he was crying too.

I had a white shirt and grey shorts on, and had packed a few clothes into a small bag. After breakfast of rice congee, Mama dipped a comb in water and carefully arranged my hair.

'Hang onto Mrs Ng and don't get lost in the big city. Macau and Hong Kong are much bigger than Shiqi,' she said, her voice trembling. 'Be careful crossing roads because there are many cars and buses there.'

I was more curious about those places than I was sad about leaving home. *Cars and buses?* I didn't think I knew what they were, for there were only carts, bicycles and, occasionally, old army trucks in town. Besides I had never been for a ride on a bus or in a car.

'Be polite to the others. Don't forget to say please and thank you. Be nice to your grandmother, and try your best to behave yourself. Don't make Mama upset.' She then hugged me close to her.

The town's only bus terminal was an ordinary hut with a large yard at the back for the two or three small buses that serviced the town and the surrounding countryside. Each bus had a large boiler at the back, and the crew of our lime-green bus were already burning coal and heating up the water in the boiler. Steam hissed out every now and then and it fascinated Flea and me. We couldn't work out how this was going to power the bus that would take us to the border.

'It's a steam-engine bus,' Baba said, 'so don't sit at the back near the hot tank.'

Now I could see Mama wiping her tears. Baba turned and pleaded with Mama, 'If he misses us badly enough and can't cope, we'll bring him home. But this is our chance for a new beginning, and we must seize it.' He then held me in his big arms and reassured me that everything would be fine as long as I was a good boy for my grandmother.

Baba's eyes shone in a new way that day. They looked determined, to the point of being stern. My heart fluttered and I didn't know how to feel.

My older sisters, rubbing their eyes, huddled against Mama. Weng wouldn't take her puzzled eyes off me; she even flashed her dimples.

We hopped onto the bus and waved goodbye. Baba had one arm around Mama and the other around my sisters, hugging the family together. Mama couldn't stop crying; she lifted her hand but seemed unsure what she should do with it. I began to feel upset as tears kept rolling down her face, and a little confused as to what was really happening. But it was too late to stop the bus now, and I was soon moving off, on my first long trip away from home.

The journey seemed to take nearly the whole day, but was broken from time to time when the driver stopped to pick up passengers or collect coal and water for the steam engine. I was most impressed by the driver, whose old PLA cap exuded revolutionary authority. Passengers obeyed his orders as they got on and off, behaving like chicks with a mother hen.

As for Flea and me, soon we became fascinated by everything, even the shaking and rattling of the bus, the dust it kicked up and the regular blasts of the horn to warn cyclists and pedestrians to get out of the way. We sang revolutionary jingles and marvelled at the green fields outside the window that stretched as far as the eye could see. It all helped make the trip less bothersome – until our stomachs began to rumble. The small buns Mrs Ng had brought along had not been enough and we didn't like her strong lychee tea. We couldn't wait to reach our destination and have some proper food.

At last, we passed through the border checkpoints on both sides and arrived in Macau. Swarms of rickshaw men rushed to offer to take us to our destination. Mrs Ng bargained the fees down to her satisfaction then occupied one rickshaw by herself while Flea and I shared another. Our rickshaws manoeuvred their way among the crowds, big buses, trucks and motorbikes that packed the streets. Flea and I were in awe of the many cars and other vehicles we didn't have in China, and delighted in the many narrow streets and alleyways, with their numerous bakeries and cake shops, from where mouth-watering aromas drifted out and tormented us – by then it was nearly late afternoon and we were starving. Eventually we arrived at Third Aunt's home. I remembered her very fondly, as before she had left Shiqi she had often fed me in her room at our house. Her fine cotton cheongsam was pretty like her face. She gave us a big smile and a warm welcome, and thanked the Goddess of Mercy and Buddha for our safe arrival. Then we had some yummy dim-sums and went for a rest while she chatted to her aunt and caught up on family matters.

After staying the night with Third Aunt, we caught a ferry to Hong Kong the next day. On arrival, we marvelled at the city and its majestic harbour, where countless boats and ocean-going ships of all shapes and sizes, many bearing colourful flags, bobbed up and down in the water. I quietly wondered which big ship had taken my grandfather overseas, and where exactly were the five dragons that lived in the South China Sea. Flea and I were bewildered. It was extraordinary that everything was so different just across the border – and chaotic. No wonder Shiqi people, my parents included, said it was a decadent world in the colonies, something I didn't understand until I was much older.

Mrs Ng delivered me to Grandmother Young, who was living in Sham-shui-po in Kowloon. A poor suburb, it was popular with Chinese transferring money from abroad, as the relatively low living costs there enabled them to pass on more to their Motherland.

I didn't even get a chance to say goodbye to Flea and Mrs Ng, and I never saw them again during my childhood, as they soon moved to another part of the colony. But Grandmother Young welcomed me warmly, offering a cup of hot chocolate and a bread roll with delicious golden butter, and as many biscuits as I liked. The oval-shaped ones she called 'Gold Mountain biscuits' were my favourite. She rented a room in a third-floor apartment at 44 Fook-wing Street, which she shared with her son Chong's mother-in-law, whom I called Grandmother Lee. They rented the room from Mrs Ho and her family, who had the whole apartment on a long-term contract and were able to sublet three rooms to supplement their income. It was already acknowledged, even in those days, that Hong Kong accommodation was exceptionally expensive.

Like Grandmother Lee, Grandmother Young had her well-lacquered hair fashioned into a bun behind her head. My grandmother was in her fifties, but she walked fast and held an upright posture, and even though she wore the plain, loose clothing typically favoured by older Chinese ladies, she looked young for her age. Her voice was loud and strong, especially when she bargained at the market, but always soft and gentle with me. I remember how she told me the rules of living in a flat in the big city: 'Be polite to the adults, keep your voice down, don't go into other tenants' rooms without letting me know, and don't ever go down to the street by yourself. And definitely no running indoors.'

Inside her room, where we all had to share a bed, she had a small altar for General Guan Gong and the Goddess of Mercy, where she burned an incense stick every morning. I particularly liked the sandalwood smell from her joss sticks, as well as the aroma of the morning coffee she brewed from grains before others woke up, and the arrowroot biscuits she soaked in hot milk for me. And I adored gentle Grandmother Lee, who went along with whatever my grandmother decided.

I soon made friends with Je Je, the daughter of the landlady and her husband, Mr Ho. An only child, Je Je had recently started high school. I had her company in the afternoons, and sometimes she took me to school and told her friends that I was her little brother. Her light blue, slightly oversized cheongsam-like school uniform reached halfway down her shins. I was amazed by her English and storytelling skills and couldn't wait for her to come home each day to listen to her reading.

But homesickness soon set in. I was overwhelmed by the pace of Hong Kong life and all the traffic noise, plus the pungent smells of diesel and garbage heaps waiting at roadsides to be collected. Worst of all, there were no playgrounds near us, and definitely no trees or levee walls to climb.

My grandmother didn't know what to do and wasn't sure whether to enrol me in the local kindergarten. She must have noticed how bored I was as I looked down at the busy street below. 'You'll just have to keep playing with Je Je when she comes home,' she said. 'You can't play in the streets, for children are often taken away and never found again.'

Children disappearing! I didn't want that to happen to me so I just sulked at home. When my grandmother ignored me, I went to seek comfort from Grandmother Lee. My grandmother didn't like that. 'I am your real grandmother,' she would remind me when the other grandmother was not around.

Despite receiving plenty of attention from the grandmothers, I desperately missed my family and friends. I also missed shouting slogans and singing revolutionary songs. I felt that I belonged in Communist China, not in dirty, capitalist Hong Kong. I also feared missing my chance to become one of Chairman Mao's loyal children and wear the coveted Red Scarf when I was old enough in primary school.

During my two months in Hong Kong, countless stories of suicide were broadcast on the radio. The hardships faced by the displaced people streaming in from China led many to jump out of the high windows of tall buildings, so the adults told me.

'I'll jump out of the window and die,' I said to Je Je one afternoon. I was looking down from the third-floor window onto Fook-wing Street, missing my family.

She was horrified and told my grandmother. The very next day my grandmother went to her trusted letter-writer around the corner and asked him to write to my parents. Grandmother Young had never been to school and she usually scrawled three Xs as her signature for everything, even when receiving money from grandfather and transferring money to Mama in Shiqi. It must have been so hard for her to navigate Hong Kong in those days.

When my mother's reply arrived, Grandmother Young had to get the letter-writer to read it out. He hesitated, then read on with a sigh: 'Maybe he is too young to leave home. Please bring him home to us ...'

The day before my grandmother took me back to Shiqi, Je Je, who had been my best and only friend in Hong Kong, said with tears in her eyes, 'I'll miss you, Ah-mun.'

'I'll miss you too,' I cried.

She gave me a small portrait of herself in her school uniform which I kept under my pillow for many months after returning home, until one day it mysteriously disappeared.

*

My parents didn't say anything hurtful on my return. Like my sisters, they were happy to have me back.

The first thing I did on arriving in Kwong Street was to run out of the house and climb onto the levee wall, where my cousins and friends from the street were waiting.

'Big Brother, tell us what it's like in Hong Kong.' Skinny, with sun-lightened hair and fair skin, Yiu-hoi was always curious about things. 'Any trains and big ships?'

'Ah-mun, any yummy food there?' Ah-dong rubbed his stomach, and the others laughed or giggled. It made me feel important, like a sojourner.

'Hong Kong is a huge place with many large double-decker buses that carry many people at once,' I said with a certain air of authority.

'What's a double-decker bus?' asked Yiu-hoi.

'They are big red buses, two storeys high. They don't have boilers or steam engines but noisy motors and are powerful enough to carry all of us and a hundred more,' I said. 'And you should see the many cars and lorries we don't have in Shiqi, running all day and night.

'And some of the ocean-going ships and boats in Hong Kong Harbour are bigger than Old Crow Hill.' I hastened to impress them and couldn't stop talking. 'And there's so much bread in different shapes and tastes. Oh, and the bakeries and cookie shops in Macau – ah, just mouth-watering.'

At home that evening Baba said we were at least fifty years behind the Western world, if not more, and stressed how important it was for us to study hard to help China catch up. 'Just be careful, son, what you say to your friends. You may get into trouble with the District Head for spreading capitalist ideas.'

But the District Head was delighted. 'You've defeated capitalism,' he said, patting me on my head, which was still reeking of VO5, a popular men's hair cream from Hong Kong that my grandmother had applied to my hair every day. 'What a good example for everyone to follow.'

Soon I was enrolled again at the First Central Primary School and Kindergarten in the old Dragon Mother's Temple. The Party Secretary and the school principal invited me onto the assembly hall stage, in front of all the students and teachers, and gave me a citation for upholding communism. I was designated a model student for the whole school to emulate because I had turned my back on Hong Kong. It felt wonderful to be a key player in the revolution despite my family's lowly classification. I marched around with my head held high like a hero.

Mama and Baba didn't share my elation. They were unusually quiet for the ensuing weeks, saying little to each other. Baba stopped reading, and Mama constantly looked for old clothes to alter for the younger children, just to keep herself occupied. But my faith in Chairman Mao and the Party had been indelibly imprinted on my mind since my memory began. I was glad that I could continue to follow their directives with earnest conviction. Along with my friends at school, I spent a lot of time singing revolutionary songs and shouting our favourite slogans:

'Down with the American capitalists and their running dogs!'

'Long live Chairman Mao! Long live! Long live!'

'Long live the Chinese Communist Party!'

CHAPTER 4

Now that Flea had gone to Hong Kong, my neighbour Ah-dong became my best friend, aside from my cousins and sisters. Before I'd been old enough to totter outside my front door, his family had moved into one of the unoccupied rooms in house Number 2 along the walled-off compound of Kwong Street.

Ah-dong's father was a senior union official, and I understood that made him an important comrade in town. We rarely saw him around. Ah-dong's mother cared for her son and his younger sisters. Ah-dong had a protruding stomach, which his mother said was full of worms that consumed almost all the food he ate, leaving him with twiggy limbs. No herbs could fix this problem. His skinniness exaggerated his big round head, which seemed ready to roll off his thin neck whenever he ran or chuckled. And he loved to chuckle; that's when his head would sway and his belly jerk.

Together with my cousins Yiu-wei, Yiu-hoi and Ah-ki (who was still a toddler), and my little sister Weng and some other younger kids in the street, we were a happy gang, minding our own business as we played together. Ping and Ying were a few years older than me and uninterested in us. Ah-dong was also two years older, but we were in the same class at school, his mother blaming the worms for his slowness in learning. However, I didn't think there was anything wrong with him: he was witty, likeable and mischievous, and brought a lot of fun to our gang.

School started at seven-thirty each morning, beginning with a political lesson on communism. So as not to be late, I'd drag Ah-dong out of bed every day. By the time we got to school, he'd be fully awake and ready to hear revolutionary words from the Party and Chairman Mao. One morning the talk was on courage and communism. We left the room glowing with patriotic fervour, and it burned deep into our hearts.

Soon enough, an opportunity to prove ourselves arrived.

*

A public execution was about to take place. These gruesome events usually occurred before important national days like May Day, the Anniversary of the Communist Party on 1 July, and of course, the most sacred 1 October commemoration of the PRC. My year level of Second Class was considered too young to bear witness; attendance would be part of our political education once we reached Fourth Class. Needless to say, it was compulsory for all the adults in town to attend as well.

An older boy at school eavesdropped on me and Ah-dong as we mulled over the idea of skipping afternoon classes to witness the execution. He challenged us to go, and offered us a biscuit if we would watch the execution up close. Without saying a word, Ah-dong grabbed the biscuit and ran off after the truck that was parading the condemned prisoner around town. I hurried after him.

Loudspeakers on the truck and on street corners blared out the prisoner's crime of spreading anti-communist thoughts, and cautioned people against such counter-revolutionary activities. The truck crawled through the main streets of town before heading towards Pig Head Hill, a small mound of red earth with clumps of desolate weeds. The hillock stuck out, resembling a pig's head, according to the adults, and was supposedly held down by the mythical tiger's claw on Pagoda Hill. Under the People's Republic, the hillock had become Shiqi's execution ground.

The truck came to a stop there. Ah-dong and I hid behind the adults, narrowing our eyes to slits and peering through the gaps to spy, for the first time, on the killing of a human being.

Sandwiched between two guards in worn PLA uniforms, the prisoner could barely stand. A rope around his neck also tied his arms firmly to his sides. Blood had drained from his face as if death had already taken possession. He was like a dog about to be slaughtered, but he made no struggle, no noise, not even a whimper. Fastened behind his head was a long picket bearing his name in black ink. A bold tick in red paint against his name symbolised that the spilling of his blood was necessary to achieve the goals of the revolution.

My heart went into a wild gallop. At the last moment I wished I wasn't there, and I'm sure my friend felt the same.

The man was dragged to a spot against a slight embankment. At the signal of the People's Militia officer-in-charge, several officers took aim with their rifles and fired.

I shook. My heart pounded harder.

Ah-dong and I covered our ears to muffle the sound of bullets thudding into the prisoner's flesh. They tore through his body, exploding organs. Some wounds oozed and others gushed red like water from a collapsed dam. Not uttering a sound, the man tumbled forward, twitching and writhing. On the ground he rattled and gasped, sucking in erratic breaths. Death came fast. The executioners looked ashen, and were as frozen as the rest of the town. With his hand shaking, the officer in charge pulled out a shiny revolver, walked over to the body and added a few more bullets, until he was satisfied that this enemy of the people could never again rise against the sacred revolution.

The rancid stench of a slaughterhouse swamped the subtropical air. Pig Head Hill slumped into dead silence.

I couldn't stop my teeth clattering, nor could I speak. My shorts were flooded.

All the townspeople stayed quiet until, after another political lecture, the People's Militia let us leave. As most people began to walk away, the prisoner's family remained, wailing and shrieking to release their grief.

At first I couldn't shift my leaden legs. The worst fear arose inside me, that I might be left there by myself with the corpse and all the angry ghosts I'd heard about from the seniors at school. There was Seven Shots, a warlord who'd needed seven bullets to put him down. Then there was the chilling presence of the ghost of a landlord's young concubine, who roamed the lonely hillock searching for her face, which had been blown off when she was executed for some unspecified reason. I wanted to cry, and regretted accepting the older boy's challenge. The stink of blood churned my stomach.

Flies gathered to feed on the congealing blood and splattered organs. Panic shot through me when I imagined that Ah-dong and I could be eaten alive by those hungry beasts once they had finished with the dead.

Somehow we managed to get away from Pig Head Hill. As we left the piercing cries of the family behind us, we entered an eerie silence that had descended on the town of Shiqi.

*

That night I jumped into my parents' bed to sleep. I was too sick to go to school the next day. When I told Baba what I'd done, he put his arm around me and said, 'It's an awful way to die, so senseless.' He lit a cigarette and told me never to witness an execution again.

Over the next few weeks I repeatedly woke from my sleep drenched in a pool of sweat. I shook and gasped, and frantically looked for bullet holes on my body; I had to stop the bleeding. Only by climbing into my parents' bed and sharing their warmth and closeness could I calm down.

I was finding it hard to wipe the scene of the execution from my memory. Shouting slogans didn't help, and neither did wishing harder that Chairman Mao would live for ten thousand years. Teachers complained that I wasn't paying enough attention.

As the year went on, political studies began to make less sense to me. It shocked me profoundly how life could be so fragile, and how easily it could be destroyed in the name of the People's Revolution. Yet I was annoyed with myself for being hopelessly weak as a revolutionary. Disappointment, fear and terror assailed me, along with perplexity at the mysteries of life. My teachers reassured me that as long as I devoted myself to Chairman Mao, I would be safe, and that the Americans and their running dogs would never harm me. But I was sick for months, while Ah-dong continued to stutter and have bad dreams.

Ah-dong's mother complained that his bedwetting had returned because of his nightmares. She filled him up with herbal concoctions that neighbours and relatives suggested might soothe him. She also burned paper money at the crossroads near Come Happiness Road to appease the spirits that she believed now haunted her son.

For many days after the execution the town was numb and lifeless. Everything had ground to a halt. No one spoke. All the adults, even Mama, chain-smoked like Baba. They kept their heads down as though they were distraught hermit crabs withdrawing from the world. The children, too, were subdued and stunned. Even the sparrows stopped chirping.

CHAPTER 5

One night in November 1956, a clatter of footsteps and the banging open of the front gate disrupted my cosy autumn sleep in the small hours of the morning. I woke to torches flashing and voices barking orders. Then a group of People's Militia officers swarmed into our room. Men and women with their shiny long rifles and well-worn PLA uniforms promptly secured their positions.

Baba had barely got himself out of bed when several officers pounced on him and pinned him to the ground. I saw that Wang Ting, one of Baba's former students, was among them. They held Baba's head down on the ground as they put a rope around his neck and tied his hands to his back. Then they sat him on a heavy rosewood chair just outside our bedroom. A few officers pushed Mama and me into the sitting room, while the rest of their party kept searching inside. My sisters ran crying from their room.

Mama was trembling. We huddled behind her.

'What's my crime?' Baba's voice was hardly audible.

'What's your crime? Fuck your mother. You fucking counter-revolutionary,' yelled the leader of the group, a pimple-faced young man, his finger pushing hard on my father's head. His bulging eyes made him look like a starving tiger wrestling its prey. 'Your father was a fucking capitalist. You fucking nationalist, so-called intellectual and scholar. You're a black element in disguise, and your whole family is fucked!'

I had never seen anyone so rudely threaten my parents. How I wished that my legs weren't weak as rice straws and I could have jumped on those nasty intruders.

'Fuck your mother,' the young leader continued to scream. 'We're here to bring you to the justice of the people.' His eyes stuck out even more, like two large lychee nuts about to burst. He cursed my parents, their parents, our ancestors and the whole family, dead and living. At each outburst I shut my eyes and cringed.

Mama held on to us tightly, even though she shook at the insults and accusations. Without her, I could have slumped to the ground like the prisoner at Pig Head Hill. The stench of blood and mangled flesh rushed at me. I wanted to vomit, but nothing came. My mouth was dry and cracked, and I had no voice. I could not move. All I could do was make weird, screechy noises like a dog begging for mercy. I pressed my hands against my ears to block out the abuse barked at Baba and the family.

Baba shuddered at each insult, but, drawing deep breaths, he somehow managed to steady himself. He shook his bowed head in disbelief. Eventually, he gathered his strength and raised his head, fixing his gaze on his ex-student with a look sterner than any I had ever seen him give before. 'Wang Ting,' said Baba in his deep voice. 'Honouring your teacher is a virtue, as much as honouring your own parents. I am here at your mercy, but there's no need to insult and dishonour the rest of my family.' His words, clear and unswerving, quietened the commotion as if spoken in a classroom. 'Don't you have parents, brothers, sisters and families? Shouldn't you treat them with honour and respect? What would you do if their honour was insulted, and their persons outrageously vilified?'

Most of the youths were taken aback, but the militia leader took over again. 'Repent and we may reduce your punishment. Fuck your mother,' he growled at Baba, his voice barely broken. He then tilted his head towards Chairman Mao's portrait on our grey brick wall, showing that Baba's words meant nothing to him.

Baba shook his head again and lowered his gaze back to the terracotta floor. He must have been aware of how frightened we were, and how futile it was to reason with the pubescent gang, let alone deny their accusations. Now a prisoner of the people, he had been banished to the lowest caste in the never-ending proletariat revolution.

By now the cold light of the broken dawn had begun filtering into the house. Our cousins were awake, and Sixth Aunt was comforting them. Yiu-hoi and Ah-ki's parents were away, working in different towns. Tenants gathered around and neighbours congregated outside the front gate to see who had been arrested. Among them were Ah-dong and the other children, including Earring – the new kid who had just moved into the street. They were stunned as we all were. Arrests were common, but knowing that my father had already been to re-education camps several times since the PRC had been proclaimed, they were surprised that he was being persecuted further.

It was a shock to the household – except for Choi-lin, who took over the scene with confidence. She kept the tenants and neighbours from blocking the front door and hindering the officers as they filed in and out of the big house. Choi-lin then approached Baba while the guards looked on, as if she was one of their members. They didn't interfere. We all knew she was a dedicated worker for the Party, a promising young comrade.

'It's time to repent,' she said to Baba. 'The people will forgive you.'

Baba kept his head down and made no response.

I recalled the many questions Choi-lin had asked us kids about Baba and Mama, and the uncles I hardly knew, while offering us lollies. I'd wondered why she was so interested in us.

Mama had stopped shaking and was still holding us close. She didn't look at Choi-lin.

The young woman tried a few more times to draw a reaction from Baba, but he didn't give her anything. She huffed and straightened herself above him, then mumbled something to the leader before marching out of the house, lips tight and face pale.

*

That morning I watched the People's Militia officers carry their shiny weapons with pride, looking solemn, tough and authoritative. Their uniforms were patched, but oh, how they prized them. I had prized them too: I'd always dearly wanted to be part of Chairman Mao's revolution and to wear that uniform when I grew up. But now my father had been arrested, I only felt pangs of hurt, and humiliation – it was clear now that Baba was definitely not a secret agent for the Party.

Some of the officers left our house, soon returning with shovels and hoes. They began digging up the tiled floor of our room, then sifted through the underlying sand to look for weapons they claimed Baba had hidden. He just looked on with quiet resignation and said to us in a strained voice, 'You have nothing to fear. Just be good children for your mother and study hard, very hard.'

He mentioned Chairman Mao, raising his voice with reverence for his captors to hear, trying to let them know that he wasn't a spiteful counter-revolutionary. But they ignored him. Their leader paced up and down the sitting room, wearing an angry expression as he drew hard on a Red Flag cigarette.

I can't recall all the words of wisdom Baba tried to pass on that day. His look of determination was etched in my memory forever, though, together with his desperate wish that we must all aim for an education.

Mama lit a cigarette and held it to his lips. The rope around his neck was so tight that veins bulged each time he drew a puff. She said nothing to him. They seemed to have accepted their fate as they submitted themselves to the authorities. The charge of counter-revolution meant the prospect of the most severe punishment from the People's Court.

Officers started pulling out our belongings and carefully examining each item. Mama looked on helplessly. I saw fear swirl in her eyes. As she began to attend to our breakfast – the usual watery rice porridge – she was in tears. We kids didn't want to eat; we wanted to stay close to Baba, who was still tied to the rosewood chair. A few young guards stood over him, solemn as ever, as their comrades extended their search to the whole house. They took away family photographs and old letters, and left the living quarters in a mess.

Baba told us to go to school and assured us that he'd still be at home when we returned. Mama agreed. She was feeding him breakfast with a spoon as the guards looked on.

With much reluctance, we went off to school. People stood outside their doors and stared at us, whispering after we walked past. Some sighed to express their sympathy for the family they had known for generations. A few bolder ones shook their heads to object to what had happened, and bowed to us. No one was bold enough to speak up.

*

Baba's arrest was on my mind all day – the longest and worst of my life. I worried about how I'd be treated as the son of the latest black element in town. Maybe other kids wouldn't ever play with me again; instead they'd taunt me with all kinds of awful names. I also worried about never earning my Red Scarf. And I'd never become a Party member as all my schoolmates would.

But worst of all were the thoughts of the public sentencing meetings that could condemn my father to be shot at Pig Head Hill or sent to a labour camp far from home for a long, long time. This idea sickened me and seized me with such terror that I lost control of my bladder again. I was ill all day.

Everyone at school seemed to be talking about us. I heard many unpleasant stories about my family – things I'd never heard before. My sisters were crying. No one dared to sympathise with us because to do so would have been counter-revolutionary.

The dream I'd long cherished of my father being on a secret mission for the revolution had collapsed into ruins around me. I felt naked before the whole town.

Finally the noon lunchbreak arrived. My sisters and I hurried home among the midday crowds of schoolchildren, pedestrians and cyclists. How we hoped we would find our father at home.

On the highest point of Come Happiness Bridge, we saw Baba and the arrest party heading towards us. A chill closed around me like a steel jacket, paralysing me.

Baba was being marched away at gunpoint on the other side of the road. The militia leader walked a few steps behind, holding the end of the rope tied around my father's neck. Baba mostly kept his head down, but from time to time he looked up as if hoping to see us among the lunchbreak crowds. He spotted us almost at the moment we saw him.

Ignoring scores of cyclists rushing about, we ran across the road. My sisters held on to Baba's legs, and I threw myself at his feet. We wept without shame. He couldn't bend over because the rope around his neck was choking him, so he lowered himself to his knees to be close to us. Tears rolled down his face.

At that moment I was no longer embarrassed about my father. I no longer cared what other children thought about me. I wouldn't even have cared if I was never awarded a Red Scarf. I didn't want that Liberation Army uniform. I only wanted Baba to be with us.

We clung to him, oblivious to the people around us. Some neighbours sobbed quietly but with their heads half-bowed, a flash of silent protest in their eyes.

Wailing, my sisters and I kept a tight grip on Baba. He made us promise to study hard and to be good, useful people. A distinctive scar in the middle of his forehead didn't mar the handsome face of a man in his prime. What's more, there wasn't a trace of fear in his eyes. His strength reached us in a way that nobody else could have detected. Passers-by paid little attention: arrests were a common sight and people tended to mind their own business for fear of attracting attention from the authorities. We were isolated in our grief, but in that instant, as a family, we were also united forever.

'Get a good education and never stop learning,' he reminded us once more. 'Keep your heads high, and don't be afraid—'

The militia leader pulled on the rope, and Baba choked.

The officers then prised us from Baba as he struggled to finish his goodbyes. They dragged him away, leaving us howling on top of Come Happiness Bridge. Loudspeakers on the street corners blared out Chairman Mao's message: 'The revolution has not completely succeeded yet. Comrades, we all have to continue to work hard for its final triumph.'

*

I didn't want to shout slogans or sing and dance to revolutionary songs anymore.

In the months that followed Baba's arrest, I had even more trouble sleeping. I often woke from a restless night filled with fear and hopelessness. Rather than staying in bed tossing and turning, I'd slip out of the house in the early hours to sit on the levee wall.

Time and again I was seized by such a state of terror that I couldn't help wondering what it would be like to be dead. At other times I would try to capture a last twinkle of hope in the stars, wishing they would keep me company a bit longer in the dark. But every dawn I was disappointed when they faded.

CHAPTER 6

What exactly was Baba's crime? I didn't know, and I couldn't understand. I asked myself, *Doesn't my family deserve to be part of the new China we're all so proud of? Aren't we all equal, as Chairman Mao tells us every day? Aren't we one people like brothers under the Party? Why do we have to eradicate people so that the revolution can go on?* I had many questions but no answers, and no one else to ask.

My teachers, knowing I was at a crossroads, tried to bolster my revolutionary spirit and guide me back to the true path. In morning political studies they repeated Chairman Mao's words to me, but I was unable to recite them with enthusiasm. Unimpressed, they stood me in front of the class and said I was the son of the latest counter-revolutionary in town; they explained how family classifications could undermine a child's desire to be a true follower of the Party, and how to overcome that. 'This is the triumph of people's vigilance under Chairman Mao,' the class teacher told the children.

When this didn't pull me out of my despondency, both teachers and schoolmates began telling me to wake up, and be strong and bold enough to denounce my father and his crime. 'You must have courage to eliminate even your own parents for the sake of the revolution,' Comrade Teacher Wong said to me every day. But I loved my parents, and the thought of betraying them never entered my mind. I lowered my gaze, wouldn't look anybody in the eye and sought solace in my own self.

On the streets some of the schoolchildren treated me and my sisters worse than beggars, and some of our friends stopped playing with us. A few nasty ones called us names. Ying and Ping often cried at school, and Weng was also sad, but too young to understand what was going on. I sat by myself and avoided others. I couldn't pay attention in class.

One day my sadness turned to anger, and I decided to fight three of the bullies. They were boys from a nearby street who wouldn't stop taunting us. That day, I replaced the books in my schoolbag with pieces of rock as big as peaches. As my sisters and I were crossing Come Happiness Bridge, the three boys appeared as usual, and began to tease us and call us names. 'Son and daughters of a counter-revolutionary, see you on Pig Head Hill,' they jeered.

When we didn't respond, one of them rubbed a handful of sand into Weng's hair and said, 'Here's something for you, capitalist piggie.'

Weng cried. The boys laughed. They followed us and kept yelling. Frightened for their own political safety, the adults on the street dared not interfere.

With rocks in my hands, I charged at the boys. They were stunned and ran off, but soon returned, threatening to beat us up. I threw a rock at the boy who'd assaulted Weng. Blood ran down his face. He cried in pain. The others ran away, for good this time.

The injured boy's father complained to the head of our street committee, who came to our house and demanded I be taught a lesson. 'I'm not leaving until you show me this brat is punished,' he snarled at Mama. 'That poor boy will carry a scar on his forehead forever.' The Street Committee Member stayed on to watch Mama discipline me.

She grabbed my wrist and hit me with a fallen gum-tree branch that I'd collected for firewood on Come Happiness Road. Her eyes were shut, but I could see pain on her face. She beat me hard, as if releasing her pent-up sorrow and anger all at once. I screamed. But she didn't stop until the stick broke into pieces.

That evening when she was attending to my bruises and welts, she wept more. 'Sorry, my son, I'm so sorry.' Mama couldn't stop sobbing as she took me into her arms.

It was the first and only time she beat one of her children.

Although Mama and I suffered for my standing up to the bullies, that was the last time those boys annoyed us. Other children also moderated their teasing, and looked on from a distance as my sisters and I walked to and from school holding hands.

*

While Baba was in prison awaiting trial, the District Head made frequent visits to see Mama, who had to be available. He wanted to make sure her political thinking was unchanged, and to urge her to take a stand against her husband. The odour of the District Head's cigarettes always heralded his entry into our home. A bulge under his patched army uniform made us suspect he wore a revolver, the type of gun often carried by comrades in town.

'Help your husband to admit he is a counter-revolutionary,' he said to Mama in the stern manner of comrades with authority. 'Help him to plead guilty for his crime against our Motherland. Help him to beg for mercy from the People's Court.'

In a timid voice Mama mumbled, 'If he didn't do any of those things, what has he got to admit to the People's Court?'

'Confess that he is a counter-revolutionary in hiding!' he shouted at her.

The District Head usually spoke to Mama in a strident official tone that frightened us children. But other times he tried to seem understanding and even friendly towards her. On those occasions he wore a silly grin that I hated, and which Ying said nauseated her – those yellow teeth and shifty eyes. Ping agreed.

One day he tried to whisper in Mama's ear while they stood in our family's shared room. I looked up at them from my homework.

Oh, how I hated him drooling over Mama. I went over and held on to her. She folded her arms across her chest and tightened her grip on the lapel of her worker's jacket. Together we edged away from the patched army uniform. I stared up at him, but Mama kept her head bowed, not daring to meet his gaze.

Every time he came to our house, the District Head delivered the same advice. And with her head lowered, my mother gave the same reply. I could feel her quiet strength as she resisted. He would become impatient, pacing inside our room and hissing at us, before marching out of the house without humming 'The East Is Red'.

*

My mother had lost her smile; a frown took over her once pretty face. Not even the mail carrying our regular allowance from Hong Kong made her beam anymore. Whenever I was at home with her, I listened to her moans and sighs from morning to night. She wept in her bed as I wept in mine. I tried not to be too loud so that she couldn't hear me – I didn't want my sadness to make her more miserable. On my mind was the constant fear that she might kill herself, like those unhappy people in Hong Kong. Before I could let myself fall asleep I listened to her breathing to make sure she was still alive.

From as early as I could remember, suicides had been common in town, and the old lychee tree not far from our house was a popular location for hangings in the night. We would never forget how two bodies were recovered one morning. My sisters, my cousin Yiu-hoi, my friends Ah-dong and Earring and I walked to school on the opposite side of the road to the tree, hurrying in case ghosts were following us. I had visions of my mother hanging from its thick, sprawling branches. I was also petrified that she might throw herself into a well, or the nearby Nine Meanders River or off Come Happiness Bridge. I ran home from school every day and was relieved to find her there, even though she always wore the same expressionless face.

During Baba's imprisonment in town she visited him every week, taking him food, personal items and, most importantly, letters from his kids, as we weren't allowed to visit him. He loved our letters and always asked how we were doing at school. He sent messages back, urging us to study hard and never to stop learning. Mama told us that though his hair had turned grey, his spirit was still strong. But each visit left her more drained and shrivelled. She could barely lift her eyes to look at us, and when she did all I saw were tears trickling down her face. It would take a few days for her to gather enough courage to visit him again.

Mama had to attend evening re-education meetings designed for spouses and families of the accused while they awaited trial. The prisoners' loved ones had to be prepared to denounce them before they were presented to the People's Court.

I went with Mama to keep her company. In the hall of the Wonder River Primary School nearby, everyone sat quietly on little stools they'd brought with them as the District Head and his committee members repeatedly encouraged the audience to be bold and patriotic, and to have the courage to stand up and denounce any criminals in their family or friendship circle. He frequently quoted Chairman Mao's assertion that the revolution was not a dinner party but 'an insurrection, an act of violence by which one class overthrows another'. Occasionally someone stood up to criticise a loved one, while the District Head and his committee members would be busy taking notes for future reference.

Mama told us that Baba, too, had to attend evening political sessions, although his were held after a long day's hard labour while he waited for his hearing. Each prisoner was routinely put through interrogations until they agreed to the confession prepared for them, which would become evidence in their trial. Baba's interrogators kept him awake for three days and nights in one grilling session; he was so exhausted that he admitted to whatever allegations they put in front of him, except for being a counter-revolutionary.

It seemed to me that Baba was in prison for months before his trial date at the People's Court was set, so he must have confessed. But I can't remember Mama denouncing him at the local meetings.

Once the date was scheduled, close to the PRC Proclamation Day of 1 October, the District Head stopped visiting Mama. And she had a break from the evening meetings, so we could all sit together at home discussing schoolwork.

Whenever she had a rare free moment, Mama went around town to find out how things were run in court and how she might lessen my father's sentence by offering gifts to certain people. The District Head indicated that he wanted a galvanised-iron basin for his children like the one we were using, so Mama insisted that he take ours, saying we had outgrown it. We used a small basin to wash ourselves after that.

CHAPTER 7

In 1956, before Baba's arrest, the authorities had told us at school and through loudspeakers that Chairman Mao had made a historic swim across the Yangtze River and had then decided to improve physical fitness across the nation. His example left all the people of China revelling for months, marvelling at and celebrating his prowess.

Overnight, swimming became popular, even in Shiqi, where drownings were common in the many waterways. Folklore had it that the spirits of the drowned would return on the anniversary of their death to look for a replacement who would free them from their torment in the clutches of the river. No matter how much paper money people burned to soothe the ghosts, together with offerings of incense sticks and prayers by the river, drownings continued.

But after the Chairman's exploits, swimming quickly came to enjoy a higher revolutionary status than all other sports. And for adults it was a respite from the endless evening political studies, campaigns and purges. I didn't blame them; they must have been so exhausted after a long day's work and, like Mama, burdened with loads of worries. People began to spend a great deal of time in the water; even older women took to the river that had frightened them since childhood. Before long, swimming became an obsession for the whole town – men and women, young and old alike, swam in

63

rivers, dams and streams. Across China, every village, town and city organised its own swimming events, such as river races, to follow Chairman Mao's call.

Ying immediately showed a talent for swimming. Her anger, sadness and dissatisfaction had finally found an outlet, Mama would say later. Ying just said she swam fast so she could get away from the District Head's smirking face.

Before long, she powered through every race, and she became the town's champion at the age of twelve. Little children followed her around, admiring her as if she were a movie star or a liberation hero. She started to smile again. Oh, how I admired my sister! With her cropped hair, big round shoulders and upright posture, she looked grown up. She trained every day before and after school in the town's brand-new pool not far from home. She stopped slamming doors and became closer to Mama.

In the spring of 1957, a special swimming event was organised in Shiqi. All those in town who were deemed physically capable would swim across the Wonder River to commemorate Chairman Mao's inaugural swim across the Yangtze the summer before.

'Attendance at this patriotic event is compulsory for everyone in Shiqi,' our teacher reminded the class the day before. 'I want all of you here first thing in the morning, and we'll go as a group.'

I was already excited. I'd been taught to swim by Baba and aspired to be a fast and powerful swimmer like my older sister. I also wanted to prove how much I still loved Chairman Mao despite what had happened to my family. 'Everything he says, I'll do,' was what I told myself all the time now that I was in a happier mood, even though Baba was then still in jail awaiting his hearing in the People's Court. I even decided to keep working hard towards my Red Scarf, hoping that this revolutionary symbol would help elevate my family's low status. It might even reduce Baba's sentence, and this was my secret obsession.

That night, I couldn't settle in my sleep. I wanted to prove myself, knowing that Baba would be so proud of me if he knew I had crossed the town's biggest river.

Early in the morning, Mama was already up and attending to the watery rice porridge. 'Ah-mun, stop,' she sang out as I rushed towards the door. 'It's only seven o'clock, too early. Eat your breakfast.'

'Not hungry,' I said, and ran next door to pull Ah-dong out of bed for the big swim. I wanted us to be the first at school before marching to the riverbank at the widest section of water near the shipyard. There, we would conquer the river together.

It was before eight when we got there.

'Wow, so many people. No room for us.' Ah-dong was now wide awake with excitement, patting his tummy of worms and ready for the challenge.

'We're swimmers, so there must be room,' I said, following our teacher as she took the class to where the whole school was assembling.

I noticed that the adult participants, dressed in swimming costumes of all kinds, appeared eager to swim as they waited with their production unit teams. Some complained of the lingering winter cold as they danced around to keep warm, while others huddled in their thin towels. Many spectators were rugged up in woollen clothes.

The starting guns fired shot after shot as team after team of swimmers dived into the rising river, the crowd of spectators cheering them on.

It was nearly noon before our turn arrived, and by then we were shivering and stiff in the icy snap, and also hungry. Standing on the makeshift bamboo platform, I saw an exceptionally high tide with swift currents jostling to get downstream. Hundreds of people were being tossed about in the wash, struggling to swim across. Some ended up drifting further downriver, and quite a few had to be rescued by fleets of sampans that dotted the Wonder River.

Spectators cheered. Drums boomed. Hundreds of red flags fluttered in the north wind.

I was a thin seven-year-old boy and small for my age compared to some of my friends, especially Ah-dong with his large tummy.

Yet we were all trembling in the cold. The waves were capped in white, a clear sign of danger according to my father who had taught me how to read the river during our fishing trips. Now I appreciated his teaching me how to float and swim at a younger age! But I couldn't see the bank on the other side and I suddenly realised it was beyond my reach as a swimmer. I feared that I might drown and be entangled with those water spirits in the bottom of the river forever.

When the starting gun fired, I decided not to dive in.

'C-c-come … my c-c-comrade …' Ah-dong motioned for me to dive with him, his voice quavering in the chill. Other schoolmates were already in. Ah-dong belly-flopped into the river, which swallowed him up in one gulp.

I now stood alone on the platform, unable to stop shivering. The icy wind howled.

The whole town burst into boos and laughter, taunting the brother of their swimming champion. I burned with embarrassment and defeat as my friends bobbed up and down, battling the waves and struggling to keep afloat. I shut my ears to the jeers and slunk away.

Later that afternoon I was sitting on the levee wall when Ah-dong walked over and told me not to worry about the debacle. I was glad he cared, at least.

'How could I not worry about it?' I replied, staring out at the lotus pond. 'What a fool I made of myself.'

Then my friend Big Eye dropped by. 'You're always my good friend, Ah-mun, no matter what. Who cares about the swim? I nearly drowned in the cold river.'

Nicknamed for his large round eyes, Big Eye had started kindergarten with me at the Dragon Mother's Temple in town and soon become one of our gang of playmates. His father was a sojourner who had recently returned after many years away in Canada. Big Eye was nearly twenty years younger than the next oldest of his two elder brothers. The family lived less than a kilometre away from us but in town.

Even with two friends supporting me, I was still disappointed in myself. But Mama wasn't. 'I'm proud of you, my son, my brave boy,' she said to me. 'You made a decision and stood by it. That's strength, not weakness.' She gripped my shoulders, her eyes meeting mine. 'And it's important to be honest with yourself. Humiliation gives you an understanding of how others feel. Humility makes you a better person.'

In the following days, her reassurance helped me to ignore the scornful stares and chicken noises from the other kids as I walked to and from school.

*

For a while I shied away from my friends and turned to comic books, simplified classics like *Journey to the West* and *Water Margin*, and practised the calligraphy Baba had taught me. I was fascinated by the Monkey King and his many adventures, the playful yet mischievous deeds that repeatedly got him into trouble with his master during their pilgrimage to the sacred centres of Buddhism. I also loved the rebels in the *Water Margin*, whose tactics in their struggle against feudalism resembled the guerrilla warfare employed by Chairman Mao in the battles that had led to his final victory.

I wrote to Baba and re-read my textbooks. When I got bored, I enjoyed doing the exercises at the end of each chapter in the maths book. This became a habit. I read all the textbooks and finished every maths exercise by the 1 October celebrations. I'd then be bored until the new term started and new textbooks arrived. I found that I always needed something to keep me occupied.

Without Baba around, I took charge of some household chores to keep busy and help Mama. As soon as I'd finished my homework, I would go out to collect the lush young grass that grew by the local farming collective's fishponds and the leftover cabbage leaves in the vegetable garden, then use them to feed our rabbits, chickens and ducks. I cleaned their cages, topped up their drinking water, recorded the quantity of eggs laid, swept up their waste and used it to fertilise the vegetable garden. Every day I scooped water from the creek that ran along the paddy field on the other side of the wall and sprinkled it on our potatoes, carrots, spinach and cabbage. On the weekends I began to fish in nearby waterways to supplement my family's diet.

When I was out on the water, I was again glad to have my cousins Yiu-hoi and Ah-ki, who was then just three years old, plus my loyal friends Ah-dong and Big Eye at my side. Together we discovered good fishing spots, and our catch was the envy of the others.

Soon more children in the street joined us, and my swimming catastrophe was forgotten. With nets we combed through the small streams, ditches and creeks for fish, small crabs, prawns and eels. The sweet fragrance of the country air and the endless birdsong followed us wherever we romped, reminding us of the Wonder River's never-ending warmth and gentleness, and its perpetual gifts to the people who have populated its banks for thousands of years.

With so much occupying me, I would forget about communism, Chairman Mao's quotations, Marxism, Stalinism and Leninism, and all the brainwashing slogans, even the American capitalists and their running dogs. The joy of a good catch was more exciting than all those added together.

Mama often said she was proud of me, and that mattered to me most of all.

*

In the summer of 1957, Mama applied for Ping, who was then nearly eleven years old, to go to Hong Kong, ostensibly to spend the long school holiday with Grandmother Young. The District Head, his mood lifted by his discovery of a swimming star in his precinct, and perhaps still impressed by my voluntary return from Hong Kong, or maybe just satisfied that Baba was in jail awaiting his sentencing and dispatch to a labour camp, signed Ping's travel documents without hesitation.

After Baba's arrest, Grandmother Young was too scared to come to collect Ping in case the authorities might not let her return to Hong Kong, so Mama asked a cousin from Hong Kong to take Ping there. Ying was busy attending swimming competitions in and out of town.

As we saw Ping off at the bus station, I was glad that she would soon meet my friends Je Je and Mrs Ho. Mama didn't seem so pleased, though: beneath a tight frown her face was devoid of expression. Clearly, Baba's upcoming sentencing was weighing on her, and now one of her daughters was leaving Shiqi. I could tell that Ping had mixed feelings about her departure: she was so fond of Grandmother and excited that she'd be living with her again, but from the way she repeatedly wiped her eyes with her handkerchief, it was also apparent that she hated to leave us. Weng meanwhile was baffled by all that was going on.

CHAPTER 8

Soon after Baba's court appearance, Mama got news that he was on the list for public sentencing. It was just a few days before 1 October 1957, the Eighth Anniversary of the PRC, the year I'd be turning eight. The pre-October sentencing was always the biggest because all the 'unwanted scum' had to be despatched before our National Day celebrations – as the street loudspeakers told us repeatedly. Mama tried many times to get information about Baba from the District Head, but he wouldn't divulge anything and told her to wait.

The day finally arrived. All production units, factories, schools and shops were closed for the occasion, and at noon the townspeople assembled at Shiqi's only sportsground. That year, the cold blast from the north had hit early. Despite the crisp air, clear sky and bright sun, there was an all-encompassing sense of gloom. It was suffocating.

Patriotic songs blasted from the many loudspeakers positioned in strategic corners. PLA soldiers were on duty, assisted by a large number of People's Militia units. With their shiny bayonets piercing the innocent sky, they looked fearsome. In contrast, the civilians were subdued, heads down, huddling close to each other on the packed oval where they either sat on their small stools or squatted – they were not allowed to stand. No one talked openly, but murmurs ebbed and flowed across the sea of people in their shades of army green and worker blue. Only the coughing of smokers and the clearing of their phlegmy throats disrupted the melancholic scene. Small clouds from cigarettes mingled to form a thin haze, delicate and directionless, hovering and drifting, as if trying to rise above the wall of imposing red flags that encircled us.

A burst of thundering drums brought everyone to attention. Even the smokers stopped coughing when the trucks carrying at least fifty prisoners screeched to a stop by the side of the concrete podium at the far end of the sportsground.

The People's Militia escorted the prisoners, with their shaved heads, onto the stage in a neat line. From a distance, I saw Baba take his position. He was the eighth-last prisoner in the line-up – and sentencing always began with the least serious offenders. Noting this, Mama shook her head in despair, mumbling to herself, 'Oh, no. Oh, no. That's the end. That's it.' Her dry lips quivered, and she began to rock back and forth. My sisters and I huddled close to her. We were all quiet. Sadness had already inflamed our eyes. Tears trickled down Mama's distorted face and were sucked up by the red earth.

The high-volume loudspeakers easily overcame any whimpers from the crowd. One by one the guards walked the prisoners to the front of the stage. They were tied up in the same way that the executed man had been, their arms bound at the back with rope that also wrapped around their necks like a noose, restricting their breathing if they moved their arms. They remained motionless, their heads bowed, as the Party Secretary of Shiqi read out their crimes. Several prisoners before Baba received ten to fifteen years in a labour camp. The townspeople shook their lowered heads in disbelief as they heard the sentences.

When Baba's turn came, he stood motionless as the accusations against him were announced. His face was paler than his newly shaven scalp, but empty of expression. He had lost weight. Buffeted by the north wind, he looked feeble. He nodded to acknowledge his accuser, then admitted to the confession that he'd signed during interrogation. They sentenced him to fifteen years in prison for re-education through labour. He nodded again to accept the punishment as fair.

Mama was weeping so much that she turned blue in the face. Ah-dong's mother put an arm around her for support, saying nothing for fear of being labelled a supporter of a disgraced family. A few neighbours shook their heads and wept in silence, showing their quiet support for the family, which we acknowledged in silence – anything more obvious might land them in trouble too.

The sound of coughing and throats clearing resumed, echoing through the packed sportsground amid sporadic whimpering from the prisoners' relatives and friends. More cigarettes were lit as people sought sanctuary in their own thoughts.

Each of the four prisoners after my father was sentenced to twenty years in prison. The last three were executed that afternoon, following the usual parade through town on the back of a truck. The prisoners already looked dead before they reached Pig Head Hill.

*

It was midwinter, January 1958, not long after my eighth birthday, when they marched Baba and hundreds of his fellow prisoners off to board a train from the provincial capital, Guangzhou, to their final destination in Heilongjiang, bordering Siberia. Mama was allowed to see him off, but we, his children, his Precious Ones, had been told we couldn't be there. The District Head didn't want us to be contaminated by the bad elements of our new society.

This must have been one of the saddest moments in Mama's life. She knew that she might never see her husband again, and that their children would all be grown up by the time he'd served his fifteen-year prison term – if he could survive it. She was withering before our eyes in her faded blue worker's tunic.

Before dawn on the morning of Baba's departure, Mama woke us and gathered us together in the third lounge room. There, she burned an entire bunch of incense sticks in one go. There was no food in her offering to our ancestors because there was none in the house. We seemed to always be looking forward to Grandmother Young's monthly living allowance from Hong Kong to buy food, although there was little rationing at the time. All we could provide in return for their blessings were three small cups of tea made from young lychee leaves that I had collected. We bowed and prayed to our ancestors for Baba's safety.

After the simple ceremony Mama rushed off, heading towards the west side of Shiqi where the Wonder River Bridge connected town to country. It began as the same road that linked Shiqi to Shenmingting, then after crossing the river it branched sharply north towards Guangzhou.

I went outside to sit on the levee wall, trying to recapture the times Baba and I had spent there together. The north wind stung my face and hands, so I pulled up the collar of my padded jacket and lowered the earflaps of my PLA-style cap. The solidity of the surrounding darkness unnerved me. The bitter wind whipped at me without mercy. I cried as I thought of the fifteen years that would have to pass before I would see Baba again. It was a long time, almost twice my lifetime. How would he be when he came home? What would I be then, as a man in my early twenties? Could we still have fun together? Would we go fishing in the lotus pond or the rivers, or even the sea that we had never managed to visit? Would he recognise me and put his strong arms around me, holding me close so I could smell his cigarettes? These questions and many others washed over me with my tears.

The first light had not yet arrived, and the frost cut into my hands as I got down from the levee wall. Despite the ban, I was determined to see Baba one last time. And perhaps he'd see me.

I caught up with Mama and followed her in the predawn darkness, keeping a good distance between us so she wouldn't know that I was disobeying the District Head's order.

The cold wind blew across town, slicing through the narrow streets and alleyways. It pierced my padded jacket and nipped at my skin. The dim light from the miserable street lights trembled.

The People's Militia guards were still on duty, cowering inside their padded PLA jackets, ever ready to defend Shiqi from would-be invaders. Dogs barked as we made our way towards the Wonder River Bridge.

Exposed debris made the river look gloomy. The water seemed frozen as it receded towards the east to join other rivers on their way to the South China Sea. A small crowd of adults had gathered along the east bank. I noticed a few older children among them, and I shared the feeble defiance in their eyes. No one was talking, but there were quiet sobs and the blowing of noses accompanied by familiar phlegmy coughs. People lowered their heads in humility to acknowledge the prisoners' wretched fates. Mama was in the crowd, unaware I was on the other side of the bridge.

Approaching footsteps thumped on the gloomy street.

We turned our heads towards the sound.

The prisoners soon appeared, walking two abreast. They wore new padded khaki jackets with large bold numbers painted on the front and back. They walked with their heads down, but from time to time their eyes searched the anxious faces of the waiting crowd for their loved ones.

As the column slowed at the Wonder River Bridge, people began to walk alongside the prisoners. And now, I noticed, Mama was by Baba's side. The backs of their hands touched as they moved in unison, tied by an invisible knot.

Much to everyone's surprise, the guards' stony faces softened. They even averted their gaze, allowing the prisoners to relish their last sensations of home: the silhouette of the Pagoda Hill in the first light, the muddy-fishy smell of the river, and the warmth of their loved ones.

Most of the prisoners were crossing the Wonder River for the last time. Heilongjiang, better known as the Great Northern Wilderness to us southerners, was a long way from home. Few would survive its severe cold to see Shiqi again.

I edged closer, trying to hear what my parents were saying to each other. Then I saw Baba take hold of Mama's free hand, while her other hand tried to wipe away those endless tears. Her small frame trembled in her worker's jacket.

I pushed through the crowd to reach Baba. I held on to him and couldn't stop crying. He bent down and picked me up. He held me close, pressing my face against his. Our tears joined together as they trickled down to my neck and onto my chest. I tasted the saltiness and locked it in my heart permanently. I felt hot and started to sweat, but I didn't care.

We walked on. Mama clung to both of us, and couldn't stop crying. The small bridge seemed to stretch out forever, exactly as I had wished for. We didn't speak, but I am sure that our hearts beat loudly as one into the silence of that morning.

It was there that I experienced the most powerful feeling of love and belonging, a moment of inexplicable magic and pain. I knew then this would remain with me all my life. At the same time, it was a moment of utter vulnerability, dejection and despondency. But there was no time to scream for justice – our remaining time together was too precious to be squandered in righteous indignation. We just kept walking in a huddle, feeling the warmth and strength of each other, so fierce that even the piercing north wind couldn't disrupt our sense of unity.

As we finished crossing the bridge, Baba promised to come home to us, and Mama pledged to stick to the plan they had hatched for the family. One day, somewhere, we would be reunited.

A light mist rose in the icy air with a fragile eeriness while the river flowed on. I saw eternity in the eddying tide under the bridge. How I wanted it to take away my family's sorrow and misfortune, but at the same time maintain our hope of a peaceful life together in a place we could call home, no matter how far away.

*

More than a month later, Baba's first letter arrived. It was brief. He sent his love to each of us and asked about our progress at school, urging us to study hard and become good citizens of New

China. He spent the larger part praising Chairman Mao for giving him the opportunity for re-education and making him realise how important it was to continue the People's Revolution. He also praised the Chinese Communist Party for its leadership. He mentioned very little about the prison camp, except that the winter snow piled high everywhere.

'The letter's been opened and resealed,' Ying said. She pressed the envelope to her cheek, savouring it as though it was Baba's touch.

'The camp authority must have inspected it,' Mama said. 'So did our local authority.' But she didn't seem to care how many times the short letter had been opened and resealed. She read it a few more times, and a faint smile rose on her face. How I wished that smile would stay there.

My sisters and I snuggled close to her and wept. We were all relieved that Baba had arrived safely at the prison, but we were worried about the extreme cold.

After that we wrote often to Baba, being careful what we said. We soon learnt to censor our expressions of affection, and to ensure that everything was politically correct. With some luck, we believed, this might count towards his re-education merit points.

*

'No, not that grinning face again,' Ying said as she noticed the District Head appear at the front of our house. She went straight to her room and slammed the door.

I overheard him telling my mother to resume evening meetings for prisoners' spouses. Three times a week, Mama would need to leave us at home while she attended these meetings under the watchful eyes of the District Head and his committee members.

'He's here to bolster our revolutionary spirits,' Mama said later to us kids. 'Just to make sure we continue to be progressive and patriotic, and don't yield to anger.'

'Hate him,' Ying said.

At school she was regularly made to stand up in class and denounce Baba. Humiliated and shamed by the teachers and classmates for being the daughter of a counter-revolutionary, she'd cry all the way home.

The street seemed to be subdued. Some neighbours talked quietly as we passed by; others looked the other way.

Mama, meanwhile, was eating little and sighing a lot. She moved about with her head down. Other times she sat alone in the dark, grasping my father's letters in her hands. She rarely spoke and didn't want to go to bed. She started a habit of smoking in Baba's favourite corner. Each time she turned to look at us, she burst into tears. We kept reminding her that Baba had done nothing wrong and that they would release him soon, even though the fifteen-year sentence seemed interminably long.

In the small hours of the morning I often went to sit on the levee wall and wait for light to arrive from the east to mark off another day of Baba's imprisonment. One time, a strange calm came over me that I found impossible to define. Maybe it was a sense of acceptance. I jumped off the wall and ran to my mother. 'Everything will be good again, Mama. Please don't be sad today.'

She looked at me and murmured, 'Yes, it'll be good one day.'

I did the same the next day, then every day after that. I felt better afterwards and reassured myself that Baba would eventually be free, and that we would live happily together as one family again.

But Mama's misery continued, especially when a letter from my father was due but didn't arrive. On those mornings she sat waiting for the postman on her little bamboo stool at the entrance to our street. She stared into the distance, an unsmoked cigarette burning between her fingers.

For her, it seemed life wasn't worth living, except for the sake of the children. A panic came over me each time I saw her stare in the direction of the old lychee tree. I put my arms around her, hoping to fend off her desperate thoughts. She stroked my hair, drenching it with tears as we hugged in silence.

*

Towards the end of 1957, Ying had been selected to train with the Guangdong Provincial Swimming Squad at the Guangzhou Sports Institute. To be included in any sporting squad meant you were among the best in the state, and the institute's intensive training was designed to improve performances further. In 1958 she represented Guangdong in the national swimming competition in Beijing, an important event held partly to commemorate our Chairman's Yangtze conquest. It was a great honour for us, and, I suspected, for the whole town of Shiqi as well, not least the District Head. Since Ying specialised in butterfly stroke and was the youngest member of the squad, they called her the Little Butterfly.

Basking in the glory of having discovered a talented swimmer, the District Head continued to pay Mama a visit from time to time. He boasted, 'Ying's fiery temper is good for sport – I spotted it and put it to good use.'

With her head lowered as usual, Mama thanked him. She never looked him in the eye, and I saw this as her way of expressing defiance, anger and sadness, rather than surrender. But she still had to be careful to defer to him.

The District Head looked smug. 'See what revolution can do for sport!' He hummed his favourite song as he left.

Now that Ying was the Little Butterfly, the small spark of hope that I'd discovered on the levee wall rekindled in my heart and grew. I kept reminding myself that life would be good again when Baba came home, one day, after serving his sentence.

CHAPTER 9

'Down with the rightists!'
'Long live Chairman Mao!'
'Down with the Americans!'
'Down with the capitalists and their running dogs!'
'Down with the Russian revisionists!'
'We'll die to protect China!'

Increasingly, we were encouraged to denounce the rightists, a new group who needed to be cleansed, as well as the usual Americans and their running dogs, whoever they were, and also now the Russian revisionists, whatever that meant. It was a confusing time for all of us in Shiqi.

Back in May 1956, a campaign from Beijing, 'Let a Hundred Flowers Bloom; Let a Hundred Thoughts Contend', had encouraged the whole country – even comrades, administrators, workers in all production units – to speak their minds about the government and the Party. Discontented citizens soon exposed their true faces. They were quickly classified as bad elements called rightists, and over the next couple of years the new Anti-Rightist Campaign began to purge them from the Party. Our town again became frantic with denunciation meetings, while Pig Head Hill was busy with more executions. Baba had deliberately steered clear of both campaigns.

With so many enemies to condemn in slogans bellowed all day long at school and often after school too, everyone had hoarse voices like our District Head.

'How do the Russians and Americans know we hate them?' Ah-dong asked me privately one day in his croaky voice.

'Not sure.' My own voice was hardly recognisable.

In spite of Ah-dong being my good friend, I was careful not to show my own true feelings to him. I wasn't prepared to risk being branded a rightist at school, as some teachers and senior students were already being tarred with this brush. It would have been a lot worse than the jeers over my failed crossing of the Wonder River.

Around this time, Aunt Wai-hung visited us with her boys, Young-young, Young-chit and Young-syn. I remember one afternoon, when I was carrying firewood from our room to the kitchen, I overheard her talking with Mama.

'Be careful, Wai-syn. Don't say anything about the Party to anyone. The Hundred Flowers Campaign is aiming at doubters. Beng'e suspects there could be a more serious campaign ahead.'

Mama attended to her cooking and didn't respond. Instead she asked me, 'How was school today?'

'Same as yesterday,' I said in my husky voice. I didn't want to say more – my throat was sore from shouting.

For a long time after that, I worried that Mama might say the wrong thing to the wrong person.

*

After Baba's appearance in the People's Court, the District Head had allocated Mama a relief job in a nursery. New mothers had to return to their production units one month after giving birth, leaving their babies in care, so there were a lot of infants to look after.

The job seemed to alleviate Mama's depression a little, though it was underpaid. Adults in town earned twenty-four yuan a month. Technical or skilled workers made thirty-two, while Party members were rewarded with forty-eight yuan because of their contribution to the revolution. Mama was paid fifteen yuan a month, the wage of an apprentice.

These meagre payments nevertheless provided Baba with some support, and also Ying, who was still in the Guangzhou Swimming Squad. But Mama often ran out of money if the payments from Hong Kong were delayed. She'd wait for the postman at the entrance to our street, the same way she'd wait for Baba's mail, at these times staring blankly in the direction of Hong Kong. Often I sat with her and we waited together. We didn't talk much but appreciated each other's company.

Mama couldn't sleep or eat when she got to her last ten-fen note, only enough for a bunch of bok choy. With reluctance, she'd write a message requesting a credit of two yuan to help us out and ask me to take it into town to Mrs Lee, my old friend Flea's aunt.

The word around town was that Mrs Lee's husband was a successful businessman in Hong Kong. Theirs was one of very few well-off families in Shiqi. For some reason, the authorities didn't seem to be too hard on them. Gossips said that her husband was sending her regular generous living allowances that also contributed to China's foreign funds, just as Grandfather Young's American money did.

With Mama's note in my pocket I'd run to Mrs Lee's house, dodging pedestrians and bicycles. Not far from Come Happiness Bridge I'd turn right into her street. Then I'd knock on the back door of the handsome two-storey house and wait patiently for someone to answer the door.

From the landing above the street, I'd see people moving about with their heads down. Their frowns were as contagious as the one Mama carried all day long. They shifted quietly along like ghostly shadows drifting in the dark, indifferent to everything around them; even the pleasant chirps of sparrows and the ringing of bicycle bells didn't make any difference.

Mrs Lee usually invited me into her house. She'd take Mama's note and return carrying two red one-yuan bills printed with

Chairman Mao's face. She was always smartly dressed in unpatched, handsome clothes. Her fair skin was unusual in Shiqi – unlike many of the townspeople, she didn't need to volunteer to work in the open. She had four children, and the two older ones had left before 1949 and lived in Hong Kong with her husband. Through the door I could often see and envy the many beautiful toys her younger children owned, but I would never stop to play.

I'd grip the money in my pocket all the way home, for fear of losing it, my hunger pangs quickening my pace, then I'd hand the moist bills to Mama and feel proud of myself for helping the family. As soon as our allowance from Grandmother arrived, Mama would dispatch me to repay our debt to the good Mrs Lee.

*

By early spring of 1958, Baba had settled into the prison in Heilongjiang and more slogans had burst into our classroom, directly from Beijing as usual. The Anti-Rightists Campaign had been a success, the adults said.

'Follow the Three Red Flags!'

'Beat the British in steel production in fifteen years!'

'Do more, do it faster, do it better and do it cheaper.'

These war cries were different: for the first time, there were no enemies to fight. This surprised us, including all the teachers at school and the adults in town. The grown-ups began to breathe a sigh of relief.

Next we plunged into the Three Red Flags Movement, aimed at rapidly industrialising China. Our District Head and his committee members eagerly advanced the new campaign, reinforcing the message of collectivism, unity and patriotism. Loudspeakers blared around town, and walls thickened with posters. A revolutionary storyteller took over the banyan tree near the school, and he told us the story of the king, his sons and their arrows – how one arrow alone was easily snapped, but not a handful of arrows bound together.

In our classroom our teacher pushed back her PLA cap, her eyes shining. 'The Three Red Flags Movement,' she explained with high spirits, 'are three directives in the implementation of the Second Five-Year Plan: first, to massively increase steel production; second, the rapid industrialisation of agriculture, our Great Leap Forward; and third, the setting up of communes all over the country. We are going to make history!'

Our teacher said this latest campaign was to reap the benefits from the 'economy of scale'. We didn't understand what that meant, but it felt important to keep chanting, 'Go all out, aim high, and build China greater, cheaper, faster, better and sooner.' So we began our industrialisation endeavour. And schoolwork could wait.

Although the slogans made our voices hoarse, they boosted our sinking spirits. When we shouted slogans with our class and then the whole school together, again with neighbours in the street, and finally with the entire town, it made us all feel we were part of the revolution. And the benefits of having more food and steel, and all our industries thriving, seemed obvious.

Suburbs in town became local communes, as did smaller towns and villages, each with their own governance and quotas to fulfil to contribute to the modernisation of the whole country. Our Wonder River District, indeed, was the first commune in Shiqi.

It had taken little time for me to feel part of the revolution once more – what I'd always wanted but lost with my father's arrest. My blood was now boiling, revving up for me to dive into this gutsy movement that would make China great by sharing the work, increasing production and hence income in the local area, for the benefit of all.

At times, I even forgot about Baba being in prison, and Mama and her misery, as I wholeheartedly embraced Chairman Mao's directives. My eyes glowed like those of the other students. Our teacher was proud of us, saying how we had truly stirred up our revolutionary spirits. 'Nothing can stop us now, even though you are only eight years old,' she often said.

How greatly we appreciated the power of comradeship under the Party. We felt invincible. The Americans and Russians were merely paper tigers, so we left them alone for the time being to concentrate on the exciting industrialisation campaign.

Before long, I put behind me the violent denouncements of the townspeople and the nightmares about Pig Head Hill. In my mind, even Baba's imprisonment had become part of the revolution. It seemed like a sacrifice my family had to make for the sake of a glorious future. I even forgave the District Head for sending Baba away to prison. I saw the radiance and pride in people rise around me, and felt closer to Chairman Mao than ever. Mama also saw a better life not far ahead for all of us, and came to believe that Baba would probably be released soon.

People went around town declaring that they weren't afraid of hard work, in the hope of receiving larger food rations and other goods, and possibly even a monthly income. Based on the collective model, the bigger the commune's production, the bigger the rewards would be for all its members. 'It's not the fifty thousand people of Shiqi alone,' I heard them saying to each other, 'but five hundred million in China all working hard together. Just imagine!'

Aha, I got it: the economy of scale.

'It'll be worth it,' I heard adults saying to each other, sounding ever so positive.

Prosperity was now within reach, more real than I had ever known.

We eagerly bellowed out our morning slogans in front of the solemn portrait of our Chairman before school began, making sure it was loud enough to reach his ears in Beijing.

Mama continued to work in the nursery, and Grandmother Young's American dollars from Hong Kong flowed in more steadily, supplementing her wage. We heard that my sister Ping had got into a good school there. I often wondered if Hong Kong had changed much since my brief stay a few years earlier. In the photos she sent, Ping had grown a lot taller and was now a pretty teenager. Like the mail from Baba, the letters from Ping had been opened and resealed. But we didn't care.

In Guangzhou, Ying had made good progress with her swimming. We were immensely proud of her, including Baba in Heilongjiang. The District Head shared in Ying's glory by telling people how he'd been the first one to recognise her talent when he selected her for the local swimming squad.

Even while buoyed by rejuvenated revolutionary spirits and the improved fortunes of my family, I still missed Baba. So did Mama and Weng and my sisters who lived away from home. When evening came and the noises of slogan-shouting and loudspeakers died down in the streets, we missed him even more. He was only into the second year of his fifteen-year sentence. I counted the days until he would be fully rehabilitated and allowed to serve communism again, while Mama never forgot to burn an incense stick every morning and pray to the ancestors for their blessings. To lessen her sadness, Weng and I tried to be good children and kind to each other. Aunt Wai-hung's visits also helped.

We found comfort in Baba's regular letters. He told us that he didn't have to work outdoors in the frozen wilderness; he had an easier job as a nurse at the prison hospital.

*

Each street within our commune was ordered to set up a communal dining room for its residents. I was excited at the thought of having my meals with my cousins and friends like Ah-dong and Earring (Big Eye belonged to a neighbouring commune, so he couldn't eat with us). The idea appealed to Mama as well: with every meal catered for, she no longer needed to wait in long queues for food every day (we had to shop daily, as nobody had a refrigerator to keep food fresh longer than a day). She also thought that she no longer needed to worry about tightening food rations, because the commune had pledged to feed all of us well, exactly as Chairman Mao had promised. She even helped promote the idea to a few sceptical neighbours.

'No such thing as a plump frog hopping into the open for you to catch,' one of the older neighbours said to her.

'Nothing comes from nothing,' was another comment.

Patiently Mama explained to them the collective possibilities for China under the Great Chairman. Her university education and her seemingly logical analysis convinced them in the end.

In order to massively increase grain production, our nation first had to contain Mother Nature's seasonal floods along the three biggest rivers in China. The Pearl was one of them, the others being the Yellow and the Yangtze. Natural disasters had long been entrenched in China's civilisation. This was all explained at my school by our teachers, who seemed to know about everything from communism to geography to history to science. We vowed to answer the call from Chairman Mao to defeat these threats and ensure strong agricultural production. 'Man can conquer nature!' I shouted with my classmates.

Ah-dong was particularly excited that we'd be spending more time away from the classroom, collecting broken tiles and bricks to build bigger roads and dams – and that there would be no more homework. His stammer was miraculously cured and he was back to his usual self, laughing and giggling, swaying his big round head from side to side, his belly jerking with each chuckle. It seemed the spell of Pig Head Hill had been finally broken.

Like my classmates, I filled my schoolbag with pieces of broken tiles and bricks I collected on the way to school. Soon there were no more classes to attend: instead, we sat around the school grounds smashing our hoard into smaller pieces. Competitions broke out between the classes to see which could produce the biggest pile of gravel, which was in great demand for building roads and dams. As we hammered, we sang revolutionary songs and chatted.

My fingers got in the way sometimes, and bruises, cuts and pain became part of the job. But I was very proud of suffering those revolutionary injuries, and most of the time they didn't seem to hurt. I was keen to compare my patriotic 'decorations' with those of my friends.

But I still felt sad sometimes when I thought of Baba. 'You must struggle against those backward thoughts and leap forward,' my teacher said to me whenever I appeared to be unsociable. 'Always put our Great Chairman ahead of all,' she advised. 'Then you'll be happy forever.'

'Stop being moody, Ah-mun,' Ah-dong said to me one day when we were smashing rocks in the school playground. 'Let's work hard now for our Red Scarf, so we'll be the first to get one next year.'

We were so eager to collect rocks, broken tiles and bricks that when we couldn't find any lying around, we simply dug up the roads. Potholes appeared on Come Happiness Road all the way to Come Happiness Bridge, upsetting many cyclists. When it was warm enough, my little gang and I dived into the rivers and waterways to search for debris from our rock-throwing contests in previous summers. We were proud as we watched the carts and bicycles with baskets arriving at the school to take away the gravel we'd collected.

I'm not sure how many months we spent smashing rocks and breaking bricks as we embraced the Great Leap Forward. Whenever I woke in the night because of pain from the bruises on my callused palms and cracked fingers, I would think of the boy in my class who'd lost his sight in one eye after it was pierced by a piece of tile. The school awarded him a white cotton T-shirt printed with 'Model Student' in bold red letters. He wore it all the time, even in winter. I was envious when he became the first in the class to be awarded the Red Scarf, before getting to Fourth Class, and I hoped they might also award me a Model Student T-shirt one day – even if I had to suffer worse injuries, like losing a finger or two. I didn't want to lose an eye, though, because when I closed one to see what it was like, I discovered that the world shrank, and everything appeared incomplete and less real. After that, I became jealous of Big Eye with his large round eyes, for I believed he must be able to see better and much more than the rest of us.

Mama warned us every morning not to try to be heroes, and that we must take good care of ourselves. 'Being cautious,' she said, 'and keeping your eyes open will help you sail safely through many storms.'

On the weekends, like all other adults, Mama and her workmates from the nursery volunteered to help construct Tiger Mouth Pond at the foot of Pagoda Hill in town. She didn't come home until dark, so I took care of Weng. The commune's kitchen, where we ate our meals, was only a few doors away. We each had a bowl of boiled rice with a serving of well-cooked vegetables and a small piece of fish. I always looked forward to the twice-weekly piece of pork, and on May Day and other national holidays we had extra meat, usually double the normal amount and sometimes a piece as big as my palm. We would praise Chairman Mao for the extras, and wish that he could live forever so that we would always have plenty to eat.

*

As well as building roads and dams, the whole population had to participate in the rapid expansion of steel production.

Our teacher taught us another slogan to shout: 'Beat the British in steel production and catch up with the Americans! If we pull together,' she danced around the classroom, beaming, 'we can do it.'

'Yes we can!' we yelled, before joining the senior students already hard at work in the school grounds.

No steelmakers lived in Shiqi, but instructions on how to build and operate furnaces soon arrived. A small furnace was set up in a corner of our school playground and junior students were assigned the important job of finding fuel to keep the furnace burning. We were also ordered to collect anything metallic that could be melted down to make steel.

Soon my schoolbag was bulging with dried leaves and fallen twigs, and the red star on its flap was stretched and grew bigger. Fired up with enthusiasm, I sometimes dragged tree branches all the way to school and delivered them to the furnace. I watched the smoke wend its way into the sky and felt the heat radiating from the big mudbrick stove. How I wished that I were in Fourth Class so I could do the night shift guarding the furnace.

Each day moved us closer to when we would beat the British in steelmaking – and moved me closer to getting a Red Scarf. The smoke from our furnace merged with smoke from all the other furnaces in town, forming a cloud that hovered over Shiqi like a huge shawl, heavy and suffocating. It concealed the crisp autumn sky from us, but this didn't matter to me. As I observed that amazing sight, my faith in Chairman Mao leapt even higher.

When waste metal became hard to find, I began scouring landfills and garbage tips with my friends. Our teachers suggested bringing items from home: bars from windows (after all, there were no more thieves under communism), old tin buckets, gutters, doorhandles, hinges, brackets. Unfortunately, the tenants at our ancestral home had already taken these items to the furnaces; they had also stripped the wooden panels that had partitioned the large house and taken them to the furnaces too. Now our home was bare and wide open. Mama and Sixth Aunt weren't pleased, but they dared not say anything to the tenants for fear of being branded counter-revolutionaries.

One day I went home and packed together Baba's few tools, tea tins, mugs and old cookware, as well as the knives and forks with ivory handles that Grandfather Young had brought home from Hawaii before I was born. Mama wasn't happy with my patriotic action, while I was disappointed that she wouldn't let me take the large pair of tailor's scissors that her father had given her on his first trip home in 1934. 'They remind me of the father I hardly knew, so you can't melt them,' she protested half-pleading and clutching the heavy scissors close to her chest. 'Besides, I need them to make or alter clothes for the family and maybe for other uses as well.' Tears welled up in her eyes. So I didn't take her scissors.

My search continued, however. One wintry Sunday in early 1959, Yiu-hoi, as he often did, had an idea: there was a half-submerged riverboat wreck by the large lotus pond not far from home, and it would have tons of big nails and other metal items. Ah-dong, Yiu-hoi, Weng and I ran off towards the wreck with our hammers and pliers, as four-year-old Ah-ki followed at his slower pace.

The riverboat had been there for months, and looked bleak in the icy water. There was little to find, because others had already been through the wreck. Balancing with difficulty on the tilted hulk, we searched everywhere in and out of the small cabin like ants exposing the skeleton of a dead fish. Ah-dong and Yiu-hoi worked hard trying to remove a large rusted nail, and Ah-ki scurried around trying to help. Weng stood by, looking into the deserted pond and daydreaming, as she often did.

It was freezing. I thought of Baba in the deep north enduring snow and ice for eight or more months a year. He would have been the right person to help us remove that big nail.

'Big brother, I've found a—'

Ah-ki's voice woke me from daydreaming – just in time to see him slip and tumble into the water.

Yiu-hoi and Ah-dong popped their heads up to check what was happening. Little Ah-ki was struggling like a kitten under the surface of the pond. The world seemed to go into slow motion as we watched him drowning. The silence was eerie.

Weng screamed.

Without thinking, I dived in to reach Ah-ki. I held his face above the surface with one hand and gripped the rough edge of the wreck with the other. The icy water cut like a million shards of glass. It was hard to breathe. But with Yiu-hoi and Ah-dong's help, we pulled Ah-ki out of the arctic pool. Weng was still screaming and frightened.

The five of us ran all the way home, arriving just before we turned into blocks of ice. Ah-ki's maternal grandmother, who was staying with us while Ah-ki's parents were away teaching in different towns, was shocked, mumbling her prayers as she rubbed colour back into him while waiting for the kettle to heat up so that she could give him a warm wash. 'Four-year-olds should never leave the house in winter,' she said to us, before giving thanks to God again for our return. We called her the God-believer; we, on the other hand, were believers in Chairman Mao.

Throughout this ordeal Ah-ki had managed to hold on to his find. Now he could proudly contribute a rusty bracket to the commune's steelmaking.

After I saved Ah-ki, he felt he owed me an immense debt, perhaps for the rest of his life. His God-believing grandmother wouldn't let him out of her sight until I was around. He followed me like my little shadow and did everything I wanted him to do; he even waited patiently for me to finish my homework. Together we attended to my chores in our vegetable patch. Then we were free to play, though we kept away from the lotus pond and the wreck, fearing the demons and spirits that had tried to take little Ah-ki.

*

For weeks we waited patiently to see the steel we'd been working so hard to make. Finally, in the spring of 1959 the day came. We took Ah-ki to school to join in the celebration. We sang and danced to revolutionary songs. Drums boomed. Trumpets blasted. There were more rounds of singing and slogan-shouting to congratulate the school on its success. Big red banners and flags fluttered in the tepid breeze. The continuous clapping hurt our hands but also kept us warm; many of our voices had already broken earlier than usual as a result of all our singing and shouting throughout the year.

The sacred moment finally arrived, but only after many speeches. By then our thin legs were buckling from hours of standing, not to mention hunger. With immense pride, the school's Party Secretary shouted, 'Long live Chairman Mao! Long live! Long live! Long live the Chinese Communist Party! Beat the British and catch up with the Americans in steel production!' His enthusiasm and revolutionary ardour reinvigorated us, and we grew even more excited as the teachers removed the safety barriers then opened the door of the furnace.

Our eyes bulged wide and we forgot to blink. There it was: the glowing liquid flowed forward like a grand character entering centre stage at the climax of an opera, unhurried and stately, and filled a rectangular mould set in a hole in the ground. We held our breaths and praised Chairman Mao for his wisdom. We had made steel. We had made history.

'Long live Chairman Mao!' we shouted with gusto. The adults told us not to touch the molten block outside the furnace, and refrain from walking or dancing on it. The holy slab, half the size of a ping-pong table, took several days to cool down before the teachers declared it safe for us to handle. We lined up. When it was my turn, the metallic block was already wet with tears, saliva from kisses, and sweat from the fondling of many excited hands. Red ribbons adorned it, turning it into a shrine we had helped create.

We didn't know then that it wasn't steel but low-quality pig iron, and that it would stay there for years to come, rusting away in the typhoons and seasonal floods of subtropical Shiqi. Nobody ever knew what to do with it.

CHAPTER 10

While the adults were enduring long hours of work for the Great Leap Forward, we children managed to have fun.

The most memorable time for me was at the end of the first big autumn harvest during the Great Leap Forward. The day after the adults finished gathering the rice, the weirs were opened to flood the paddies between the commune's lotus pond and fishponds, just opposite Kwong Street. Thousands of ducks kept for export waddled in to pick up worms, insects, snails and bits of grain that had been left behind. After the ducks had feasted for a few days, the field was allowed to rest and dry in the sun. Once the muddy surface was firm enough, it became our playing field, one many times larger than a football oval. There we held all types of games that city children could only dream of having space for. To me, kite-flying was the most enjoyable.

Our kites weren't decorative – they were fighters, regularly doing battle with other people's kites. The aim of a kite fight was to cut your opponent's string with yours. To be king of the sky, a kite had to be agile and responsive, and fast and accurate in its attack, and have a razor-sharp line coated with shards of glass. Often we had to build several kites before we were satisfied that we had a champion fighter. The rejected kites were decorated with long colourful tails and given to Ah-ki and Weng.

While the ducks were in the paddies, we busied ourselves making the kites, using delicate rice paper and bamboo skins taken from the district's plentiful bamboo stalks and dried in the sun on top of the levee wall.

'Ah-dong,' I said one day, 'it's your turn to bring some rice to make kites today.'

'Do I have to?' Ah-dong replied, rubbing his big tummy of worms. 'Still hungry,' he complained. He was always hungry. He was always tempted to gobble up the last few grains of rice when his stomach continued to rumble; however, the magical lure of kite-flying lessened the pain.

'We need to make the best fighter kite ever,' I said. 'Earring will get the sap from the peach trees, and Yiu-hoi and I will be responsible for grinding up the broken lightbulb glass to glue onto the string.' Yiu-hoi was the best in our gang at making things, regularly crafting toy cranes, and bamboo swords for warding off the nasty geese that chased us on our way to school, and I envied him for all the things he could make.

We sat on the levee wall with our pocketknives, working away on the bamboo sticks, shaping them bit by bit into the exact suppleness, length and size we needed for our sky fighters. At this time of the year the humidity had vanished and the air was crisp. Endless breezes replaced the dreaded typhoons and heat. We pulled Ah-ki up to sit with us on the levee wall as we planned our exciting fighting strategies. Then we carefully cut some fine rice paper in the shape we wanted, before gluing mashed-up cooked rice onto two carefully crafted sticks, one vertical, the other bent to form the frame of the kite.

A few days later, we came home from school to find Ah-ki sitting on the other side of the levee wall, crying. He told us that a kite from the neighbouring street had cut loose the one we'd made for him. We looked up to see a blue kite hovering high above us, soaring from one direction to another, showing off its intimidating skills and asserting its dominance of the whole sky. The menacing noises it made when diving and scooping were scaring the dozen or more little children in our street; they clutched their precious kites and ran for cover. They wouldn't launch them into the perfect breeze of the season, for fear of the blue monster.

'Let's go!' I shouted to Ah-dong, Earring and Yiu-hoi. 'The fight is on.'

We dropped our schoolbags and ran to get our kite in the air.

Our supreme fighter was painted with a bold red star. We launched it by climbing onto the levee wall to catch a stronger breeze. Our Red Star had a soaring take-off and quickly gained altitude. It pulled on the spool, hungry for more string. We could hear the razor-sharp line cutting into the crisp autumn air.

Ah-ki stopped crying and held his breath. Weng stood with her arm around him. All our necks stretched high. The enemy kite disappeared into the blue distance but soon returned, seeming to sense the presence of Red Star just as a hungry beast smells blood. It turned, took aim, and dived straight towards our rising kite before it had gained enough height and power.

Ah-dong and Earring cried out. Ah-ki and Weng closed their eyes. I tucked the spool to the left, then tightened hard to steer our kite into a half-dive, keeping it clear of the attacker. Letting more line to Red Star as it began to swerve, I sent it into a fast roll. The breeze was strong up there; Red Star soon caught it full on, pulling harder now. More line sliced into the air. We stopped breathing. Silence all around. I could feel the vibration in the spool and hear the eager rustle of the rice paper. Red Star was keen to go into battle.

It continued to roll, taking more line with it – and headed right for the tall gum trees along the road on the other side of the lotus pond, with the blue kite in pursuit.

'Big Brother!' Yiu-hoi screamed, and Earring nearly fell off the wall.

'Watch out!' Ah-dong yelled at the top of his voice.

The blue kite regained its dominance in height and shot to the left, then to the right, and patiently waited for its prey.

'Are we ready?' I shouted to Ah-dong and Earring behind and Yiu-hoi in front of me.

'Yes!' they cried out.

Ah-dong and Earring ran away from me on the wall, leaving me room to manoeuvre. Yiu-hoi stepped back from the sharp line.

I spun the spool hard, sending Red Star into an upward swoop just before it touched the treetops. This was the biggest gamble in my life that day – I knew even the slightest misjudgement would see Red Star crash into the trees, and the fight would be over. But the endless line I was feeding the kite allowed it to climb high into the sky, where the powerful pull of the stronger breeze would give me the upper hand.

I ran along the wall, holding the spool high, and watched our kite surge. *Fast.*

Red Star shot up like an arrow, straight and clean, tearing high into the air. Passers-by got off their bicycles to watch by the roadside. Ah-ki, Weng and all the little children clapped. All of a sudden, Red Star was above the blue kite with little room to spare. Wasting no time, I sent it into a dive straight at the aggressor, thirsty for its blood.

The blue kite dodged to the left and began spinning to gain more line. Red Star spun with it, but continued to maintain its superior position. Then the two kites climbed, racing to beat each other to greater heights. Our enemy was catching up. It was neck and neck. I prayed for a stronger breeze to fill our kite. I spun in the line to send it higher. Now Red Star was almost directly above us, with the blue kite in pursuit.

It fell into my trap.

'Great!' Ah-hoi shouted.

Ah-dong grunted. Earring cried out in awe. The little children on the ground screamed, their faces upturned to keep their gaze on our warrior. I pulled and spun in hard at the same time, sending Red Star into a slicing dive, catching its pursuer at the jugular. Crisp and clean. I felt it cut right through our helpless enemy's line.

Ah-dong, Earring and Yiu-hoi were already off the wall, running after the drifting blue kite. A whole bunch of children followed behind them, screaming and screeching with great joy.

I took a breath and praised Red Star for a job well done. People looked up in admiration. Children's laughter returned as their kites emerged, soon dotting the neighbourhood sky with many shapes and colours. Red Star, the king of the sky, hovered above them like a guardian angel, regal and proud.

Before long, Ah-dong, Earring and Yiu-hoi returned, gasping for breath, overcome by excitement and pride. In their hands was the blue kite. As I'd sensed, it was cleanly cut, leaving less than a metre of line, which made us marvel at Red Star's accuracy.

We sat on the wall for the rest of the day swinging our legs, clapping our hands and singing 'The East Is Red', our favourite song.

*

I now felt completely part of the Great Leap Forward and more confident than ever about life, especially after beating the aggressive blue kite. At school we continued to promise ourselves that we could beat the British and catch up with the Americans in steel production. Life must be like kite-flying, I thought: be prepared, be bold and take risks in order to be successful.

My determination to succeed became an obsession. I'd never won any prizes at school, but now I was desperate to win one to cheer up Mama. When a new command came from Beijing to eradicate flies and mosquitoes to improve hygiene, I wanted to win the Kill Flies Prize, and Ah-ki became my number one comrade-in-arms.

As the competition intensified, every day before school we set water traps around the house to catch flies, and after school we collected the dead insects in matchboxes. I gave Ah-ki a flyswatter and some empty matchboxes, and told him to fill them with dead flies while I was at school. Ah-ki had sturdy hands. He not only chased flies with his swatter in the house, but he also began killing them on the street; he seemed to know where to find them, unlike other kids his age. I then offered to do Ah-dong's calculation assignments in exchange for three boxes of dead flies each time. Together we filled 238 matchboxes and I won the class Kill Flies Prize for Mama.

'I'm very proud of you, Ah-mun,' Mama said to me when she heard of my triumph. She hugged me close to her. I could feel her trembling with emotion.

Everywhere I went I repeated my favourite slogan – 'Do more. Do it faster. Do it better. Do it cheaper!' I was thrilled by my prize: a large poster of Chairman Mao surrounded by cheerful children belonging to the Red Scarf Brigade. I wanted very much to be one of those children. I had dreamed about it and saw myself there among the beaming faces of the Precious Ones. Sometimes when I sat on the levee wall, those hazy images appeared in my mind in the predawn obscurity, and I watched them disappear in the early light.

One morning I realised I had to be content that having the poster was the closest I would ever get to Chairman Mao. So I stopped fantasising. I took down my grandparents' portraits and hung the poster with great respect on the main wall inside our room, decorating it with bold red ribbons. I promised myself to follow whatever Chairman Mao taught. His words resonated within me wherever I went: 'To ride the wind and pierce the waves to realise the Great Leap Forward in all fields.'

With the Kill Flies Prize under my belt, and even without the Model Student T-shirt or the Red Scarf, I felt tall around the schoolyard and on the street. Two hundred and thirty-eight matchboxes of dead flies in one month was no mean feat. I realised that determination and an effective team of helpers, especially Ah-ki, were the reasons for my success. Would it be the same in life?

One bonus of winning the Kill Flies Prize was that more of the local children began talking to me. My little gang of friends grew beyond Ah-dong, Earring, Yiu-hoi, Ah-ki and Weng. Now Ah-bil, Hui and Big Eye from town came to play with us more regularly.

*

I'd lived two summers without Baba, two kite-flying seasons with many victories, and a third winter was near. His regular letters revealed only glimpses of what life was like in the extreme north of the Great Northern Wilderness. It was frightening but fascinating to read about wolves howling in the night, and sometimes we even heard the Siberian tigers roaring in his letters. He also wrote about his joy in seeing the frozen ground erupt into life in spring. He described how the many colourful wildflowers raced to bloom in the desolate wasteland, which he and thousands of intellectuals laboured to turn into productive farmland while they strove to be re-educated so they could participate in the revolutionary society, one day.

'When winter is with us we have spring to look forward to,' he wrote, keeping our hopes high.

*

Late in 1959, food rations were tightened because, according to the adults, the harvest hadn't been as good as the previous year's, and people began to go hungry. Everyone in the Wonder River District was ordered to perform a new activity for the Great Leap Forward – to reduce grain consumption by getting rid of the plentiful sparrows that were said to be eating a lot of the rice in the paddies. We dropped the hunt for mosquitoes and flies, and turned our attention to killing sparrows.

Like my friends, over time, I'd become used to the many government campaigns and treated them like the waterways of the Wonder River – I just went with the flow and swam with the current. But this plan upset me. While I knew I had to follow the Party's directives without question, deep down I had a soft spot for sparrows. I loved their happy dispositions, and their chirps had helped me through many of my saddest days; they reminded everyone that there was always fun to be had in life. With enviable precision, they caught insects, grasshoppers, moths, worms and dragonflies – they didn't just steal our grain. As soon as they had eaten, they danced in the sun as if they owned the universe. Easily satisfied, heartily contented, they seemed always optimistic.

Little did they know how precarious life was to become when the Great Leap Forward swung into its second year and grain production took a dramatic dive.

'We must get rid of every sparrow in Shiqi,' our teacher declared in class. 'They are worse than the flies, mosquitoes and rats. They have eaten too much of our valuable grain, and that's why the ration went down, and you are starving. We must get rid of them and save our food.'

Together, the sparrows, flies, mosquitoes and rats were known as the Four Pests. They had to be eradicated, like all the unwanted human elements in town.

Our teacher had told us previously that the Russians also contributed to China's food shortage by insisting on repayment of debts from the Korean War. I wanted to know more about that but didn't dare ask – it was unthinkable that the son of an unwanted Shiqi man would have the cheek to question the orders of the authorities. I had learnt to keep my mouth shut and not discuss my own thoughts, hopes and dreams with anyone. Yet there were so many questions I had no answers for, and there was no Baba to ask.

Early one morning, I sat on the levee wall watching the red glow rise and thinking of Baba in Heilongjiang prison. The predawn light had begun to capture my whole world with its reach – the lotus pond and fishponds, the Wonder River and its many tributaries, the gum trees along Come Happiness Road, the lychee trees, the dreary roofs and grey walls of the ten houses in Kwong Street, the vast rice paddies surrounding Old Crow Hill and beyond. The glow even reached further across Come Happiness Bridge into town where Pagoda Hill perched in its somnolence on the flat landscape, near the dreaded Pig Head Hill, and further ... as far as my eyes could see. There and then, I decided I shouldn't feel sorry for the sparrows and would go along with the rest of the class. There was no escape for anyone. It was futile to resist. It was better to be part of it. The choice was clear: fewer sparrows meant more food for us humans as Chairman Mao had promised. Perhaps I could obtain another Great Leap Forward prize.

Later that day after school, I sat on the levee wall with a big group of my friends, trying to work out the best way to help eradicate the sparrows in Shiqi.

'What about the fortress, the derelict place by the river?' Yiu-hoi suggested, brimming with ideas as ever. 'It's full of sparrows and their nests.' This ruin, near Old Crow Hill, was just ten minutes from home. But it was also the place where the townspeople had resisted the British Navy as it sailed up the river during the Opium Wars; British cannonballs had killed many young volunteer fighters from the district, and locals said the fortress had been haunted ever since.

Ah-dong turned pale. 'The, ah, ghosts. No … no one wants … to get near it, at, at … night.' His large round head swung from side to side in obvious distress.

'There are lots of us,' I said, reassuring him. 'If we stick together, we'll be fine. We'll be strong like a bundle of arrows bound together,' I added, quoting the revolutionary storyteller from under the banyan tree.

It was dark by seven o'clock, when we met at the end of Kwong Street with our torches and fishing baskets. Only Ah-dong and Yiu-hoi turned up. Undaunted, we headed towards Old Crow Hill along the narrow track that separated the paddies from the vegetable gardens. At times, a small glimpse of a new moon peeked from the clouds, which were as dark as the night itself. There were no lights once we left the last street in town, but we knew how to make our way, even in near-darkness, along this narrow path we romped on every day.

We had to be wary, though, of the small but venomous South China snakes, which were plentiful in the Pearl Delta. As we walked we clapped our hands and talked loudly to shoo them away. Frogs stopped croaking and dived off into irrigation ditches. Swarms of insects paused their humming as we approached, only to resume after we passed. Not a star shone that night. But we were at ease with the cosy scent of the countryside, and the muddy smell of the Wonder River not far away.

Yiu-hoi pushed open the heavy wooden door of the fortress. It creaked. A scraping noise sounded from the large beams high up. Ah-dong and I quivered, but we followed Yiu-hoi inside. My friends and I often marvelled at his boldness, and now we felt strangely safe with him, even though, at seven, he was the youngest of the three of us.

'Ssshhh,' said Yiu-hoi. Ah-dong was trembling and his teeth chattered, echoing mine. 'I'll count to three and we'll flash our torches up at the sparrows. Swing your torches from side to side and shout loudly to frighten them, then they'll start flying and knock themselves silly. Ah-dong, you pick them up and secure them in the fishing basket, while Big Brother and I keep upsetting them.' Yiu-hoi was reiterating what the teachers had told us about catching sparrows. The leader of our expedition had spoken, and we went into action.

Yiu-hoi and I swung hard and fast with our torches, spinning them in arcs of brightness, terrifying the hapless sparrows huddling high on the beams. Dazzled by the light and noise, they started flying around in all directions, hitting the walls and knocking themselves out as they shrieked in alarm, their wings flapping but going nowhere.

'Ha, ha, ha ...!' a stranger's voice cried out.

Yiu-hoi dropped his torch.

'Ouch, ouch, ouch ...' came the echoes from deep inside the derelict building.

Ah-dong shrieked. I turned to see what in my frenzied state I thought might be a ghostly face towering over him. He dropped his basket and closed his eyes.

Yiu-hoi and I screamed. We took off for the front door, dropping our torches and tripping over a pile of bricks. We landed in a heap and squealed our hearts out.

We managed to get ourselves up and run.

Splash. Yiu-hoi fell into a ditch. We stopped to drag him out. Slippery mud made the uneven path hard to negotiate. We stumbled and cried but managed to make it home, covered in dirt.

The next day, we sat on the levee wall and didn't want to talk about what had happened. A few sparrows flitted overhead, chirping.

We decided it would be easier to join the rest of our neighbours beating their pots and pans in the evenings. Sparrows took flight and bashed themselves against tree trunks and brick walls in the dark, knocking themselves unconscious. We kids ran around with our fishing baskets and picked them up by the score. My mother spent a whole night killing, plucking and cooking them. She kept the claws for me to take to school for the Kill Sparrows competition.

This went on for weeks until the song of the sparrows died in Shiqi.

Ah-dong took many pairs of sparrow claws to school, and he won the Kill Sparrows Prize that autumn. He ate so many sparrows that he was the only one on our street with good colour in his face, and his skinny legs began to fill up. He was chirpier than ever, and cocky.

CHAPTER 11

Towards the end of 1959 the greatest piece of news in the gloomiest days of my life arrived: my father was being released on the grounds of his 'complete re-education and good behaviour'.

Over three years had passed since his imprisonment. In his regular letters, he'd told us how grateful he was to Chairman Mao for the opportunity to redeem himself along with many of his academic colleagues, fellow intellectuals and other prisoners in Heilongjiang. He was learning more about communism and socialism every day, and felt proud to be part of the revolution and rising PRC. He wanted to serve the nation under the District Head. Now, more than ever, he pledged to devote his life to serving China and working for a better future for our people. I was proud of Baba – although later I overheard him telling Mama that the government hadn't been able to feed all the prisoners, so some of them just had to be released.

On the day we received his brief letter announcing his freedom, Mama read and re-read it, her face contorted with indescribable emotions as her tears flowed. We huddled together. No words were necessary; no words were adequate to describe how we felt.

The next morning, Mama wrote a long message for me to deliver in town. 'This is very important, my son,' she said. 'Take this to the good Mrs Lee to ask for a loan. Baba needs money to fund his journey home. It's a large sum, so you must be most careful. Come home with it immediately.' Her face was glowing, and I suddenly noticed how pretty my mama had become again.

I sprang to my feet and ran into town along Come Happiness Road, then crossed Come Happiness Bridge over the Nine Meanders River onto Come Happiness Street. I turned right into the road where Mrs Lee lived, knocked on her back door and waited. My heart was racing, and the entire town seemed to reverberate with my excitement.

'Oh, that's a lot,' Mrs Lee exclaimed on reading the message.

'Baba is on his way home,' I blurted out. I couldn't wait to announce the big news, even though Mama had probably told Mrs Lee in the note.

Her face brightened with a big smile, then, lost for words, she briefly disappeared into the house before returning with the money.

'Be careful, Ah-mun, this is more than two months' wages for many people,' she advised.

I sprinted home with one hand holding the money in my pocket, and proudly gave Mama the sweaty notes. She then took the money to the bank in town and sent it to Baba.

I was confident that with Baba home we wouldn't starve. He would have many ways of finding food; we might even go fishing in the South China Sea, as he'd said we would. It was wonderful to be alive, even with a grumbling stomach.

As Mama, Ying (recently returned home from the swimming squad), Weng and I waited patiently for Baba's homecoming, we burned an incense stick every day to show our gratitude. It seemed to take months for Baba to make his journey. Mama kept reassuring us with his frequent letters from famous historic sites, including the palaces in Beijing, the Great Wall, the Yangtze River, and many of the places mentioned in the famed literary works that Baba loved. It looked as if he was indulging himself with the money from Mrs Lee and soaking up as much culture as he could while he had the chance.

We plotted Baba's journey home like it was a lesson in geography, history and literature. Diligently, we marked his whereabouts on the map, beginning at the Great Northern Wilderness bordering Russian Siberia, continuing down the tortuous east coast, west along the Yangtze River and on to inland places such as the ancient mountains of Huangshan and the Great Wall of Badaling, as well as many other locations that we'd never heard of before. Mama, ever a good teacher, explained the cultural significance of each of these locations. And whenever a letter from Baba arrived, we charted his whereabouts on the vast continent and estimated how many days it would be before he arrived home.

Mama now often danced around the house, humming and singing. We all talked about the many things we were going to do with Baba. We laughed until our jaws ached. It was the happiest time I'd ever experienced as a child in Shiqi. I slept in most days, and Mama had to wake me up for school. We praised Chairman Mao and burned more incense sticks to show our gratitude to the ancestors, and waited with great patience. We wrote to Ping.

'My Baba will be home soon,' I hurried to announce to my friends as we sat on the levee wall. Yiu-hoi's face brightened and he said, 'That means we'll catch more fish. My Seventh Uncle knows all the best fishing spots in Shiqi!' Ah-dong and Earring nodded in agreement and clapped.

*

One day, I was about to pack away my homework and attend to the usual chores of feeding the only two chickens we could afford and watering our small vegetable garden when a man, with his bedroll slung over his shoulders, marched into our open house.

At first glance, he looked like a new tenant. What a tramp, I thought.

It took a second look before I realised he was my dearly missed baba. He was tanned, healthier-looking and more solid than when I'd last walked with him, over the Wonder River Bridge. He also seemed shorter. His hair was long and flowing from months of neglect, but a broad smile hung on his face, and tears glinted in his eyes.

He hugged us all in his big arms, and we cried and laughed in a huddle. The large numbers stamped in white on his jacket identified him as a prisoner of New China, but with his newly authorised pass, he could show that he was now a reformed citizen. The odd smell oozing from his uniform didn't stop us from snuggling close to him. Weng couldn't stop peeping at the man she barely knew; she smiled at him, flashing her beautiful dimples. There was a lot of catching up to do.

We were the happiest family in the whole of Shiqi, but the bigger of the two chickens was not so fortunate that day. After offering it to our ancestors for their blessings, we ate it in celebration. Incense smoke filled the happy household in Number 1 Kwong Street.

Baba brought with him gifts he'd collected on his long way home. The honey melon from some remote place was priceless, according to him, and we kept it for so long that it rotted before we could bear to cut it up. The apples he brought were going brown, but we enjoyed parts of them; we couldn't make their seeds germinate, though. The wildflower seeds from the Great Northern Wilderness also failed in our humid climate.

'This is for you, Ah-mun,' Baba said to me that evening he arrived home, as he handed me a copper-handled pocketknife. 'My friend in the Northern Wilderness prison made it for me as a gift. He said I might need it on the long hike to the train station.'

It was a crude little knife with a rather sharp ten-centimetre blade, just perfect for working those tough bamboo skins when kite-making. It was the most memorable gift I'd ever been given.

The news of Baba's return reached the District Head, and he paid us a visit the next morning. He asked why it had taken Baba so long to get home, but commended him on his effort to undergo full rehabilitation. 'Attend the evening meetings from tomorrow. The revolution is continual. Never stop learning communism, and don't leave the street without my permission.' With that, he marched off to the beat of 'The East Is Red'.

*

With gusto I again shouted the Great Leap Forward slogans: 'Do more. Do it faster. Do it better. Do it cheaper!' until my voice became hoarse and my throat hurt. My schoolteachers were more than pleased with my reinvigorated enthusiasm. I told my friends on the levee wall that I would die for communism if I had to, now that Baba was home.

'But would you die happy if your stomach hurts and rumbles?' Ah-dong asked.

'If it's for Chairman Mao's revolution, I would,' I said without a second thought. I had already made up my mind as I fixed my gaze on the rising sun that morning from the levee wall before heading off to school. I was used to the gnawing pain in my stomach and didn't remember what it was like to have it filled with food. I'd probably be sick, I thought.

Within days of his return, anxious to make a contribution to the Great Leap Forward, Baba threw himself into the rope-making enterprise in our street commune. It was his volunteer job. I was quietly pleased and outwardly proud that he'd been fully reformed, whatever that meant. To me, he was now a progressive man, almost a comrade in the sacred revolution, exactly what I had been secretly wishing for all these years. He joined the commune workers in flaying palm stalks on rows of long sharp nails to extract the fibres for rope-making. Every day he came home with fresh wounds on his hands.

Baba soon invented a fibre-extracting machine using old bicycle chains, paddles and other odd mechanical parts to turn a large drum spiked with nails. His fellow workers were delighted by this much safer and faster method. Before long, with several machines operating at full capacity, the Kwong Street Rope-Making Brigade had more than tripled its output. Baba was awarded a white T-shirt with 'Model Worker' printed on it boldly in red, symbolising the spirit of the sacred Great Leap Forward. The District Head was pleased and even smiled at us sometimes.

In the dining hall, Baba never once complained. With relish he devoured his allocated bowl of rice with soggy vegetables and a small piece of fish fried in black oil.

'We are lucky here in the commune.' He spoke loud enough for others to hear. 'Up north we ate rice only once a month, and on national holidays. It was corn and sweet potatoes at all other times. Together with black mantou buns, that was our staple diet in prison.'

I couldn't hold in my curiosity and asked him, 'But why were they black?' The mantou, I knew from propaganda posters and books, were white steamed buns served at New Year celebrations or on special occasions in the cold northern provinces. I had always aspired to eat one but had never even seen one.

'The grains were ground with the husks and maybe straw too, plus other unknown additives, to bulk it up,' explained Baba. 'We rarely had fish or meat but soon learnt how to trap squirrels and other little animals to supplement our diet.' He stopped short of saying prisoners had been released early because there were too many mouths to feed.

Baba told vivid stories, attracting people from streets away. We gathered around him, listening to his retellings of legends and other historical happenings. In private, he told us that when he had visited those historical sites on his long journey home, he'd tried to envisage the thoughts and emotions of the great poets and authors who had created literary masterpieces, thus deepening his interpretations of their work and enriching his experiences. Apart from smoking and going fishing in the waterways, storytelling was Baba's favourite activity.

When telling stories to a crowd, Baba was careful to embellish them with appropriate revolutionary colours to ensure he wouldn't be accused of spreading counter-revolutionary ideas. One of his most popular tales was that of the heroic exploits of Commander Yang and his children, who defended the Song Dynasty against the onslaught of the mighty Mongolian armies. They died martyrs, and became symbols of resistance against foreign invaders. We also loved his yarns from novels like *Water Margin* and *Romance of the Three Kingdoms*, no matter how many times we heard them.

Baba's audience had listened to the narratives many times over the years without tiring of them, even before he was sent to prison. The same old stories were now told with fresh passion, emotion and respect. To the adults, they seemed more interesting than the monotonous revolutionary slogans and the compulsory political meetings. Many in the audience were illiterate, so these legends were all they knew and were familiar with. Generations of storytellers had passed them down. To us kids, revolutionary and political items already filled our curriculum; there was no time left at school for the legendary stories we loved.

The hour between six and seven in the evening was Baba's storytelling time. It never seemed long enough. After that, he had to attend his political re-education a few houses down the street. There, under the watchful eye of the District Head and his committee members, Baba and his fellow undesirables faced another barrage of self-criticism, thought-cleansing and even denouncement.

CHAPTER 12

Ah-dong's mother frowned. 'What? Another cut? How are we going to tell the people?' She was talking to the two women who worked in the kitchen of our commune dining room.

Inside, there was a huge wok so big that I could have bathed in it. (How I missed our galvanised-iron basin that the District Head's children now enjoyed.) The wok sat on a specially constructed brick stove with a hand-operated ventilation fan on one side. One of the women was pulling and pushing it, feeding rice shells into the glowing fire. The kitchen had the earthy but comforting smell of cooked rice.

It was early in 1960, still winter, and the cold gnawed at our empty, rumbling stomachs. Ah-dong and I were there hoping to get a sweet potato to share after school.

Ah-dong's mother was in charge of feeding the whole street. She had to divide carefully, month by month, the dwindling rations of rice, oil, meat, fish and vegetables that were delivered to all the dining rooms in our commune, the amounts of each based on the number of residents. I was pleased that she was in charge of ours; she often slipped an extra spoonful of rice into my bowl and pressed hard to hide it when no one was looking.

'Drought in the north and floods in the south have destroyed a lot of crops,' Ah-dong's mother said, reiterating what the street-corner loudspeakers had been telling us since before the New Year.

'Someone said too many people are building dams and making steel, and not enough are working in the fields,' one woman mumbled.

'I wouldn't say that if I were you,' said Ah-dong's mother, as she washed a large basket of vegetables. 'You could get yourself into trouble.'

The woman wouldn't stop. 'That's just what I hear some young people are saying. They go to high school. Intellectuals. They should know.'

'Maybe we had it too good last year.' Ah-dong's mother seemed confident. 'We ate too much, but it was a good harvest the year before, they said. Nature isn't helping us now. Don't forget, we had the Russian debt to repay, and we have to support our comrades in Africa and Cuba.'

Ah-dong's mother seemed to know more than others in the street. She worried when people in the dining room complained about the decreasing portions of food. As their main meal of the day, working adult men now got a bowl of boiled rice that Ah-dong's mother weighed carefully on a scale in front of them, just to show they were getting the right amount, plus a serving of overcooked vegetables and a small piece of fish. Women and children received a smaller bowl of rice with smaller portions of the same accompaniments. The vegetables were boiled in water with salt; there wasn't a trace of oil or garnish. Once a week we were each allocated a serving of meat as big as two adult fingers put together.

'Remember how the heroes of the Long March overcame their challenges,' our teacher reminded us every morning at political studies – our first lesson of the day, which was now all about the soldiers of the civil war. 'Our heroes and martyrs often had nothing to eat, yet they trekked ten thousand li [five thousand kilometres] and overcame the snow, mountains, rivers and desert to dodge the enemy's pursuit, and reached Yan'an, our holy destination, and final victory.' She beamed with pride and emotion, but couldn't hide her thin, jaundiced face. 'We can do the same with less food.'

We tried not to complain and kept our spirits high, knowing that we were taking part in Chairman Mao's sacred revolution. Some adults quietly voiced their concerns, but many merely shook their heads and kept quiet, fearful of punishment for speaking up.

'Even with an empty stomach, man can overcome nature,' Chairman Mao told us every day through the street loudspeakers. 'Let's tighten our belts.'

*

Rations were steadily reduced. Every day we felt the hunger pangs. My mother sent us to bed early to save kerosene for our one little lamp, which was often needed for the frequent power disruptions. Each of us wore an extra woollen jumper and a pair of thick socks, and she insisted we put on our sandshoes to go to school in winter, instead of going barefoot as we did in the warmer months.

'When Grandmother comes from Hong Kong, she'll bring us food,' Mama said as she tucked me into bed. Every night I rubbed my empty stomach and pretended I was on the Long March, and looked forward to Grandmother Young's arrival.

Relatives in Hong Kong and Macau began bringing food to Shiqi to help their starving families. Grandmother Young started making a monthly trip, even though adults at home always seemed to fear that she might be detained by the authorities, for whatever reason.

Grandmother's matrimonial home in Shenmingting was just around the corner from the Young's ancestral home where Great-Grandfather Fu-chiu had married the maiden who'd fallen out of her bridal sedan. Each time my grandmother visited, we'd go there to get our share of food. It was a good five kilometres west of Shiqi. To save us the long walk, Mama paid ten fen for each bicycle courier who had a seat attached to the back wheel. Ying and Weng would take one bicycle, Mama and I another. With our District Head's permission we often stayed at Grandmother's house for a couple of nights and had fun with Aunt Wai-hung's sons, our cousins Young-young, Young-chit and Young-syn. Though he was just three or four years old, Young-syn insisted on hanging around with us older kids and was determined not to miss any of our games.

Grandmother Young brought the monthly customs quota of ten kilos of food. It usually included two tins of Spam, three cans of Eagle Brand sweetened condensed milk, several baguettes that saw us through a day (maybe two), a can of peanut oil, brown sugar in long blocks, and sometimes cooked and salted pork that lasted us a week if we ate small amounts at a time. She also brought us our favourite Arnott's arrowroot biscuits, Wrigley's chewing gum, and Adler pencils and erasers. What luxuries in those days. She'd put all these in a big bag made from four layers of tough cloth; it would be unpacked later, then Aunt Wai-hung and my mother shared the fabric to make clothes for us. If Grandmother remembered, there might even be fishing lines and hooks for me, meaning I didn't have to heat my mother's needles to bend them into hooks that couldn't catch fish longer than ten centimetres.

Laughter and excitement reappeared in our lives whenever my grandmother travelled home. She would laugh with us, and her well-powdered face glowed. But soon it would darken. 'You're all too thin,' she'd sigh, frowning at us. Her voice was always loud and clear: my mother said Grandmother had needed to shout so that Great-Grandmother Good Arrival could hear her, and it had become a habit. Now maybe Grandmother was going deaf, because her daughters had to shout back at her to make her hear. But she didn't seem to want to know exactly what we kids were talking about, so she just said 'Oh, yes' to everything and smiled.

When we stayed with Grandmother Young in Shenmingting, I would climb out of bed at five in the morning to watch her light incense sticks and offer prayers to the ancestors for their blessings. I'd sit quietly in the dark corner of the front room and listen to her mumbling, unable to make out what she was saying. Sometimes she half-turned her head and noticed me, before she turned back to her prayers. The aroma of slowly brewing coffee from the kitchen and the sandalwood scent of her incense sticks permeated the cold house, turning it into a warm and welcoming home. The fragrance surrounding her hadn't changed since I'd lived with her back in the summer of 1955 in Hong Kong.

Memories of that time returned to me. I thought of good Mr and Mrs Ho, and their daughter Je Je, whom I had missed badly, and gentle Grandmother Lee, my grandmother's room-mate. I wasn't sure if my grandmother had forgiven me for giving her such a hard time by threatening to kill myself, and I couldn't remember if I had ever apologised to her for being such a brat. I was full of admiration for her and most thankful for the food she brought to ease our hunger.

After her prayers, I would follow her into the kitchen. She'd pour herself a cup of her favourite dark brew and a small cup for me, just as she'd done in Hong Kong. Mine was diluted with hot water but the fragrance was still strong. I sipped my coffee quietly with Grandmother Young in the front room. Many times I was close to saying, 'I am sorry, Grandma, for what I did,' but I never summoned the courage.

One morning Grandmother Young smiled at me and slipped two biscuits into my hand, and I knew I'd been forgiven. 'Your favourite, remember?' She looked at me from across the table as she spoke, then she went on drinking her black coffee mixed with sugar and a raw egg. Her kind face gleamed like her lacquered hair. She was wearing a high-collar traditional-style gown with knotted fabric buttons running in a slant from the neck to under her left armpit, and then straight down the length to the hem.

'Have some more, Ah-mun,' she said, just as she had in Hong Kong. But now she followed up with, 'These arrowroot biscuits are from Sydney in the New Gold Mountain, and you can't even buy them in Hong Kong. Our old neighbour recently brought them all the way from Australia to Hong Kong when he came looking for a wife. He'd been away since around the time your grandfather went back to Hawaii in 1935.' She sighed and shifted her gaze to a big photo hanging on the wall; it showed a man in a cowboy hat riding a white horse. 'That's your grandfather,' she said, looking at the husband she hadn't seen for over twenty years.

I leant closer to her across the rosewood table and held her hand. I felt the soothing coolness of the smooth hardwood. This table and the matrimonial bed were the only pieces of furniture the rampaging mobs hadn't confiscated during the anti-landlord years.

Grandmother said, 'We are well off today because we are here together as a family. We owe it to that white horse.'

I already knew the story well, because she and Mama had told it many times, but I was happy to hear it again.

My grandfather had first arrived in Honolulu, on the island of Oahu, officially as Gut Young, supposed to be one of the sons of a Mr Ki Young, who was a neighbour from Shenmingting. Years later I found out that Grandfather, like many sojourners in those days, had bought travel documents to enter Hawaii illegally as an indentured labourer.

In the late 1920s, after he had fulfilled his obligation, he left Ah-ki Store, a thriving business next to the Honolulu Market, and he went to work at the Dole Pineapple Cannery in Honolulu Harbor, where he worked long hours to raise money to try to bring his four younger brothers to Honolulu. Unfortunately, constant exposure to chemicals inflicted bad burns and dermatitis on his hands, and for many months he was unable to work. He ended up doing odd jobs to earn his keep at a farm near Waikele, not far from Pearl Harbor, while waiting for his hands to heal properly. There, he became attached to an old white farm horse, and took her out for exercise during the magnificent Hawaiian dawns and sunsets.

He wondered how he could earn enough money to feed his family in China, who were relying on him. He remembered the promises he'd made years earlier to his parents, his brothers and his young wife. His small savings were fast disappearing.

One evening Gut Young was riding the white horse as the sun dallied on the horizon, its warm glow turning pink, scarlet and then purple. Yet another day had gone by, and his hands still cracked and bled easily. The Hawaiian remedy of bathing in a potion made from well-boiled young eucalyptus shoots, native plumeria (frangipani) flowers and other herbs hadn't worked. His worries were constantly on his mind.

The last light was leaving the shallow valley of Waikele and receding to the mountain ridges, where ocean mist gathered and an evening shower loomed. He hastily turned his mount to head home.

On the way, the horse was startled by something, reared and almost threw him off. The reflected light from the ocean revealed a parcel by the roadside. Gut Young dismounted. He found a canvas bag. When he opened it, bundles of money – American dollars in cash – spilled out. He lost his breath, and his head spun. No one was around, not even the spirit of a local god. The sparkling Hawaiian cosmos had already blurred into another night that guaranteed a promising tomorrow.

Dizzy and scared, Gut Young paced up and down the volcanic road trying to decide what to do. All his worries would be over with such a large sum of money. Life would be like the glorious sunshine following a Hawaiian shower, with no more hard labour in a foreign land. He could send his family money and bring his brothers to Hawaii. Or, basking in glory, he could go home to Shenmingting and buy up all the available good land, along with any businesses he fancied. He could then employ many servants and have a comfortable life for years to come. He could easily be the richest man around, including in the bigger town of Shiqi.

'But your grandfather had already made up his mind before the last rainbow retreated to the mountains – he would wait with the money for its rightful owner to return,' my grandmother said with pride.

Her voice softened as she kept her gaze on grandfather's handsome portrait: a serious young man looking into the distance, his back straight and shoulders squarely in control of a white horse that always turned into a white dragon in my dreams, just as my grandfather became a knight in silver armour.

'Needless to say, the owner was most grateful,' said Grandmother. 'He set your grandfather up with a small business in downtown Honolulu.'

Sam-wo, or Harmonious Three, was the name of the delicatessen in the Honolulu Market that my grandfather came to own. He eventually saved enough money to buy travel documents for his brothers, Dai-ung, Dai-lum and Dai-hin, to join him in Hawaii (but sadly not his other brother, Dai-fook, whose papers were rejected twice at the Chinese border). The three eldest brothers ran the business, which in turn supported their families in Shenmingting for many years, while Dai-hin, the youngest brother, was sent to school. Grandfather also returned to Shenmingting for a year-long vacation in 1934. Denis, my mother's youngest brother, was born the following year.

'By returning the money he found to its rightful owner, your grandfather brought great good fortune to the whole family,' my grandmother added.

But her eyes showed she was recalling what had happened next: her traumatic persecution as a landlord during the land reforms, before she went to Hong Kong. Only by borrowing a large sum of money to compensate the new government as demanded by the local authorities, so the family story goes, did my grandfather manage to avert the threat of imprisonment or even capital punishment. 'It would've been a lot worse if your grandfather had returned home with his riches,' Grandmother Young would say. 'The mobs would have executed the whole family.' She made a sign with her hand swiftly across her throat. I trembled and heard the thud of bullets at Pig Head Hill, before Grandmother Young hastened to end her story the way she had begun. 'That's why we're well off now. We are safe because we have our family together – the best thing in life.'

*

Having been discharged from the provincial swimming squad after failing to gain a position in the national swimming competition, Ying was now living at home full time. Mama was thrilled and Weng and I were super-excited to have our big sister back. Now sixteen, Ying wore her hair short and had the strong physique of an athlete, much to the envy of many of the townspeople. For a while she was the healthiest-looking person in town, with good colour in her face and her body bursting with energy. But that wasn't to last, as she now had to endure starvation like the rest of us. She enrolled at Shiqi's Number One High School and settled back into student life.

By then, mid-1960, famine had well and truly set in. The commune kitchens were finding it hard to manage the increasing number of people; complaints proliferated as rations shrank. There were more children and babies than adults as a result of the Party's successful call, several years earlier, to increase the population. Many parents were working long hours as volunteer labourers building dams and roads away from home, so we were left to fend for ourselves most of the time. Some of my friends had to care for their younger siblings after school, as I did with Weng, so our gang grew even bigger. But that made it harder to manage slightly dangerous activities such as kite-flying; whatever we did, we had to consider the younger ones in our care.

With less food, we exhausted ourselves easily. Hunger pangs lasted all day long, from breakfast to lunch to bedtime. Our skinny legs couldn't carry on as we wanted, and we ran out of puff so quickly that we simply had to slow down. We sat more often and for longer on the levee wall in Kwong Street, talking and dreaming of food. Eventually we would even tire of talking and sit silently instead, looking towards the motionless horizon and imagining what a feast would be like.

Ah-dong's father, being a union official in town and a comrade, had larger food rations than other regular civilians. Still, this didn't sate Ah-dong's hunger. His potbelly grew bigger. His mother said you could hear the worms from across the room; she said the food he ate fed the worms before him. He carried his stomach around with increasing difficulty, and he puffed more than any of us. Sometimes he seemed dazed, sweat dripping from his face, grey as the old bricks of the Kwong Street houses. When he began to sway, his eyes turned dull like those of a dead fish. We would rush to wet his face with cold water and to squeeze lychee or sugarcane juice into his mouth or give him a bite of a biscuit – anything sweet to revive him enough to take him home to his mother. Sometimes we suspected he just wanted a treat, especially if he knew someone had half a biscuit in their pocket. We'd get our reward when we took him home limp as a wilted lotus leaf: his mother would hand each of us half a biscuit. Then a much-revived Ah-dong would run off with us to celebrate on the levee wall. He was generous that way, and I still can't help wondering how genuine those fainting attacks were – maybe he just wanted to share his privileges as the son of a Party cadre.

We kids noticed that adults had lost their smiles. Their faces turned dark yellow, and some of their swollen legs oozed odorous liquid. They grumbled and complained that we children had no idea of the dire situation we were in. They no longer worried about informants lurking in the crowd; some even started to complain on the streets in loud whispers. A few bold ones swore and cursed to release their frustration. All were overcome by lethargy and starvation.

One day the authorities introduced a bright new idea to make us feel like we were getting more food: twice-cooked rice. After rice was cooked, it was stirred while more water was added, and then cooked a second time. This resulted in puffed-up rice that took up more space in our bowls. That meant the same quantity of uncooked rice could now feed more people. (Or so it seemed. In fact, we were all getting less rice than before.) It was an exciting concept, and for a short time our spirits were buoyed again, and we believed we could conquer anything, even hunger. But the puffed-up rice failed to satisfy hungry stomachs and revitalise depleted bodies, which led to more grumbling. One heroic comrade introduced thrice-cooked rice, promising an even bigger serving for each person. But that didn't work either. More people complained. We were all rickety and thin.

My grandmother's regular visits did little to relieve our increasing hunger, due to the strict monthly quota of ten kilograms of food for each visitor from the colonies. Baba said this was to discourage the now-thriving black market. I overheard Mama wishing my sister Ping could visit too. Given the family's unfavourable classification, Mama feared they would detain my sister on her return, as had happened to a few unlucky people in town. Mama agonised for weeks. I heard her talking about it with Ah-dong's mother, who always had a sympathetic ear for her.

One day Mama gathered enough courage to seek assurance from the District Head. She took me to keep her company. The District Head, once a strutting fellow, now appeared like one of us. His head hung low; he looked increasingly sallow, thin and tired. I hadn't heard him hum 'The East Is Red' in months. He told Mama that the country was in a dire situation because of the drought in the north, floods in the south, and the outstanding Korean War debts. 'Ping would be doing a patriotic job if she could bring food home to help the revolution,' he said to Mama, who bowed her head. 'The Eagle Brand sweetened condensed milk is the best. Our children love it. And the American Camel cigarettes are the richest tobacco, with a smooth, lingering aftertaste.' He gave Mama a faint smile. Mama nodded.

She wrote to Ping immediately and told her to come home with Grandmother Young on the next trip. She reminded her to bring the cigarettes and condensed milk.

My sister then began to make regular trips with food, just as many other relatives were doing for their families in Shiqi. Whenever Ping came home, Mama would register her arrival with the District Security Officer. That evening the District Head would pay us a visit, and Mama would offer him a tin of condensed milk, a toy or two for his children, and a packet of imported cigarettes.

I remember watching him place the goods inside his old army uniform, a feeble smile rising to the corners of his mouth. Then he nodded to Mama, and left without looking at us.

'We must share in these bad times,' Mama said without malice. 'A bright moon will shine again one day, after the clouds disperse.'

*

To impress the District Head, Baba had volunteered to work on the construction of a hydroelectric dam when the call for labour arrived.

The small coal-fired generator not far from our home had long been struggling to provide households in town with their one-per-family fifteen-watt lighting. Blackouts were common and kerosene lamps were essential backups. The light inside our room quivered most of the time.

In the hills many kilometres from our town, outcasts from the new society gathered to build the Changjiang Dam to generate more electricity for Shiqi. Some were, like Baba, unsuitable, unwanted or unqualified for any jobs in the new nation. Huts sprang up on the hillside to accommodate these otherwise unemployable people who received no remuneration apart from three modest meals a day. Baba's food ration was transferred to the dam site, where extra food in the form of sweet potatoes for the labourers served as an incentive. Political education was to continue for Baba and his fellow labourers in the evenings.

Building the dam required moving mountains of earth across a valley. The volunteer labourers used their spades and hoes to break the virgin ground. They carried the rocks and soil on their backs in sacks and baskets, or in carts pulled by teams of other workers and an occasional water buffalo or two.

Every Monday before sunrise, Baba set out on foot for another week at the dam site. Before he left home he would stroke our faces and kiss us goodbye while we were still asleep. He usually returned home on Saturday evenings, wheeling an empty wooden tank to collect nightsoil from residents in the street; he and his fellow workers transported this human fertiliser to the hills, where they grew vegetables to supplement their diet. This was their extra contribution to the Great Leap Forward. Baba told us how the red earth at the dam site was clay-ridden and dry, only good for weeds and the tough pines. It took him months to loosen and prepare the soil near his hut before he could grow sweet potatoes and other hardy vegetables. He tended to his small garden with the little spare time he had between his daily ten hours of volunteer labour and his evening meetings. 'It gives me respite watching the vegetables grow,' I overheard him tell Mama.

At bedtime I often listened to the quiet rumbles of their voices in our shared room. They discussed how the family would survive the unpredictable continual revolution Chairman Mao demanded, and now the worsening starvation as well. I had no idea what they meant by surviving something unpredictable, but from their tone and the way they whispered during the day, they seemed to be concerned that something serious and urgent was imminent. I wasn't sure if it was revolutionary or counter-revolutionary. Whenever I turned to listen, they changed the subject and smiled to show their contentment that we were together. That togetherness was important for our happiness, even though it didn't completely reassure me. It seemed to be the most important thing the family possessed, and it helped me feel more confident as I worked hard towards finally getting my Red Scarf at school.

CHAPTER 13

At the height of the famine in 1960, we arrived home from school to find our Street Committee Member supervising a gang of workers who were building brick walls against one side of the levee wall to create a series of rectangular, one-metre-deep reservoirs; these would be subsequently filled with water. Even though we could still reach the top of the levee wall by climbing onto the reservoir walls first, they dramatically shrank our playground.

We heard the workers saying how the smooth concrete surface of the street was ideal for holding water. The Street Committee Member was excited about cultivating some green algae in these ponds; she said that brilliant scientists somewhere up north had discovered rich protein in this algae that would supplement our diet. It looked as though our hunger might soon be over. Our hopes surged once more, like Red Star, our champion kite, soaring into the bright sky.

Ah-dong rubbed his big tummy with his skinny hand. 'It's a shame about the wall, but think about the food, my friends.'

'Yeah, anything for more food,' I agreed, wondering exactly what, how and when.

Every day we fastened our gaze on the new ugly structures that had taken over our street, hoping to witness the promised revolutionary phenomenon erupting soon in Kwong Street. The water was greening rapidly before our eyes with billions of tiny particles. There we hung our hope.

'See, we'll be big and strong one day,' said Ah-dong, flexing his tiny arms and straightening his back to look taller, though he couldn't tuck in his belly. Yiu-hoi was too tired to talk. Others nodded.

Each day we sat on the levee wall, breathing in the faint but nauseating smell of the concentrated algae, and felt proud to have made sacrifices for the revolution.

One day, curiosity overtook us. When those in charge weren't looking, we jumped off the wall, scooped up the thickened green muck and examined it closely. It smelled almost like Ah-ki when he'd slipped into the sewer pit when he was younger, after using the public lavatory near the commune's vegetable garden.

We screwed up our noses and yelled out, 'Yuck, how can we eat this?'

'No way would I eat this,' said Ah-dong, trying to expel the odour from his lungs. Yiu-hoi and Earring nodded. Weng and Ah-ki just stared, too lethargic to be bothered.

'Me neither,' said Yiu-hoi. 'I'd rather eat rats.'

'Ah-dong,' I said, 'why don't you go and ask your mother how she'll cook this stuff?'

So Ah-dong headed off and soon returned holding a piece of cake. 'My mother said this is how you cook with the algae: you put it in anything from rice to cake, even biscuits,' he declared, trying to look authoritative.

Even from ten steps away, the scent of the cake's burnt crust was mouth-watering. My stomach rumbled in a frenzy, aching and cramping more than ever. I was ready to offer Ah-dong my leadership of the gang in return for the cake.

'Great Leap Forward cake,' he affirmed, his sallow face beaming with pride, albeit faintly.

He broke it into small pieces, one each, and I gulped mine down in one mouthful. The burnt crust was tarry and bitter. It stuck to my throat like the black oil used for cooking vegetables, almost suffocating me. But at least it was soft and edible: a mixture of pumpkin, sweet potato, lentils and the algae, all bound together with a coarse, greasy flour made from rice husks.

We stayed on the wall and swung our legs, and thanked Chairman Mao for the treat.

'My mother told me they used to feed this stuff to the pigs,' Ah-dong said with a devilish grin. 'But it's really good for us to eat it now.'

'Then what do we feed the pigs with?' Yiu-hoi asked. The forward-thinker in the gang, he was concerned there would be no pork on public holidays.

'Don't worry,' Ah-dong said, 'Chairman Mao will guide us.'

We nodded in agreement, happy that we didn't need to care about such things as food: we had our Great Leader to lean on.

'And if things get worse ...' Ah-dong mumbled unexpectedly as we stared into the east. He said it with a solemn tone that was most unusual from him. 'I'll sell myself to child-eaters for one hundred yuan to feed my family,' he declared.

A chill rose like a glacial bath in the lotus pond. I trembled.

In those days, there were no newspapers or radio broadcasts about what was happening in the PRC, let alone the rest of the world, just Party propaganda. However, as the famine grew worse, news of increasing hardship circulated among the adults in Shiqi from those who had travelled to other provinces on government business; they said the worst-affected places were inland villages and towns where natural disasters had wiped out the harvest. But the hushed news that many people had starved to death was too hard for us children to comprehend. There were also stories of people eating the flesh of those who'd died – and, later, of abducted young children. I shivered each time I heard those stories, and began to think of death again.

Death was the man shot at Pig Head Hill, his body spurting blood in every direction, slumping, writhing and then not moving. Or it was those unhappy people who had jumped off tall buildings in Hong Kong, or leapt into wells or the Wonder River, or hanged themselves on the lychee trees at night. Death was also the many heroes and martyrs of the Long March and the Korean War who'd died for the revolution, and whose names would live on forever.

But when I had visualised my own death in the predawn darkness, while sitting alone on the wall, it had involved a surreal sense of peace and rebirth. There, darkness was always followed by light; as winter is followed by spring, morning would come again, and the dragon boats return with the seasons, year after year.

Ah-dong's idea of selling himself to be eaten was a big shock to me. From that moment, my understanding of death changed completely. To be eaten meant an end, a disappearance, a no-return, like the deaths of the frogs, fish, rats and sparrows we ate.

'No, Ah-dong,' I hastened to say to him on hearing his morbid declaration, 'I wouldn't do it unless someone paid my mother a thousand yuan.' I had no idea how much that was: to me, the one-yuan bill was a large amount, enough for my family to carry on for a few more days while waiting for our living allowances from Hong Kong. A thousand yuan would last us a lot, lot longer and definitely ease Mama's constant financial worries.

Yiu-hoi agreed, but with despair on his face. We then looked at one another and said nothing for a long while. When the dinner bell rang, we jumped off the levee wall and headed for our street's dining room.

My bowl was full of fluffy, tasteless thrice-cooked rice mixed with slimy algae, and some soggy brown cabbage with a hint of soy. There was a small piece of fish fried in black oil that always burned my throat, so to soothe it I gulped down a few big mouthfuls of rice.

Weng screwed up her face and complained that it was awful.

'Eat up,' Ying told her. 'It will make you grow, and stop your hunger pangs.' Then she added: 'You wouldn't want to eat dead people's flesh, would you?'

Shutting my eyes and trying not to smell it, I concentrated on shoving what was left in my bowl into my eager mouth with my chopsticks. I kept wondering just how quickly the algae protein would make me grow bigger and stronger.

*

In the weeks that followed, we spent a lot of time debating the nutritional value of green algae. We measured the width of our arms every day, and tried to forget our screams of pain when we strained hard to defecate, sometimes bleeding as we excreted the algae in black lumps into the toilet over the fishpond. Our faeces sank like rocks, and the fish didn't rush for them like they used to.

The Street Committee Member diligently assessed the algae crop to make sure it would provide enough sustenance. 'Precious Ones,' she sang out to us one day, 'I want you boys to pee into each pond every day to help the algae grow faster.'

'What?' we replied.

'Yes, a wee a day in each pond by each of you will make the plants multiply quickly and grow faster. Kwong Street will produce the best crop in the whole of Shiqi. Virgin boys' pee is the best.' The woman's tired eyes were vague, her jaundiced face glowing greener by the pond. Her voice had lost the authority it once commanded.

Ah-dong jumped off the wall and took the lead. 'Come on, boys, let's see whose wee shoots the farthest.'

We all stood up.

'One. Two. Three. Go!' When Ah-dong gave the order, a dozen boys pissed into the pond.

When I told Weng and Ying what we'd done, they refused to eat their dinner.

'I'd rather be eating grass roots,' said Ying. 'At least they don't smell like your pee.'

She was talking about the kikuyu grass with its long white roots, which the boys and I had already been eating as a snack; it was sweet and easy to chew, as were the tiny, sour, turnip-like roots of the clovers. My family was fortunate: with the money sent and food brought from Hong Kong, we didn't have to eat grass roots to survive – not yet. But many townspeople did, and the roots were getting scarce.

'Suppose we're lucky,' Ying said later at home, after retelling some stories she'd heard of children being eaten in provinces not far away.

My legs trembled when I heard those stories, and they nauseated me. No wonder Mama was worried about us going to and from school, especially little Weng, who at eight looked more like a five-year-old. Her big round eyes now appeared even bigger on her shrinking face.

*

One evening not long after Baba's release, Ah-dong's mother announced that the commune dining hall would be closed for good. 'We're going back to the old system of rations and vouchers for rice, meat, oil and kerosene,' she told us.

After nearly three years of eating with the people in our street every day, Mama felt uneasy about taking on the cooking and budgeting again, and dreaded lining up in those long queues to buy food. She also worried about how the rations of fourteen kilograms of rice a month for each adult (half of that for each child), thirty millilitres of black cooking oil (the lowest grade of oil, which Baba called leftovers), and 250 grams of meat per person would see us through the long month. One consolation might be greater variety of vegetables, although everything was in short supply.

Broadcasts from the street-corner loudspeakers blared from morning to night to inform us that this wasn't starvation, just rationing to share the burden equally. The authorities continued to blame the food shortages on natural disasters and the theft of grain by sparrows, mice, locusts and rats, as well as the Russian debts.

Baba made no comment about any of this. Instead, he obtained permission from the District Head to fish in waterways further away from home, after sharing his Red Flag cigarettes with the good comrade.

*

Whenever we were desperate for food, Ping and Grandmother Young would take turns to come home with their quota of provisions.

Sometimes they would travel together, especially during longer school vacations. Mama and Aunt Wai-hung always waited at the bus stop for their arrival, frightened that they would be robbed on their way to us. Weng, Ying and I would join our mother and aunt after finishing school. What scared us most was the recent story of two bicycle couriers who'd killed their passengers from Macau for the food they carried; when the murderers were caught, they were promptly taken to Pig Head Hill.

Although the town's small fleet of buses had grown, the operators found it hard to transport the increasing number of people from Hong Kong and Macau who brought food for their starving relatives. The buses ran late into the night, and on several occasions Ping and Grandmother Young didn't arrive until after midnight. I would wait with Mama, Weng and Ying at the bus station until they turned up, then we'd head home together through the dark and narrow streets of Shiqi, feeling more secure as a crowd.

The District Head continued to pay a visit each time Ping or Grandmother Young came home. He was thankful for each tin of sweetened condensed milk, and the Camel cigarettes. Our tin of condensed milk lasted three or four days with careful rationing and diluting. Mama insisted that we drink it inside our room, but I often snuck my cupful out to the levee wall where Ah-dong waited. We'd share it and feel better together. Other times, it would be Yiu-wei, Yiu-hoi or Ah-ki's turn.

Even with extra food, we were always hungry. We were small and thin like the others in Shiqi. Only our bellies grew bigger, until we all looked like Ah-dong. Mama tried various herbal remedies to clear our infestations; nothing helped. Whenever Ping and Grandmother brought food, the tinges of green and yellow in our sallow complexions would disappear for a few days, but it didn't take long for them to reappear.

*

By late 1960, people had begun dying in the streets of Shiqi, and the situation got much worse over the following months. It terrified me to watch sanitation workers collecting the corpses of the sick and homeless from the streets in the early mornings. A few days later, newcomers would occupy the places of the dead, and a few days later their bodies would be collected.

It was even worse in winter, when Shiqi trembled in darkness. The dim streetlights flickered in the chilly north wind. When it howled, the town rattled. In the dark people tripped over bodies and let out screams. We all kept our eyes wide open as we walked holding hands. Ah-dong's mother was worried when even the Party members' rations were cut, even though they were still better off than the rest of us.

As the winter deepened, at school we shouted our slogans with less conviction, and political studies lost their meaning. We were still studying the hardship and endeavour of the Long March, hoping to find inspiration, but it failed to drive away our hunger and lift our spirits. I was petrified by the thought that Ah-dong might offer to sell himself for a hundred yuan.

The dam-building slowed down in winter, but Mama was still working at the nursery, and on weekday evenings she did volunteer work, making string from hemp and palm fibres. She soaked the dried material in water for days until it was soft, then she removed the hard skin and peeled the fibres into long, fine pieces. Holding three at a time, she twisted them together to form one long string that she pressed and rolled on her thigh. As the string grew in length it was collected in a straw tray, and when dry it was reeled into a big ball. She delivered the string to the commune hall, where it was spun into small ropes by other workers. The skin of my mother's thigh turned brown, the colour of the raw fibres. It was callused and dry, and would crack and bleed in winter. She changed to rolling the strings on the other thigh until it, too, cracked and bled. By then the other thigh had healed. She kept on making string, and never complained. The lonely shadow of her thin figure under the kerosene lamp moved back and forth on the wall late into the night. As well, she still managed occasional Tiger Mouth Pond building duties but said most people were too weak and lethargic to continue.

'I'm not well tonight, no appetite,' I remember Mama often said to Ying. 'Divide the food among yourselves. Don't waste any, not even one grain.' She then went to bed without making string.

It took little time for us to gobble up every grain of rice in her bowl. But it took a long time for us to realise that she didn't eat so she could feed her starving children.

CHAPTER 14

On the eve of Chinese New Year in early 1961, an army truck full of festivity supplies struck the manure tub Baba was wheeling home. The impact smashed the tub into splinters and threw him onto the narrow gravel road. He sustained a serious injury to his right hip and had to be carried home in a cart by his fellow dam-building volunteers. A huge bruise covered his buttocks and spread down his right thigh to below his knee. He was in agony and unable to move, let alone bear any weight. Mama called for the town's herbalist, who had a reputation for treating fractures, and under his direction she boiled herbs and made poultices. We kids helped by collecting wild herbs from the countryside, as well as from neighbours and friends.

According to the herbalist, Baba hadn't broken any bones, yet for months he couldn't walk, even after the bruises had disappeared. The herbalist visited regularly but refused to accept any fees. He said he wouldn't have been there caring for Baba had it not been for my Grandfather Kwong helping his family to survive when he was a young boy during the Great Depression. Later Baba told us that the herbalist was from a very poor family in town, and that on the eves of major festivals my grandfather had always distributed the unsold grains from his rice mill to the poor families in Shiqi.

Baba had many months off work to recover, and he earned another Model Worker T-shirt in recognition of his injuries and dam-building.

After the summer of 1961, even though the Mid-Autumn Festival with its cooler days was near, dam-building ground to a standstill because many labourers became so weak and sick that they deserted their jobs; and even the comrades themselves were too tired to round up the workers and return them to the work sites.

*

Although he'd twice been hailed as a Model Worker, Baba was still under some form of street arrest, supervised by the District Head. On warm and humid days, wearing one of his prized white T-shirts, he sat on the levee wall catching the cool breeze from the lotus pond. I often found him staring at the horizon, drawing hard on his cigarettes, his eyes glinting in the receding light.

I know now that at such times he must have been transporting himself over the border to the east where the colonies were, imaging a life for us across the South China Sea. I hadn't been able to cope with living there in the past, but now I sometimes began to feel I'd like to try again. Baba and I didn't talk about my failure to stay in Hong Kong, and he never raised his disappointment with me. Perhaps he sensed that I'd come to understand what it meant to fail to grasp an opportunity, and that I'd learnt one of my first life lessons.

'Let's look to the future and make the best of it,' Baba often said to me when we shared our moments on the wall.

I was always puzzled as to how we could make the best of something that wasn't there, but I would nod and shift my gaze past my favourite playgrounds – the fishponds, the lotus pond, the paddies and Come Happiness Road – to the clear sky stretching eastward towards the South China Sea, dreaming, wishing, wondering. I tried hard to resist the thought that Baba had had enough of the revolution we were all so proud of, even though we were dispirited by hunger that seemed to go on forever.

Shiqi was prone to typhoons, so at an early age we'd learnt how to tell when one was approaching. The chickens stopped clucking and the dogs became restless, looking for somewhere to hide. Sparrows, dragonflies and butterflies disappeared, and even the normally aggressive geese huddled together hissing timidly, their feathers trembling. The sky turned black in minutes, and clouds gathered at great pace. Just moments before a typhoon struck, an eerie silence descended.

Then the blows hit. The mighty wind uprooted trees and crushed buildings effortlessly, while thunder and lightning split the sky. Rain filled the waterways, spilling over onto the flatland. If the tide happened to be in, the whole of Shiqi would be under water, and the levee wall wouldn't stop the schools of fish, eels and poisonous snakes swimming in and out of our house through the open front door. We'd have to stay home until the floods subsided, during which time we'd swim in our lounge room and fish from the top step of our bedroom. Afterwards, we'd have to help the adults with a lot of cleaning up.

One hot day after school, Ah-dong, Yiu-hoi, my classmate Hui and I were rowing a small wooden boat downstream into the countryside, looking for somewhere to have a cool swim. Without much warning, clouds rushed and tumbled, turning day into night. Fearful, we turned the boat around and headed for home against the strong wind from the sea. We pulled hard on the oars to get to the bank before the typhoon struck. Everyone else had already deserted the river as quickly as mourners leave a cemetery after a funeral.

As soon as we touched the bank, Yiu-hoi and Ah-dong jumped from each end of the boat, unwittingly pushing it back into the rising water. At that very moment, Hui jumped from the middle of the boat. The two other boys ran off, not realising that Hui had fallen into the river. He struggled in a frenzy to free himself from the swollen tide, his arms flailing in useless attempts to lift his head above water. His eyes were closed, and his face was grotesquely distorted.

Left alone in the boat, I was gripped by terror and panic. Hui must be fighting the river ghosts and spirits, I thought; he must be so frightened. I shouted for the boys to come back, but the storm drowned out my voice and they kept on running.

With a deafening howl, the big wind bore down. I didn't know what to do except try to keep the boat afloat. I screamed. I cried. I didn't want to desert my friend, or to watch him being pulled to the bottom and drowned. If Hui died, I'd have to face his father, a comrade in town; what would I tell him? How would I explain the accident to Hui's mother, the kind lady who had at times tried to slip more food into my bowl like Ah-dong's mother did in the dining room? But if I reached out to Hui, he might pull me in, and I wanted to die only for communism and Chairman Mao.

Hui was looking more desperate and ghastly by the second, gulping in water and air as he rose and sank, unable to keep afloat. Then his thrashing got slower and weaker till he was just writhing and jerking.

Lightning tore at the sky, and thunder shook the earth. It felt like the end of the world was near. Rain started to pour down. The little boat began to fill up with water.

Hui was losing the battle but still trying to get to the surface. His face was horror itself. And that horror has never left my memory. His eyes opened wide, staring at me, pleading, and perhaps accusing me for not helping. He began to sink. It looked like the battle would soon be over. How disappointed he must have been with me as he gave in to the river ghosts.

At that very moment, some unknown force pushed me to hold out an oar to him. He grabbed it and pulled his whole head and shoulders above water. He took one big gurgling breath after another, coughing and choking. He vomited. He gasped and tried to suck in air. His purple face went green, yellow and then crimson and grey, like a dead fish in the sun. He pulled himself onto the side of the boat, grunting and crying. But the boat was tipping into the rising current. Water was rushing in. I yelled at him to ease off as I tried to balance the boat.

Just then, Yiu-hoi returned with Ah-dong crying behind him. Somehow we kept the boat afloat and pulled Hui to safety. The crushing wind beat down with great force, trying to smash the ground and everything on it. Huddled together, we made our way home. As the rain bucketed down without mercy, it washed away our tears.

The next day Hui's mother burned bundles of incense and paper money at the spot where her son had almost drowned, to thank the spirits and ghosts of the river for not taking him. She didn't allow Hui near the waterways for months, not until after September, when it was too cold for swimming.

'They should thank you for saving their son,' Ying said.

'How could they?' Mama replied. 'His father is a comrade and his uncle is a senior official, and our family has a dubious background.' She lowered her gaze to the ground.

I didn't care. I just wanted to forget the whole thing, and I felt greatly relieved that I didn't have to face an important man to explain how his son had drowned.

*

After Hui's near drowning, Baba was concerned about my safety around the many waterways in Shiqi. He also worried about my stunted growth and physical weakness from poor nutrition. I heard him discussing this with Mama. 'Can't keep him away from the water,' Baba told her. 'So we've got to make sure he becomes a better swimmer, a stronger one. There's more than just the Wonder River to conquer one day ...'

After returning from Guangzhou, Ying hadn't stopped swimming. She'd kept up her training with the local squad under a Russian-trained instructor, Mr Lee, who was well known around town. In fact, the young man was a local celebrity due to his swimming prowess and amazing physique. (He wasn't related to the good Mrs Lee; there were many Lee families in Zhongshan.)

Baba would go along to watch Ying train, making the half-a-kilometre walk his daily exercise as he recuperated from his injury, still relying on a bamboo cane. Having been a physical education teacher in his younger days in Macau, Baba knew a lot about sports. He and Mr Lee chatted and shared their ideas about training. Before long, they struck up a friendship. Mr Lee began visiting my father on a regular basis, often after the squad had finished for the day. Kids in Kwong Street would hang around outside our door to catch a glimpse of the man, hoping they would be picked for his squad. We children admired him, worshipping him almost like a god.

One day I announced to Ah-dong and the rest of the gang on the levee wall that Mr Lee had accepted me as an associate member of his squad. Their jaws dropped, and they nearly fell off the wall.

'You didn't cross the Wonder River,' Ah-dong reminded me with disbelief. 'You're too skinny.' His remarks didn't upset me. Ah-dong was never a jealous person, and despite the fact that some kids called him an imbecile behind his back, he knew a lot more than the others thought he did.

Yiu-hoi jumped off the wall and went to ask my father if it was true.

'Yes,' Baba said, leaning on his bamboo walking stick, 'I've asked Mr Lee to teach Ah-mun how to swim properly. Then he can conquer the Wonder River one day.'

In the squad line-up, I peeped from the end of the line, past the big boys and girls, at Mr Lee, and listened to his every word. The round muscles in his arms and shoulders were easily as big as Ah-dong's head. No wonder people in town looked up to him, the District Head included. I was more than a foot shorter than the shortest kid in the team and self-conscious about my bony frame. But although I couldn't complete the required number of laps each session, I felt proud to carry my towel on my shoulder, making sure the red imprint of 'Shiqi Swimming Squad' was visible to everyone around. I hoped it would help erase my failure to cross the Wonder River.

My friends waited on the levee wall for me to return after swimming sessions and tell them what I'd been taught. When the weekend came, I shared the techniques with my gang in the Wonder River. Except for Hui, whose mother kept him out of the water, we all seemed to be swimming better and faster by autumn that year. How I enjoyed the envy and admiration in the eyes of the other Kwong Street children, while Ah-dong and Yiu-hoi grinned at me with pride and stuck by my side.

Baba was recovering well, but I noticed he hid it from the District Head. And when Mr Lee stopped by our place, he and Baba leant close to each other when they chatted, their voices hardly audible. If a tenant approached, they'd sit back in their chairs and talk in a louder tone on completely different matters. Occasionally they appeared to be absorbed in some serious conversations that were of little interest or relevance to us children. Later I would hear my parents whispering in bed. I was too tired to take much notice, though I understood that their conversations related to what the men had been discussing earlier.

Ying became suspicious of Mr Lee's frequent visits – she thought he and Baba were debating the prospect of her marrying him. After all, she was seventeen, nearly the revolutionary age to marry and have many sons to join the People's Liberation Army and protect China. Each time he appeared Ying went to her room, slammed the door and stayed there. She remained surly even after he'd left; she wouldn't talk to anyone. For a while the ancestral home eddied with the gossip that Mr Lee was interested in her, like the constant murmuring of the nearby Nine Meanders River. My parents didn't publicly dismiss or validate the rumour, although inside our room they tried to reassure Ying it wasn't the case.

Around this time, Baba also took a sportsman under his wing. A young track sprinter called Ho-bun had begun training by himself on Come Happiness Road and had captured Baba's attention. He would nod with approval at the young man's start, and how he held his arms, and he would mumble to himself when he noticed the young man was not sprinting with the right posture or attaining sufficient speed. After some weeks he couldn't help himself and went up to Ho-bun and offered to be his coach. Ho-bun never looked back from that day on, and he went on to become the town's champion sprinter. He also began to take a keen interest in my sister Ying.

CHAPTER 15

When hunger pangs woke me before dawn, I would creep outside to sit on the levee wall. There I thought of food and the challenges facing my family, and waited for the sun to rise. To me, sunrise was the best time of day in any season. The whole universe stood still as the magic of the sun's rays filtered through the thick lychee branches onto the banks of the lotus pond and over the weary houses that lined our street. The soft light dressed the dreary grey bricks and weather-beaten tiles in a warm salmon gleam, and it covered the ponds with a smooth emerald sheen. Peace at dawn softened the contradictions of life, enticing me to look forward to a new day. No wonder we were told that Chairman Mao was our rising sun.

Like Baba, I now looked to the east when sitting on the wall, and my thoughts carried me all the way to Hong Kong and Macau. Earlier I'd turned my back on those places, but now in my mind's eye I saw children enjoy dim sums, or butter and jam on toast for breakfast. I could smell the dim sums being steamed. I could feel the crunch of the toast as it crumbled between my teeth. The creamy taste of butter lingered on my tongue. It soothed my hunger. But the feeling never lasted long enough. Soon I would drink a cup of hot water, pretending it was my breakfast, and go off to school.

Starvation hurt more in the winter. On the levee wall I had to pull up the collar of my padded jacket to stop the chill biting the back of my neck. I rubbed my numb face with numb hands, and gazed towards the commune's vegetable garden, looking for a mature cabbage, hoping its disappearance wouldn't cast suspicion on my family. When darkness came I slipped out of the house into the night, pulled a cabbage from the cold earth, shook the mud from its roots and carried it home. I was always very careful to stay out of sight of the People's Militia officers who guarded the farm and would belt me if they caught me, and stop me from ever getting the Red Scarf.

I didn't feel too guilty, as it seemed unfair to me that most of the vegetables were being either exported for foreign currencies or distributed to comrades, Party members and officials, and that only a few would be sent to the vegetable market for the benefit of the commune. The same applied to the fish kept in the commune ponds. There, using roasted cockroaches as bait, I planted my line and waited quietly in the dark for a carp or any fish that would help feed my family. With Baba unemployed, there was no choice: we had to look everywhere for food. The algae ponds had long been abandoned; now only mosquitoes flourished there.

One wintry day after school late in 1961, Ah-dong, Yiu-hoi and I decided to try our luck catching wild prawns from the commune's fishpond just off Come Happiness Road. Ah-dong said as long as we threw any fish we caught back into the pond, the guards probably wouldn't mind. He pushed his chest forward to show off his Red Scarf. Besides, our homemade sewing-needle hooks were too small to catch any fish.

Crouching on the muddy bank, our tiny hooks baited with earthworms, we brought in prawn after prawn in a short time. They jumped and jerked inside our fishing baskets, trying to get back to the water. We chatted away, feeling happy – until some big hands landed on us.

Two stern-faced militia officers lifted the three of us from the embankment onto Come Happiness Road. Ah-dong burst into tears, his ear twisted and pinched by one of the guards.

It was early evening, the light turning dim. People were on their way home from their production units after a twelve-hour working day, and they stopped to watch the commotion as we begged for mercy. Stealing commune property would surely jeopardise our chances of being accepted for high school, and that was bad enough. Worse still was the thought of being trussed up and marched off, to be locked away for the night with the water buffalos. But worst of all was the thought of missing the only meal of the day. Hunger cramps were like wrenches tightening around my stomach, and my legs were shaky and weak. Sweat soaked my clothes. I felt cold.

I dreaded people judging us as bad elements. I'd just got into Sixth Class in September 1961 and hadn't yet been awarded the prized Red Scarf. The prestige I had gained from being in Mr Lee's swimming squad didn't seem to count enough to outweigh my family's low status. Ah-dong, Hui, Ah-bil, Big Eye and Earring had already earned their scarves, and it would be shameful to start high school without one. Even though hunger was hard to bear, I still yearned to be one of Chairman Mao's obedient children.

Ah-dong hung on to his Red Scarf with both hands, and I was sure he was prepared to martyr himself for it. 'The ... they are oh ... only ... wild prr ... prawns.' He was speaking to the guards but couldn't meet their stern eyes.

'They are commune property,' shouted a guard, his eyes fearsome as he tightened his grip on Ah-dong's ear. 'Shame on your Red Scarf!'

Ah-dong shook and cried more. He gripped his Red Scarf even tighter. His stutter had become worse than ever, and his big head flopped to his chest. Yiu-hoi looked petrified, and I felt sick with fear.

'Let the kids go,' pleaded a woman in the crowd. 'It's only a few wild prawns.'

A few people nodded. 'Yeah, yeah.'

Then a loud voice called from the crowd, 'If they weren't hungry, they wouldn't—'

'Commune property is sacred!' one of the guards yelled back. 'We'd rather starve to death than steal from the people.'

'But they are hungry kids, and there's no food,' came another civilian voice. 'And we're all hungry!'

'Yeah, yeah,' echoed the crowd, getting louder as more people surrounded us.

Both guards now turned to face the crowd, and one shouted, 'They're to be punished!'

The people were jostling as others joined in, gathering around us. Come Happiness Road was blocked. What had started as a timid protest grew as people spoke louder and louder over each other, soon shouting, arguing against the injustice of the dire situation they were in, their own lot in life. The guards struggled to quell their anger.

I felt a tug on my arm. 'Go, now,' whispered the woman who'd first spoken up.

I ran off. Yiu-hoi followed, with Ah-dong staggering behind. We got Ah-dong home to his mother in time for some sweets she kept locked away for his funny turns.

After that incident, when we sat on the levee wall we'd often talk about our close encounter with the People's Militia. Ah-dong couldn't stop laughing, his eyes gleaming and face beaming; his head seemed to get even bigger as he retold the story without his stutter. We would then plan our next move to find food for another day.

*

As we grew older, we were becoming more aware of the reality of our situation. We grumbled about the fact we couldn't afford to buy food in the black market to help our hungry families, and we dreamed about getting rich. It saddened me to hear Ah-dong say how he was still waiting for someone to offer him a hundred yuan to die so his family could afford to buy extra food; he said he didn't care anymore if he was eaten. Yiu-hoi echoed me, insisting that he wouldn't do it for less than a thousand yuan. I began to consider selling myself again, even though my father had come home and things were looking better. Thinking back now, I don't believe we really wanted to sell ourselves, but at the time we felt prepared to do anything to save our families.

One day we sat on the levee wall jealously watching the commune ducks pick up the leftover grain in the paddies. After this, the birds would be force-fed balls of cooked greens and rice husks to speed up their growth – while we didn't even have rice husks.

Without a word to each other, we knew exactly what we were going to do.

Quacking merrily, the ducks poked their heads into the shallow water to gobble up the loose grains. I stood on the wall holding a piece of broken brick behind my back. Ah-dong watched as my eyes focused on the fattest duck closest to the wall.

'Go Big Brother,' said Yiu-hoi, as soon as the duck keepers weren't looking our way and no one was watching from Kwong Street.

I hit my target. The other ducks dashed for cover while their mate struggled, but within seconds they were all back, eagerly feeding as if nothing had happened. We were frozen on the wall. My heart skipped out and took off. My hands and lips went cold. Then I began to tremble.

The dying bird also trembled and couldn't raise its head above water. Soon the flapping stopped. Silence hit as we watched the duck stretch its legs for the last time. The other ducks kept looking for food around its floating body.

'You look awful,' Ah-dong said to me. 'The colour of death is on your face.'

I didn't like hearing that, though I usually appreciated his honesty.

'Shut up, Ah-dong,' said Yiu-hoi, ever so loyal to his older cousin.

Before long, the ducks were moved on to another field. Yiu-hoi jumped off the wall and weighed down the dead bird with a large ball of mud, hiding it beneath the surface.

'You look a bit better now, Ah-mun,' said Ah-dong, patting me on my shoulder. 'The colour of death has gone. You'll live a long, long life, but I bet you'll never forget this.'

I'd never thought about what a long life meant, or what it would be like. Life in those days was too much like living with death wrapped around your throat, tightening at its will and suffocating you at its pleasure. Death meant little, so little that at that point I didn't care if I was to die, but I did hope for at least a thousand yuan for the family. I could only free myself from these ill thoughts when I was doing things with my friends, or when Mama and Baba hugged me close, or when Ping and Grandmother Young brought food home.

'Let's fly our new Red Star tomorrow,' I said to Ah-dong and Yiu-hoi. 'I'm not sure if it'll last the season.'

The boys agreed, and we started to talk about other things, trying not to regret what we had done.

When evening came, I retrieved the duck and took it home. Mama boiled water and soaked the bird for nearly half an hour, then plucked it. She cooked it in our room without any herbs or spices, for fear of the tenants smelling it. She then woke the family in the small hours, and we sat around and ate the duck after saving the drumsticks for Ah-dong and Yiu-hoi. I slept a lot better after that.

Before dawn, I got up to bury the duck's feathers and bones in the family's small vegetable patch. Just that extra bit of food seemed to restore me, or at least strengthen me enough to plot another day's survival.

*

Food rations were cut even further, and rice for unemployed adults went down to twelve kilos a month. Essentially, that meant you had about four cups of cooked rice for every three meals, with very little other food such as meat, fish or vegetables. Sugar and black oil were also in short supply. Yet loudspeakers in the street kept urging us to tighten our belts to repay the Russian debts.

I was pleased that Baba had finally recovered from his injuries, but he smoked more in his dark corner and seldom talked. We knew he was planning how to persuade the District Head to allocate him a job so that he could help feed his starving family.

Ping and Grandmother still visited every month, and the District Head continued to collect his share. One day he shook Baba's hand to express his gratitude for the extra goods. Baba seized the moment. 'I need a job, comrade. Any job.'

The District Head took a long sniff at the small handful of Camel cigarettes Baba had given him. He kept his head down and avoided looking at Baba.

Then he nodded.

'The weight of the world is on his shoulders,' said Baba, after the man in charge of us had left.

'Times are hard.' Mama's voice was subdued, tender and soft.

I remember clearly Baba's excitement when he got his first paid job, after being unemployed for so long. Finally, after all these years of re-education and imprisonment, he was qualified to work as an apprentice to a pot and kettle repairer. I suspect he'd finally ceased to regard himself as an academic, an intellectual, knowing his education was useless.

'Look what I've earned today!' he called out as he bounced into the house after his first day at work, waving five ten-fen notes in the air. Cuts glistened on his hands in the evening light, but he didn't seem to care.

Mama cried. She rushed to make bandages from an old sheet and fetch clean water to tend the wounds. Baba's face was beaming, red as the bright blood stains on the notes flapping in front of us. My sisters and I danced around him, singing our favourite song:

I am not a parasite, and I work hard to rebuild China
Soon we'll rise, and soon we'll be a great, great nation
Under our dear Chairman's guiding light
La, la, la, la, la, la, la ...

Baba gave each of us kids a two-fen aluminium coin – a small fortune for us in those days. We were very happy, and Mama was smiling again, so prettily.

Baba was also pleased that he now knew how to replace a pot's burnt-out bottom with another piece of tin. He even brought one home to show us how it was done. However, he cautioned us against limiting our learning to simple tasks and didn't stop stressing the importance of a good education. 'Always utilise your brainpower,' he reminded us as he often did, pointing to his head. 'It is unlimited.'

I heard him mumble to himself one day while sitting in his favourite cane chair smoking his cigarette, 'While I ride on a buffalo, I am looking out for a horse.'

*

In late winter 1961, strangers with sunken, wrinkled faces, like dried melons, drifted into town, begging for food in peculiar dialects I had never heard before. They horrified us with their dark yellow skin and lifeless eyes. Their bulging bellies were nearly too heavy for them to carry. They panted as they dragged their exhausted bodies along, fluids oozing from their swollen legs, soaking their makeshift bandages. Flies swarmed around them, but they had no strength to drive them away. Even from a distance the stench was awful.

Baba said these people were from the poorer inland provinces where the famine had hit the hardest. They were not far from dying of starvation and the smell of death clung to them.

Although awareness of the famine had spread, there was no mention of it in the official newspapers, radio broadcasts or over the loudspeakers, which continued to praise Chairman Mao and the Party as our saviours, and remind us of the success of the Great Leap Forward. As well, there were new slogans, along with accusations against the Russians, who it was said were causing all our troubles. We began to hate the Russians even more.

'Hold hands on the way to school,' Mama reminded us every morning. 'Never let Weng walk home by herself.'

Most days Mama walked halfway into town with us and met us near the school when it finished, just to be sure we were safe. For the first time in years my family locked our front door and bedroom door every night, and we kids wouldn't sleep unless our parents were in the room with us.

'Have you eaten today?' friends and relatives grimly asked when they greeted each other with concern, but that was as far as it went. Nobody could spare any food.

We used the manure from our chickens to fertilise our vegetable patch, and we saved a few eggs for hatching. Baba taught me how to identify the fertile eggs under our kerosene lamp: they have a dot in the middle of the yolk. Nothing was more exciting than watching the tiny chicks peck their way out into the world. The balls of squirming slime soon dried and turned into fluffy, golden, chirpy creatures. We fed them grass seeds. When they grew up, we exchanged some of them for other necessities. It was never a happy time when we had to eat the biggest of the flock.

One morning in winter, my pet rooster refused to feed. It was on my mind all day at school, a bleak midwinter's day with clouds hanging low and the north wind howling. As soon as class finished, I rushed home; I couldn't wait around for Ah-dong to come out of detention class. While the chickens went about the yard looking for insects and worms, my little rooster was left behind. He tottered out of the pen and settled a short distance away where he dozed, his heavy eyelids slowly opening and shutting. Baba shook his head, expecting the worst – a nodding chicken was a bad sign, and chicken flu hit without warning every few winters.

I gently held my little rooster in my hands, no longer the bold and handsome bird he used to be. His shiny bronze and red feathers had lost their lustre. He could no longer hold his head high and march around the yard, asserting his authority. His body felt like a hot water bottle and he couldn't stop trembling. His eyes were half-shut, but I was sure he knew I was there.

Then he began to shake violently. Minutes later he stretched out his long legs, threw back his head and died in my palms.

For days I was very upset. Worse still, we had to eat him.

The following week, the rest of our small flock of chickens died, one after the other, and so did others in the neighbourhood. We had chicken for dinner every night of the week because there was no refrigerator.

After the chickens had died and fish became harder to find in the rivers and waterways around the town, we saw much more worry on our parents' faces. Baba's eyebrows now knotted in the middle as he sat in his corner, deep in his thoughts, drawing hard on his cigarettes.

'The bright moon will shine again one day when the clouds disperse,' Mama said softly to us when we sat with Baba. There was no anger in her voice, just fatigue. We believed everything she told us and went to bed hungry, hoping to see a clear sky in the morning.

*

Mr Lee continued to visit Baba at our house. He didn't smoke, though, for he took good care in maintaining his legendary lung capacity. We called him Comrade Instructor, but Baba always called him by his given name, Ding-yan. A quiet rumour around town was that his father had been taken up to Pig Head Hill as an enemy of the revolution as soon as the PRC was proclaimed.

One day after school, I walked into our room to find Baba carefully cleaning a piece of bloodstained meat Mr Lee had given him, the size and shape of a small cauliflower. Baba, who seemed very excited by the gift, cooked it with some herbs and half a bowl of cheap rice wine. The smell of the concoction wafted through the whole house while it simmered for hours. He delegated us kids to keep the fire going and to guard the gift. Later that evening we each had a small bowl of broth with cut-up pieces of meat.

This happened a few more times. We kids were most surprised to receive such a big piece of meat without needing ration vouchers. It was unbelievable.

'It's human placenta,' Baba eventually confessed. Mama nodded, and explained to us what that was. 'It's all right to eat it. They use it in medicine. Many animals eat their own afterbirths.' She told us it was rich in protein, what we needed the most to stay alive.

Ying felt sick and said she wanted to vomit, but Weng and I appreciated the extra food and didn't care where it came from.

'When you are starving, you will eat anything to stay alive,' Baba said. He told us how desperate people up north would eat white clay, called Goddess of Mercy's clay, to relieve their hunger. It was usually their last meal, as the clay clogged up their fragile bowels.

Suddenly the supply of placentas ended. I found out later that senior members of the maternity hospital took priority over others like Mr Lee's sister, who was a midwife, in securing them for consumption.

I impressed my friends by saying I had eaten human placentas. But we only wanted a biscuit or two, or a sweet of some sort. We didn't want to steal food from the commune. We really didn't want to eat human afterbirths, and definitely not human flesh. So we continued to sit on the levee wall, dreaming of food.

CHAPTER 16

One unusually warm day at the peak of the famine in late 1961, I returned from school and smelled food in our street, something tantalising – an unforgettable moment. It wasn't a scent from our daily fantasies on the levee wall. It wasn't the fragrance of ripening rice that always made me drunk with delight, and it wasn't the bland smell from huge woks in the commune kitchen. It was the delicate whiff of sugar, milk and flour all mingled together – an aroma treasured in my hungry mind, and associated with the yummy oval 'Gold Mountain' arrowroot biscuits my grandmother sometimes brought from Hong Kong.

At first I thought the smell could have been my wishful imagination, even a hallucination. But then I remembered it was related to something we'd been talking about and expecting for days.

'A man from the New Gold Mountain is looking for a wife,' Ah-dong had said to us on the levee wall the week before. Like his mother, he always seemed to know what was going on in the street.

'How do you know?' Yiu-hoi asked, eyes widening.

'I always know these things,' said Ah-dong, 'because my baba told my mama.'

My parents had long told us stories of sojourners who'd spent decades abroad toiling for families they'd left behind. After squirrelling away some wealth, many returned to find a wife and start a family, but by that time, they were often elderly.

A few of my cousins, like Third Aunt's daughter, had married sojourners, and their families lived more comfortably than others; having girls in the family could be a blessing in this time of starvation. But my older sisters swore that they would never marry old men, even if they were from the goldfields. The slightest mention of it made Ying slam doors even harder.

Baba had told us that in the early days of the PRC many sojourners were fearful of returning home because of the sanctions against China and the risk of losing their residential rights in foreign countries; they were also afraid of being detained under the PRC. So they had usually looked for wives in Hong Kong or Macau instead. But since the sojourners had been reclassified as patriotic because they helped increase foreign currencies for China's rebuilding program, a few more had started to return to seek a wife.

This one would be negotiating with a family in Kwong Street. The thought of witnessing such an unusual event had us buzzing with excitement for days before his arrival. The go-between, who had recently returned from a re-education camp, had received approval from the street committee and the District Head to help with the negotiations.

The young woman was still unmarried at the age of twenty, a great concern to her parents, and the street committee wasn't happy with the family because she hadn't answered the government's call to get married at the age of eighteen and have babies to rebuild China.

Mama had often said that the young woman's mother worried a lot about her daughter's future and those of her other four children. Like my parents, she was unemployed because her parents were from a now-disparaged class, in their case the landlords. Luckily, the daughter had somehow obtained an indoor job in a lightbulb factory. She was once friendly with a young man, a son of a Party member, in her production unit. But the comrade in charge of the factory promptly put a stop to the acquaintance, telling her she was unworthy of the young man.

At least having an indoor job had benefited the young woman's marriage prospects: she'd retained a fair complexion, which the go-between emphasised during the negotiations.

'Sojourners like fair-skinned women to be their wives,' Baba explained to me. 'And there aren't many fair-skinned women left in Shiqi. They have to work in the fields, or build roads and dams.'

Whether such negotiations were successful or not, they always involved the distribution of special treats for us children. The thought of foreign sweets and biscuits had us drooling for days. Indeed, in the lead-up to the sojourner's arrival everyone was wondering what gifts he would bring, what clothes he'd be wearing and even how he would smell – the event evoked visions of foreign countries and their bountiful opportunities. I sat with my friends, inventing tales of what it would have been like for us if we'd gone to live in a foreign land. How would our families cope? How old would we be when we returned? Would people in the street recognise us? Would we ever make it home again? These thoughts lifted our spirits.

That afternoon we felt the sojourner's presence in the street. People were already crowded around the front door of the prospective bride's house. Instead of heading off to do my homework, I ran with Ah-dong to see for myself. Although the bigger children blocked most of my view, I could just glimpse the man from the New Gold Mountain. He looked older than my father.

He was wearing a crisp white shirt, stiff as cardboard, nicely ironed trousers, a leather belt with a gold buckle that flashed like a small sun, and shiny leather shoes. His thinning hair, neatly combed and tamed with cream, shone like his expansive forehead. From time to time, he took a handkerchief from his trouser pocket to dab away the little mist of sweat from his full face. Ah-dong said it looked as if negotiations were drawing to a head, for the man was getting more restless in his seat.

'His face is bigger and fuller than all the men's in town,' Ah-dong whispered to me. 'Including those of the comrades. Wow, and his fat belly! He must be wealthy.' The man's big stomach bounced when he coughed. I tried to imagine what this man had been like before he went away to Australia to make his fortune; he'd probably been young, wild and carefree like us.

I elbowed my way out of the crowd to get some fresh air. I felt sad. Why did life have to be like that? Why did families have to be separated? Why did young men have to leave home and not return until they were old?

Ah-dong, who'd followed me, looked at me with a faint grin. He knew how I often struggled with the many unanswered questions about life, and how it seemed no answers would make me happy. 'Give up,' he said, rubbing his potbelly of worms. 'You think too much and worry too much. Think about yummy biscuits now, my friend.'

He understood me better than the others. In the unseasonable heat, sweat oozed from his patched singlet, dripping onto his dirty feet, thin as joss sticks. I became aware of my own patched T-shirt and grubby feet with mucky toes hanging like undernourished potatoes. How I wished we had shoes like the man from the New Gold Mountain.

'We are grubby!' I said.

But who cared how we looked? We only wanted the treats. With barely a nod, we dived back into the crowd.

Laughter rang out of the house, boosting our hopes. The negotiation seemed to be drawing to an end. The young woman's father had a big smile that took over the whole of his shrunken face. Years of working outdoors had aged him, but the lines on his skin couldn't mask the happiness and pride in his eyes that day. He looked older than his possibly older prospective son-in-law. His stained teeth rattled when he talked, and cigarette smoke hissed through the gaps left by the ones he had lost. Now he was laughing so heartily that I feared he might lose all of his teeth. But this was his big day, a day he'd been hoping for in between political studies, work and volunteer jobs. It was the day the fortune of his family might turn for the better: regular foreign currency would be secured, along with food from the black market for his family. And there was one less mouth to worry about.

The young woman sat quietly behind her father with her head down. She glanced at us every now and then, while stealing looks at her future husband. The flush on her face grew, making her smile look awkward, until she became as red as the large flag that her father had borrowed to cover the dreary brick wall long before the sojourner arrived. The imposing golden stars on the flag seemed to gleam with approval for the parents' patriotic act of arranging a marriage for their daughter with a sojourner from Australia, viewed as less hostile than the United States. The young woman nervously covered the small tear near the elbow of her faded floral blouse, a less proletarian outfit that made her stand out, like the sojourner, among the grey and blue, and those dirty feet in her house.

As I looked at her, I wondered again what would happen if one of my sisters married a sojourner. Would that give me the opportunity to become one myself? I thought if that could relieve my family's hunger, I would certainly do it, even if it meant missing all of my loved ones. If I had the opportunity to go overseas, I'd work hard to earn money and send it home to my parents so they wouldn't have to work long hours building dams and roads, making strings, or repairing pots and pans. They wouldn't need to worry about food anymore, for I would send enough money to keep them. And it would be a lot better than selling myself to child-eaters for a thousand yuan.

The crowd shifted, pushing me forward. Negotiations were favourable for all parties. Ah-dong urged me to get closer to the door, where fortune smiled on us too. We moaned with excitement the moment the young woman's mother got up from her chair. She took the colourful tin that had been sitting on top of the family's small tea table since negotiations had begun. She was glowing as she walked towards us with a warm smile. Our stomachs rumbled in a mad frenzy. We edged closer. What was inside the tin? Sweets? Biscuits?

Blood rushed back to Ah-dong's sallow face as the lid popped open. Sitting neatly inside were rows of oval biscuits with foreign words on each of them. The sweet smell of sugar, milk and flour hit us head on. 'Me, me, me,' Ah-dong cried out, standing on his toes and reaching out.

I struggled to attract her attention too. 'Me, me, me!'

'One each,' the young woman's mother said as she handed out the biscuits with the biggest smile I'd ever seen. 'And an extra one for you for taking care of the little ones in the street,' she said to me, as our gang's leader.

I sank my teeth into my biscuit. It felt and tasted so different from the hard-to-come-by 'Great Leap Forward biscuits' on sale from time to time for a precious food voucher. They were almost unbreakable: we had to smash them into small pieces with a hammer. Even then they were too hard to chew, so we sucked the sweet taste one piece at a time. Ah-dong once took a bet that he could bite off a piece, and he lost a tooth.

I ate my arrowroot biscuits in tiny bites over many days, sharing them with my sisters. As I savoured them, I remembered the ones Grandmother had soaked in milk when I was in Hong Kong with her. Once the biscuits were gone, I kept pulling out my pocket to catch a whiff of their wonderful and now fading aroma, and I waited patiently for the wedding, when more biscuits would be distributed to neighbours.

CHAPTER 17

'Ideology is destroying China,' my parents mumbled to each other, in pain as they watched the decline around us. They gazed out of the house, past the levee wall, the vegetable gardens and Come Happiness Road, and over the gum trees all the way towards the South China Sea.

By now the Great Leap Forward was well into its fourth year. Things were getting worse by the day, and starvation had become deeply entrenched. Our rations hardly lasted us three weeks each month, even with my mother's strict planning. People regularly grumbled in public: some were angry, but most were too frightened to make a scene.

My cousins Young-young and Young-chit, my Aunt Wai-hung's older sons, rode for half an hour on their antiquated bicycles all the way from Shenmingting into town, to see if Mama might have some food for them. She always made sure she had a sweet potato or two for the boys, and she told us we all had to share. Sometimes they stayed a few days, and Mama had to arrange for their rations to be transferred to Shiqi. Not only did my gang enjoy their company, but we also had more productive food-finding expeditions because of the boys' knowledge of fishing holes and how to evade commune guards.

Most of the rats and sparrows had been killed during the campaigns to eradicate the Four Pests, or eaten by hungry people during the previous summer. Without these predators, rice-paddy beetles and grasshoppers became bigger, fatter and more plentiful. They tasted all right when roasted in a fire, but we got sick with nausea, stomach cramps and diarrhoea if we ate too many. Baba said our digestive systems were now used to low- or non-nutritious food, and they could no longer cope with even the slightly rich fare of beetles and grasshoppers.

We were all thin and sallow. Our ribs threatened to push through our chests. They squeaked like worn-out spokes on old bicycle wheels as we moved. We lost our breath easily and struggled to keep our balance. We noticed the ankles and feet of many people around us began to swell. Baba said once this happened, the swelling would advance to the knees, then, in a short time, the stomach, and finally the chest and face, wringing the air out of the person. Then they would die an awful death of suffocation. I started checking my ankles and feet many times a day. I couldn't keep my eyes from my friends' feet and stomachs, especially Ah-dong's. He was dear to me like a brother.

More and more people in Shiqi were looking like the waves of outsiders who had previously poured into town in search of food. Some older people developed blisters of all sizes, and a clear fluid, the colour of dried rice straw, oozed from their legs. It trickled all day long, soaking through bandages and sending out an unpleasant odour. The sicker people panted as they moved, trying to keep away the flies that gathered to suck the fluids on their skin. Later their breaths became more laboured and rattly, and flies swarmed on them like leeches as they drew their last breaths.

Baba told us to collect beetles and grasshoppers from the fields, and even to trap field rats. He carefully prepared and roasted the grubs we caught, before letting us eat them in small amounts. The years in Heilongjiang had turned him into some kind of health expert in our eyes – better still, a survivalist, determined and obsessed, unyielding. But there wasn't much more he could do to remedy the situation. He became more apprehensive by the day, probably more than the other adults, who didn't know what was happening to them.

Apart from the few rice distribution centres, hardly any other commune-run shops were open in Shiqi. Those that were had scarcely any goods to sell; they were mostly empty shops with empty shelves. Shopkeepers were idle, taking long naps during the day, even at work. And of course there were no private enterprises, as those were illegal in the PRC, although we heard from the adults about the black market stirring in the background. With that mostly hidden from view, the town was turning into a ghostly place like Pig Head Hill.

*

During 1961, Grandfather Gut Young had retired due to poor health and gone to Hong Kong to recuperate – as an American citizen, he was fearful of how the authorities might treat him if he visited Shenmingting. My parents seized this rare opportunity to apply to the District Head for a visa for Mama, Weng and me to go to Hong Kong. My mother's reasons were to help Grandmother nurse Grandfather back to health, and for us kids to meet him for the first time. (Ying, being more patriotic than the rest of us, refused to travel abroad.) Mama hadn't seen her father in many years, and she hoped the authorities would consider the application with compassion. Aunt Wai-hung, who was then living in a different administrative district, also applied to leave, giving similar reasons.

This time if we were allowed to leave, we would not return. The family was quietly excited, having something to look forward to. But the possibility of success was slim. The District Head knew we'd probably not return, and in due course he rejected our application.

Mama tried again and again. After each rejection, she'd wait outside the district security office early the next morning to collect another application form. For people in Shiqi, securing even one of these forms was a triumph – an opportunity to be considered for an exit visa, even if approval was unlikely. Baba said that the Hong Kong goods we gave regularly to the District Head moved him to give Mama an application form each time – but nothing more. Aunt Wai-hung, on the other hand, was permitted by her local District Head to leave with her youngest son, Young-syn. For reasons since forgotten, they ended up staying in Macau instead of proceeding on to Hong Kong.

*

'Living without freedom is like a living death, and now with starvation it is a certain death,' Baba grumbled to Mama inside our room, with the door shut so the tenants couldn't hear. Stated publicly, that comment would have landed him a long prison term in a worse place than Heilongjiang.

I sensed that he could no longer tolerate his situation – that he was getting ready to run away to Hong Kong or Macau, as some townspeople had recently done. His attempt would mean risking his life, and it would involve more denunciation and criticism of our family. The fear of Pig Head Hill began to hover in my dreams again. Yet escape seemed to be the only way out for us. I began to wish Baba would just do that: run away and live. If he could make it out of China, we might all have a chance; then one day the family might be together again. I was sure Baba would try his very best to get us out, no matter how many years it might take.

One day in late 1961, I overheard Baba telling Mama that he had made a pact with Mr Lee to escape China, and that was what they had been plotting. It took little time for her to agree to this. She had seen the man she loved being punished, denigrated and shamed – not for committing crimes, but for his education. While Baba remained under watch by the neighbours, especially by Choi-lin, Mr Lee had been planning how to get out of Shiqi. The deal was that Baba would take care of Mr Lee when they got to Macau, and perhaps eventually Hong Kong, both places my father knew very well and Mr Lee did not.

Through the rest of the year and into the spring of 1962, while Baba and Mr Lee refined their plan, Mama kept applying for an exit visa, but the District Head rejected every application. She was losing

Mama, Wai-syn Young, and Baba, Shek-tong Kwong, in 1961 after Baba's release from prison. Baba and Mama had both trained as teachers, and fell in love on a ferry on their way to Hong Kong before the People's Republic of China was proclaimed in 1949.

In 1955, when I was just six years old, I was sent to Hong Kong, where I lived with my maternal grandmother, Grandmother Young. This photograph of the two of us was taken during my brief stay, before I became homesick and asked to be allowed to go back to Shiqi.

A 1959 propaganda poster promoting the Great Leap Forward, Mao Tse-tung's plan to modernise and collectivise China's agricultural production. *(Alamy)*

Mao in 1959, surrounded by adoring children. He is wearing the Red Scarf, an honour awarded to young people who had proved themselves to be loyal communists. *(Getty Images)*

A photograph of my primary-school year group, circa 1959, after we won a 'Model Class' prize for assisting efforts to boost steelmaking during the Great Leap Forward. I am fifth from the left in the back row. My friend Big Eye is third from the left in the second back row.

A family portrait taken just after Baba returned home from prison in early 1960. Back row: me, Ying and Ping. Front row: Mama, Baba and Weng. Ying is still wearing her provincial swimming squad uniform. Mama and Baba both look anxious – not surprising given that the family was by then having to deal with major food shortages exacerbated by the government's economic policies.

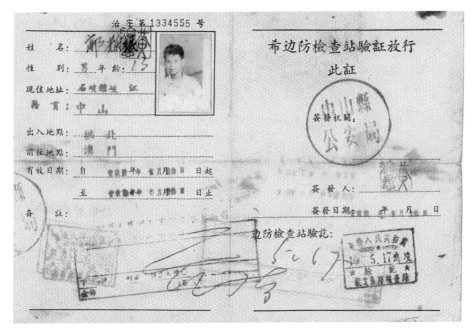

The visa that was approved and stamped by the District Head, allowing me to leave China. The photograph was cut from a larger image of Mama, Weng and me. Mama later submitted the other part of the photo with an application for her and Weng to leave, which was rejected.

A studio shot of Ping, Baba and me, taken not long after Baba and I arrived in Hong Kong, in late 1962. Baba's renewed optimism is clear. Every year from then on, we would dress in our best clothes and have photographs of ourselves taken to send to Mama and our sisters in Shiqi.

Fly, young eagle, fly! Me on arrival at Sydney Kingsford Smith Airport on 31 January 1969. My Pan Am bag and typewriter stand beside my suitcase. As it turned out, I had a long wait here, but fortunately was quickly befriended by other newly arrived Chinese students.

At Holy Cross College, Ryde, with fellow students Tony Chen (at left) and Peter Wong (at right). For me and many others, Holy Cross provided a safe and happy entrée to Australian society.

After passing my final-year medical exams in 1976, I took a trip back to Hong Kong to see Baba. He looks so happy, and I was clearly very proud of my University of NSW sweatshirt!

I was sad that Baba and Mama couldn't be at my University of NSW graduation in January 1977, but delighted to have other family in attendance, including my sister Ping, Grandmother Young, and my Aunt Bertha and Uncle Chong Young from Hawaii (at far left and far right, respectively).

Sheree and I were thrilled to have Ping and Baba as our 'guests of honour' at our wedding in Sydney in 1977. We sent photographs of our happy day to Mama and my other sisters, and even managed to smuggle some of the wedding cake to them in Shiqi.

Baba and Mama during their first trip to Sydney in 1983. It was thrilling for me to finally see them together again and to show them around my new home city.

Our family reunion in Washington, DC, in 1989 was the fulfilment of a long-held dream, bringing together three generations and our entire immediate family. I'm standing at top left next to Baba and Mama; Ping is second from right in the back row; Weng is second from left in the second back row; and Ying is second from right in the second row, in the blue dress.

Walking down memory lane in Shiqi in 2018, with my lifelong friend Ah-dong. Despite the loss of our old playground in Kwong Street, we were delighted and amazed by Shiqi's transformation from a quiet riverside town to a thriving, cosmopolitan and environmentally friendly city of three million people.

With my family at home on the Central Coast of New South Wales. From left to right: my daughter Harmony, me, Sheree, daughter Serena and son Andrew-James.

hope – like the townspeople as they became even more emaciated – and becoming desperate. I heard her say she would be content even if Baba was the only one in our family to make it to the free world, away from starvation, persecution and looming death. She said she was prepared to put up with the inevitable consequences from the authorities after my father's escape. There was nothing left for her to hang on to except the tiny glimmer of hope that, perhaps, one day they might be reunited. Success depended on blessings from the ancestors and the gods, so she continued to light an incense stick each morning to keep her hopes alive.

*

I have scant memories of how we survived the winter of 1961–62, but I recall how grateful we were when the warmer weather returned. Early May 1962 was like the previous late springs, hot and humid. We took respite in the swollen rivers and enjoyed the sounds of the dragon boats practising for the annual race. Although the drumbeats sounded weary, they still managed to spark our imaginations, reminding us of life, of hope, and of the big river flowing eternally into the South China Sea. We couldn't help but stop and listen to those strange, almost supernatural sounds that returned year after year without fail, in good times and bad, booming like a beating heart. They also reminded me of an incident that had occurred during the previous year's boat race.

On the day of the festival, Yiu-hoi and I had squeezed between other spectators who, like us, thought the best vantage point for watching the race was the lifesaver's tower at the swimming pool by the river. Too short to see properly, we climbed onto the plank that stabilised the posts under the tower. It was still high enough there; the view was spectacular. Thousands of people were crammed on both sides of the Wonder River.

Dozens of dragon boats had gathered, decorated with many colourful flags and streamers representing different villages, towns and organisations. The drums boomed, and the men moaned with great effort as they rowed. We cheered, shouted and clapped to the vibrations of the race. The boats skimmed along, hovering on the surface of the swollen river. The excitement took us away, momentarily, from the misery of the famine.

The race was reaching its highest point. The currents gathered force, and the loaded tower began to move in the burgeoning river. It swayed as the spectators shifted with the motion of the boats. Crouching beneath the tower, I remembered what Baba had often taught me about risk-taking: never stand under an unsafe wall. I became nervous. Instinctively I pulled Yiu-hoi to the outermost pole that supported the tower. We clung on, hanging free from the spectators above us, feeling wonderful and enjoying a particularly superb view of the whole Wonder River. The cool summer breeze caressed us as we shouted and cheered with the crowds who were equally excited, even though all our stomachs were empty and rumbling with cramps.

Suddenly the entire tower tumbled with one big clunk. It plunged into the rising river, taking with it planks of wood and all its spectators, except Yiu-hoi and me. It fell so fast that people had no time to scream; they were gone in a gulp. All seemed quiet in that instant, despite the commotion around us. Yiu-hoi and I dangled on the lone stable pole, watching scores of spectators struggling to keep afloat. It was a miracle no one drowned.

*

Now with another summer approaching, another season of hope had begun.

'The sea takes all that flows into it from the river,' Baba said as Mama walked past him without taking her watery breakfast, heading to the District Head's office for another application form.

For some reason I still don't understand, I followed her out of the house that day.

The District Head was now just a shell of the man he used to be. He didn't look Mama in the eye; he didn't seem to notice my presence either – although from time to time, I thought his eyes slid in my direction.

'Put your son on one,' he said, as he handed Mama two application forms instead of the usual one. Then he mumbled something incoherent.

'But he's only a young child,' she replied, struggling to understand the meaning behind the District Head's unusual offer.

'Just do it for luck,' he said with his head down, his voice soft and surprisingly gentle. 'He did it before, didn't he?'

My head began to spin as I also tried to understand. The tiny spark of hope I had nurtured all through these lean times was twinkling inside me like a glow-worm. We'd heard of a few more people being permitted to leave for Hong Kong or Macau since the Qingming Remembrance earlier that year. Mama said that maybe the District Head was finally touched by the plight of his people. Or perhaps it was the sight of my pitiful shrivelled body that had moved him – or a touch of humanity, Baba would say later.

That evening, my parents asked me if I would apply to leave China by myself.

'Yes, I want to go,' I said.

I had no second thoughts about leaving home alone. Nearly thirteen, I was more than twice the age I'd been when I'd left home with Flea and Mrs Ng. Now it seemed to be the right thing to do. After all, Grandfather Young and his brothers had left home when they were young men; so had Grandfather Woon-duk when he lost his father at the age of twelve. I might become a sojourner one day. And for now, I might be living with Third Aunt in Macau, then Grandmother Young and Ping in Hong Kong.

'No one knows what the future holds,' Baba said to me that night, 'but we must seize any opportunity to get us out of our lot in life. With some luck, I may see you in Macau soon.'

There was little time for further discussion. Baba pulled out his treasured fountain pen, a Hero brand he'd taken all the way to Heilongjiang and back. He looked unsure about the whole matter as he printed my name on one of the application forms. He paused to suck on his cigarette, glanced at me for a brief moment and shook his head, before filling in both forms.

Mama sat motionless, staring at a photo in front of her for what seemed to me a long time. In the photo she was sitting with Weng and me on either side. She took out the tailor's scissors that she had refused to turn into steel. She looked at me. Her lips quivered as if she was going to say something but couldn't. Tears welled up in her eyes, and her hands were shaking. Baba and I watched as she cut me out of the photo. The tears now rolled down her face. I sat close to Mama and held on to her. I don't remember if I was crying. The uncertainty ahead was all too much for me to fathom; my mind went blank, and I felt numb.

Baba lit another cigarette. He went to sit in his dim corner and fell back into his thoughts.

'I'll save some rice tomorrow to glue the photos to the forms,' said Mama.

I could feel the fragile hope, the timid longing, that sprang up in my parents and grew each time they filled in an application form. Seemingly from nowhere a burst of energy would come, enough for them to put forward another application, enough to carry us through to the next rejection.

I heard my parents consoling each other that night, as they often did while hanging on to every little shred of optimism until the next refusal slammed them down. 'We have to be thankful even if only one of us makes it out,' they said.

CHAPTER 18

On 15 May 1962, two days after Mama had handed in the application forms to the District Head, my friends and I were on our way home from school for our lunchbreak. My class had recently turned its attention from the black elements – landlords, capitalists, counter-revolutionaries, Americans, rightists and even the Russians – in order to concentrate on revitalising the fast-declining Great Leap Forward spirit and fending off starvation. We continued to salute Chairman Mao and wish for him to live ten thousand years and ten thousand more – as well as pledging our support to Liu Shaoqi, our new chairman, who had admitted the famine was a man-made disaster and promised a new deal to end starvation. To us at school, the Party was still the only way forward, our only hope, and we rallied to overcome hunger and bring prosperity to China.

When my friends and I got to the end of Come Happiness Street, we perched in the last bit of shade to gather our dissipated strength before our midday bridge challenge. This was always a formidable task in summer: without shoes we had to sprint as fast as we could over the bridge to save our feet from being fried on the hot planks. I clearly remember how the heat smouldered from the slats that day, blurring the view to the other side of the river where the country began, as did Come Happiness Road. I tried to imagine pleasant things on the country side to take my mind off the challenge: those juicy lychees that were ripe for stealing when the guards weren't watching, then something to eat at home, followed by a swim in the cool river, and, of course, the chance to catch a glimpse of the dragon boats practising.

The granite slabs we sat on were rough but cool in front of the unappealing Come Happiness Bridge. Ah-dong slumped onto the shady footpath and was prepared to stay there until the sun dropped out of the sky. But the lychees were on the other side, ripening, enticing us. All of a sudden, Ah-dong got up and gave the signal to charge. A bunch of barefoot kids took to the simmering bridge. We ran as fast as we could, screaming and cursing as we leapt from hot plank to hot plank.

Suddenly my tall Eighth Uncle was there in the middle of the bridge, pulling me to an abrupt halt. The others ran past. Yiu-hoi called out to his father, and Eighth Uncle told him to go home.

As I danced up and down to ease the rising pain in my feet, my uncle bent over and whispered to me, 'Ah-mun, you are going to Macau!' His voice trembled with obvious joy, along with some strange, mingled emotions. He looked at me closely and muttered the same words a little louder. His eyes glinted.

I was confused. *How does my uncle know our plan?* I stood still on the hot planks with my feet burning, not knowing what to do. My feet still sizzle every time I recall that remarkable moment.

I ran back towards the shady footpath while my tall uncle marched behind me. By that time Yiu-hoi and my friends had reached the other side and plunged their burning feet into the cool stream. They couldn't be bothered with what Eighth Uncle was telling me.

'The authorities approved your application,' he said, his voice still distorted with joy.

'But what about Mama and Weng?' I asked, unsure if Ying was included in the plan. I sensed that her patriotism worried my parents.

'That may take a few more days.'

'Oh, does that mean we can all go together?'

'Not sure. But you must leave as soon as you can.'

'Why?'

'Your parents asked me to get a bus ticket for you so as not to arouse the neighbours' attention. An ex-student of mine works at the bus station.' My uncle's hushed voice was just loud enough for me to hear. Any neighbour's objection could mean suspension or cancellation of the approval: people power in a totalitarian society, Baba often said. Eighth Uncle was on his monthly weekend off work and had gladly taken on the job of securing a bus ticket to the border. 'You mustn't tell any of your friends, not even your cousins at home,' he made me promise.

Without delay, we headed towards the bus station, located on the west side of town. We kept our voices low as we walked on, even though by then hardly anyone was around in the narrow, humid streets. Eighth Uncle walked triumphantly on his lanky legs a little ahead of me. It was obvious that he was very excited, as if he was the one leaving. The truth was that he wouldn't even dare contemplate applying for an exit visa and thereby risk persecution as an admirer of the capitalist West. But I could feel his happiness for me, palpable and vibrant, carrying me along like a chariot. If it wasn't for the fear that the authorities might change their minds, I was sure he'd have loudly sung the great news to let the whole of Shiqi know. As for me, many feelings rushed about in my head like a flight of lost sparrows, noisy and directionless.

The bus terminal was deserted except for a few comrades sound asleep and snoring on the only two benches against the wall. My uncle headed swiftly to the little window and called out for somebody, who respectfully addressed him as Teacher Kwong. Only one bus went to the border each day, at six in the morning; the next day's was already full. Eighth Uncle settled for the following day. A young face popped through the window. 'Be here early to get a good seat,' she advised, staring at me with envy.

On our way home, my uncle offered me a lot of advice. 'Seize the opportunity. Work hard for whatever you do. Never stop learning. Never be complacent or take things for granted. Be respectful to others and they'll respect you ... And one day, you'll make a glorious return ...'

A glorious return like that of the sojourners? My mind was still circling in confusion. In less than two days, I might never be hungry again. I tried to count the hours until I left for Macau, where, in my memory, food was in abundance. My mouth watered, and I swallowed the saliva to ease my hunger pangs. I was happy to leave the starvation behind, but I was already starting to miss home, my parents and sisters and friends. How I wished they could leave with me. I didn't hear much of what my uncle was saying. Incoherent thoughts kept ringing in my head until the hunger cramps took over. Usually this didn't bother me, as I was used to hunger; however, it was different that day when I became so tangled with excitement, relief, worry, anxiety and, now, fear – that I might fail as I had seven years earlier. I hoped it would be different this time. In silence I walked on behind my uncle, who kept reminding me to keep my trip a secret from all my friends, including his sons, Yiu-hoi and Ah-ki.

The lunchtime crowds had abandoned the lethargic town for their much-needed food, meagre though it was, and a siesta to replenish their fast-dissipating stamina. The few surviving sparrows hid in the shade and were quiet. My uncle and I stopped outside the noodle shop, the only eatery that was still open. It too was deserted. It catered mainly for the town's Party officials and comrades. 'It's bourgeois and extravagant to eat out,' my father often said. The shop operated every day until they sold out of the only item on the menu: plain noodles in watery prawn-shell broth, garnished with a small pinch of finely chopped shallots. Each bowl cost ten fen plus a 250-gram food voucher. That day, the scent of boiling prawn shells made my mouth water. I couldn't resist my uncle's invitation. We sat down, and – not caring who would be the lucky ones to eat the prawn meat, which, like many foods China produced, was probably exported for foreign currencies – I enjoyed the most delicious bowl of noodles I'd ever eaten.

*

When I got home, Mama immediately took me to the black market and bought a live young carp with her last yuan. We headed to the banks of the Wonder River and released it into the water. The carp lingered in the shallows, confused, disorientated and not knowing what to do. It flapped its fins and swam in circles on its side. Mama bent over, caressed it and calmed it, just as she did to us when we suffered from hunger pains. 'Now go; far away you must go,' she said. Before long, the young carp recovered and swam into the deep of the river, to safety. We stayed on to make sure no one would recapture it for food.

That evening my family celebrated behind closed doors, without making too much noise. Ying was excited that I would soon be eating many baguettes with butter. It was hard to keep our elation to whispers. We laughed. We cried. We huddled together and made lots of promises. Even Baba shed tears for the great news.

'You now have a bright future ahead of you,' he said to me.

I'll never forget the sparkle in my parents' eyes as they held me long and hard, and told me what to do and what not to do after leaving home. They made me promise to keep quiet to protect our good fortune until I had finally crossed the border – the District Head could change his mind at the last minute.

Mama kept flapping a dried palm leaf in the shape of a fan at us to drive away the mosquitoes and keep us cool. There were no cakes, not even a biscuit – no food at all. There were no soft drinks, only lychee tea. Yet, we were glowing with radiant joy under the fifteen-watt globe that repeatedly blinked and dimmed.

*

The next morning I went to school as usual. My parents had reminded me a few more times not to say goodbye to any of my friends and schoolmates, just in case. We were still at the mercy of the District Head.

At lunchtime I took my last bridge challenge. 'I'll wear a pair of shiny leather shoes to walk over this bridge next time,' I boasted to my friends as we paused to rest in the shade of Come Happiness Street. I wasn't sure why I'd made such an audacious prediction when everything around us was so gloomy – maybe to stop the burning under my feet I already felt in anticipation of running. Perhaps I was thinking of the sojourner from the Gold Mountain with his shiny leather shoes. Or perhaps I was delirious as a result of the most unexpected opportunity that had been handed to me by the District Head.

The boys burst out laughing. Ah-dong's big head swung so much, I was sure it would drop off that day. Then I realised I'd blundered, unable to contain my excitement.

'That'll be the day,' Ah-dong said, straightening himself up, patting his stretched tummy. 'A shirt and tie would look good on you too. Ha, ha, ha ...' He must have been remembering that same sojourner, and those yummy biscuits.

I looked at our soiled feet. Grime and dirt mixed with sweat had coated our skin from our toes to halfway up our shins. Hardly anyone in Shiqi could afford proper shoes, even the comrades, though at least they had khaki cloth sandals issued to them by the Party. The few families like ours who had regular across-the-border visitors might get a new pair of sandshoes very occasionally; but when that happened to me I would refuse to wear them because they looked too new and therefore not revolutionary – I didn't want to stand out in the crowd for fear of being called a bourgeois or even a capitalist. Even fewer people, only the likes of the good Mrs Lee, had proper shoes.

With my new eyes I saw that our clothes, our patched T-shirts and torn shorts, were in need of a good wash. *Yes, I'll be wearing neat clothes and shoes after tomorrow, but I'll be missing all of you*, I thought as I stood on Come Happiness Bridge watching my friends soak their feet in the running water while ignoring the rising heat in my own feet.

'Come join us and stop dreaming, Ah-mun,' Ah-dong sang out. 'You think too much. You worry too much, and you dream too much. When you become rich one day and wear leather shoes and a tie, I'll come visit you.' He looked at me and laughed again. 'Will you still remember me?'

'Of course,' I said, kicking gravel at my friends on the riverbank. 'I promise.'

More laughter broke out. But Ah-dong stopped his giggling, and his stare was unusually pensive. He seemed to know I was serious.

CHAPTER 19

The night before I left for Macau, my parents invited me to sleep in their bed. We talked and cuddled and made promises and didn't sleep much. We got up at four the next morning. The universe was at peace; nothing made a sound in the stillness outside, not even a dog barking.

Mama checked the small grey leather case a final time. It had once belonged to Grandfather Young, and he'd given it to Mama on one of his two visits back to China after his departure for Hawaii in 1921. The letters GY embossed on one corner in gold gleamed under the dim globe in our room that day. Mama had stored her tailor's scissors in it. She gave it to me for the journey, packed with a few clothes Ping had brought back from Hong Kong – clothes I'd refused to wear because they were new and not revolutionary enough.

My parents could offer me nothing more. Mama had already carefully prepared my grey cotton pants by leaving them pressed overnight under a heavy rosewood Mandarin stool turned upside down on another. With her charcoal-heated iron, she pressed the white shirt Ping had brought home on one of her trips.

'The shirt looks smart on you,' Baba said as he fixed up the collar the way it should be: buttoned all the way to the top, even without a tie. Mama looked on with a sad smile.

Dawn arrived, splashing a warm glow on the terracotta tiles in the front hall. Ying and Weng were up, as were Eighth Uncle and

Sixth Aunt. My aunt said what good fortune it was for the family to have a young child leaving starvation and hardship.

Baba had lit three incense sticks in front of the ancestors' plaques in the third lounge room. Three small cups of tea stood in a neat row on the large rosewood table. They looked lonely to me, although three of everything was the custom in paying respect to our ancestors. '"Three" sounds like the word "life",' Baba would explain, even though I doubted he believed it. He also often said these things were superstitions, nothing more. But that morning, I think he believed in them. As the most senior male at home, he took the lead, standing solemnly in front of the table as he offered respect and gratitude to the ancestors and other deities. He requested forgiveness for the lean offering, which was all that we could afford. He then asked for their blessings for me as I left home for good. My uncle followed, then my aunt and Mama. Then I too offered my sincere respect and thanks to the ancestors. A strange feeling rushed through me as I stood in front of the rosewood table. I was now ready to become a man, ready to take what fate would bring, with blessings from my ancestors and my family. The doubt and fear of being away from home began to dissipate.

'Oh, Ah-mun, don't forget to pay respect to Guan Gong, our guardian angel,' Mama reminded me. I wasn't sure exactly when Mama had become so superstitious.

I went into Yiu-hoi and Ah-ki's room to say goodbye. They were sound asleep, so I woke Yiu-hoi. Still half-asleep, he realised I was going to Macau, where a thousand toys and many games were available, and plenty of food. Envious, he wished he too could go there so he wouldn't have to make his own toys anymore. I promised him I'd come home one day and bring him toys, fishhooks, chewing gum, biscuits and sweets. I gave him my precious bamboo sword, which I used for fending off aggressive geese. I gave all my toys, including my favourite kites and fishing gear, to him and Ah-ki. I then made Yiu-hoi promise to help Weng care for the new chickens and my goldfish. And he was to take charge of our little gang, with

Ah-dong. I told him the pocketknife I had received from my father after his return from prison was to go to Ah-dong.

Yiu-hoi got out of bed, now fully awake and upset by the realisation that he would miss me. He insisted on seeing me off at the bus station, and we decided to let Ah-ki sleep.

Then I went to be with Mama in the kitchen, watching her quietly cook my breakfast. Her face glowed with each burst of flame as the rice husks crackled and burned, a handful at a time, keeping the fire going. Her undernourished figure was unyielding and determined, cherishing every bit of hope as mothers do for their children. The struggle to survive in a ruthless revolution had exhausted her, but not the dreams she had been nurturing for me all these years. Yet my rare opportunity hadn't elated her to the point of excitement, as there were still so many uncertainties and worries ahead. She and the rest of our family had to live in fear and hunger as the famine savaged them with no end in sight. And now our separation.

'The journey is going to be long, and you must take good care of yourself,' she said to me, fighting back tears. 'Write home regularly and don't keep me waiting for your news.'

Images of Mama waiting outside the gate for the postman to come with our living allowance from Hong Kong, her longing for Baba's mail when he was away in Heilongjiang, and her anxious waits at the bus station for Ping or Grandmother to arrive, all passed in slow motion through my mind. Every one of her words etched itself in my heart that morning.

'Study hard if you have a chance to go to school,' she said. 'Work hard if you have to work for a living. You must promise me that you'll attend evening school. You must learn English well – it is your passport to the world beyond Shiqi, the Wonder River and even the South China Sea. When you can read and write it well, it becomes your foundation for success in life beyond China. Education is our only hope to change our destiny. So work hard, my son. My blessings will be with you always. My thoughts will be with you every minute of your life until my last breath. Forever.'

She kept her eyes on the fire as I felt her heart being shredded into pieces. 'I'll pray to the ancestors and the gods to protect you on your life's journey. It has now begun.'

Mama then turned to face me and held me closely to her bosom for the last time, trembling but firm. Teardrops hit the large terracotta tiles of the kitchen floor. I hung on to my mother and wouldn't let go. All of a sudden, I dreaded the inevitable and imminent severing of our togetherness, as much as the unknown world ahead.

The steamy hot rice was a luxury. I couldn't eat it – I wanted to save it for my starving family. I was already missing them. I tried to give the bowl of rice to Ying, but she started to sob, eyes red and blurry. Weng cried too as I made her take it. 'There's a lot of food in Macau, and I'm saving my tummy for a big feast when I get there,' I said to her, with the courage of a big brother. She looked at me with her large trusting eyes and took the food.

*

As we made the fifteen-minute walk to the bus station, the reddening sky changed to a mixture of orange and pale-pink. Shiqi was waking up to another hot and humid day. Some dogs barked as we navigated through the backstreets and little alleyways that led to the west side of town. The soothing cool of early morning reflected from the large, rough slabs of grey granite, which were as ancient as the town itself, was welcoming. My parents talked softly as they walked on each side of me, holding my hands, reminding me once more of all the things to do and not to do, and to be nice to Third Aunt in Macau, as I might have to stay with her for a while, and to my grandmother if and when I got to Hong Kong. There wasn't much of a plan, as my parents didn't know what would happen after I left. My exit visa allowed me to travel only to Macau.

The gentle sound of our footsteps on those centuries-old stones did little to disturb the peace of Shiqi, just as had been the case for the past thousand years of pedestrians before us. Only an occasional bicycle interrupted the calm of the dim and narrow streets. By the time we reached the Wonder River Bridge, the sky had overcome the fast-fading glow. A few more pedestrians hurried by on their way to their production units. The People's Militia officers at the bridge had gone off duty and were heading home.

As I looked at the rising tide, it reminded me that I would miss the coming dragon boat race. But I had no time to brood over this now. And I had no real regret in leaving Shiqi, where my family and I weren't wanted.

It was time for me to go.

The bus stood ready to receive passengers for the slow trip to the border. The town's buses ran on diesel now and were slightly faster than the old ones, but my parents had told me it was still a six-hour trip with many stops along the way. Clouds gathered, and it started to drizzle. My family lined up at the door of the bus, so I walked past each of them to say goodbye. My sisters wept. Mama had no more tears to shed, but I knew she was crying inside, her joy and sadness intertwined.

Baba held my hands in his. I could feel his hardened skin and healing wounds. His white Model Worker T-shirt gleamed in the morning light, making me proud of my father, the so-called high intellectual who'd become an assistant pot repairer.

He said to me, 'Son, see these hands? Make the best use of them. For no matter where you go from now on, you will have no more fear of hunger. Your hands will make a living for you. Work hard. For the energy in you is endless. Be fearless. The world is yours to enjoy and experience. Also, don't forget that you have two eyes to see, a mouth to ask questions and two ears to listen, so make good use of them. Learn from others. Things are going to be tough ahead but they can't be worse than they are now. Always remember, challenges are there to test our strength and to bring out our best qualities. They are not there to stop us from fulfilling our dreams,' he reassured me as our eyes met.

I had seen Baba suffer. I had witnessed him being denounced in public, convicted and imprisoned by the authorities for doubting the revolution. I felt his courage surge inside me as his eyes glimmered with hope in the morning glow. I nodded, holding back my tears. The knot in my chest tightened. I couldn't speak.

I stepped onto the small bus and took the single seat behind the folding door. My family, still standing in a line, waved goodbye to me. I waved back as the bus slowly pulled away from the station, heading east. I took one more look at my weeping family before turning in the direction of my journey. I couldn't feel, I couldn't hear, and I couldn't see. For a moment I didn't even care what was happening to my family and home; I just wanted the bus to take me away, far away from it all. Only when the bus started to make a left turn towards the bridge over the Wonder River did I begin to feel uneasy, and I couldn't resist turning to look at my family again. They huddled together, crying, as Sixth Aunt, Baba and my tall uncle tried to console them.

'Big brother, I want to come with you,' Yiu-hoi called out, wiping his tears as he ran alongside the sluggish bus. Leaning out of the small window, I promised to come home and help him escape too.

In the brightening light, I could already feel the day's heat. I began to perspire. A warm swell gathered around my eyes; my vision blurred. Dark diesel smoke and the red dust kicked up by the bus soon engulfed Yiu-hoi and our family. A thick lump rose to my throat, and it exploded as the bus hit a pothole.

I wept.

The bus drove past Kwong Street to reach the road that led east towards the South China Sea. I wiped away my tears and stared at the neat street where I'd spent my childhood with my gang of friends. The grey-brick houses with the smart levee wall perched squarely behind the orderly jade-green young rice plants – how they glowed in the morning radiance.

Ah-dong, Ah-bil, Hui, Big Eye, Earring and my other friends were waking up to face another day, another bridge challenge. When they found out I had gone, they would miss me, as I already missed them. By the side of the road, the gum trees we'd planted in answer to Chairman Mao's call to make sleepers for railway tracks rustled as the bus picked up speed. Before long, Shiqi, the town where I was born, disappeared behind a haze of red dust. There was no turning back.

PART II

Snake Business

CHAPTER 20

The slow bus was full to capacity, with more people standing than sitting. All the windows were open to ease the heat generated by the passengers. The sky was clear but steely pale, and I knew the glow from the east would soon make it worse. Country air wafted through my small window as the bus struggled along the gravel road. Although polluted by burnt diesel, the breeze was refreshing. It cleared my head but not the heavy dread that I might not see my family and friends for a long time – maybe never again. I tried to concentrate on the whiffs of sweet air from the peaceful landscape to lessen the sadness of leaving home, a little at a time.

I started to perspire. I knew I had to grow quickly from a child to a man. I could feel the plight of my family, their anguish and pain. There was no room for failure.

The bus continued to chew up the distance.

From the conversations the other passengers shouted at each other, and their blue or khaki tunics, I could tell that most of them were reporting to their production units. Others were returning to their towns or villages along the coast. A lucky few of us were heading out of China for a new life. From our more presentable clothes and proper shoes, it was obvious to the others that we were leaving for Macau. The envy from those not leaving was hard to bear. Any eye contact would surely make them feel worse.

The road to the border hadn't changed since the last time I'd travelled on it with Flea and the good Mrs Ng. And it was the same kind of warm, humid day. The main difference this time was that this bus didn't have a big boiler hanging behind it, so the driver didn't have to keep making stops to shovel coal. However, his face was still red from the abundant dust that came through the window, and he wore a faded PLA cap and exuded an air of progressiveness. He seemed communistic and revolutionary, and proud of his plum job. Baba had told me that there were very few bus driver jobs in our town, and that we were fifty years behind Hong Kong and Macau in transportation, and in many other industries and technologies.

For some reason I began humming my favourite revolutionary song, etched in my brain since my first days at kindergarten:

Eighteen-year-old girls go get married soon,
Bring up your sons, and quickly will they grow
To be men and liberation heroes,
Defend our Motherland bravely will they go ...

Was I a coward for running away to the capitalist world? Was I a deserter from communism? Such questions ran through my mind and I wondered why things were so sad; why did my family have to split up to survive?

*

It was mid-afternoon when we finally arrived at the border. A large Chinese national emblem in red and gold with five golden stars adorned the main entry to a plain two-storey building. Solemn guards in green PLA uniforms were everywhere, separating men, women and children into closely watched waiting areas. They then began to body-search every one of us in dim and humid rooms. They asked many questions, the same kind as they had when I'd entered Macau all those years ago.

The first question: 'Why are you leaving our Motherland?'

I stared at the guard and didn't attempt to answer.

He didn't even bother to look at me and went on to ask more questions. 'Have you got any money with you?'

'Twenty fen.'

'Have you got more than that? You know you are not allowed to take more than one yuan out of China.'

I showed him the two ten-fen notes my father had given me for an emergency.

'Did anyone ask you to take anything out of China, like newspapers or revolutionary books?'

'No.'

'Any antiques?'

I didn't know what he meant.

At different times other guards asked the same questions, then they went off to confer with each other. They repeated them a few more times, exactly as my parents had predicted. I wondered how Mama and Baba knew all these things – probably from Ping and Grandmother Young.

The guards eventually went away for a final discussion, just to be sure about me, before subjecting a few people to further interrogations as I was kept waiting.

After I'd passed many hours in that border building they finally gave my papers back and allowed me to cross over to Macau. Hastily I strode through with the lucky ones, on what seemed to be an endless walkway, under the stares of more sombre guards. I wasted no time in sympathising with those detained behind me.

The building on the Macau side of the border was equally plain, a large hall opening out into several rooms. No one was around apart from my fellow travellers and a few customs officers. The big difference was the Macau guards were relaxed, even friendly. They checked my papers and asked a couple of questions. I must have looked weary, if not pitiful and spent.

A khaki-uniformed officer with a high-bridged nose, tanned skin, wavy brown hair and large deep-set eyes, a gweilo – foreign devil –

offered me a drink of cool Sunkist Orange. I couldn't remember ever being so close to a gweilo before, but I was distracted by the drink, delicious and much needed, my first refreshment for the day. My chest had been aching when I thought of the family I had left behind, but the chilled drink numbed my pain in one big gulp. It was magical. The exhaustion from the long trip left me, and I was ready to move on.

I followed the others into the streets of Macau.

*

As soon as we stepped out of the border building, dozens of men pulling rickshaws swarmed around us, offering to take us to our destinations. But now everything seemed hazy and uncertain and I just stood there, looking around in some confusion.

Then I noticed a man approaching me with a big smile on his face. He was a distant cousin who'd once lived a few houses away from us on Kwong Street and had come to Macau months earlier. He explained that he'd spotted me as soon as I stepped out of the building. 'Must have been a tiring trip,' he said as he took my little leather case. 'Lucky I got your Baba's letter this morning about your arrival.'

'So glad to see you cousin. You look so much stronger than before,' I said.

'Must be the good food here,' he said, grinning and patting his stomach.

My cousin and I walked through many shop-lined streets in order to get to Third Aunt's house. We went past stores laden with big colourful fruits – lychees, bananas and apples, and golden oranges I had never seen before. How I wanted to linger at the many cake shops and bakeries to take in the abundant mouth-watering smells of those freshly baked cookies, biscuits and cakes of all kinds. I also marvelled at the many stores filled with thousands and thousands of items for sale, from watches and cameras to a host of fashionable clothes, to shiny leather shoes and a seemingly endless variety of toys. The goods spilled over onto the footpaths where many little stands and carts competed under numerous signs and billboards drawing attention to their merchandise and produce.

My eyes popped wide open as my cousin navigated us through the razzamatazz. How quickly my world had changed.

As we approached the gentle incline that led to a small hill on the southern side of the Macau peninsula, the shops petered out. Soon there were no stores and very few pedestrians along a taxing slope lined with tall banyan trees, and I started to droop with fatigue.

'Just a little further to go.' My cousin coaxed me on.

We finally stopped outside a single-level, flat-roofed bungalow on a road that led to Macau's Guia Hill district. The sunset cast a welcoming flush onto the front courtyard of the whitewashed building. My cousin checked the address on a small piece of paper and nodded. I opened the gate and stepped in.

Third Aunt appeared on the front porch, cooling herself with a small hand-fan that gave off a sweet, soothing sandalwood scent. Her well-combed hair was fashioned into a big bun behind her head like Grandmother Young's, and a few streaks of grey seemed to emphasise her seniority in the family. Her fine aqua-blue satin cheongsam made her look very dignified as she welcomed me into her home.

'Do come on in,' she said to my cousin. 'You must need a good drink now.'

She then turned to me and said, 'I'd begun to worry about you, my dear boy, and wondered if they had detained you at the border.' Her loud clear voice rang through the courtyard. 'How's your father? Poor man, I'm sure he's had enough of the revolution. Lucky he survived the Great Northern Wilderness – not many did. Oh, Buddha please have mercy. Goddess of Mercy, please have mercy.' She made half a bow towards a corner of the courtyard, where three big incense sticks were burning in front of a statue of General Guan Gong, the Goddess of Mercy and the other deities. Then Third Aunt patted me on the shoulder and looked closely at me with her large eyes that gleamed with intelligence. 'My poor boy, just skin and bones … I'll fatten you up and make you strong again. The blessings of the ancestors are with you. Oh, Buddha please have mercy,' she repeated, holding back her tears and counting the traditional Buddhist mala beads she wore on a small chain and thanking the gods for my safe arrival.

I took off my dirty shoes and dusty socks, and walked on the polished floor that glowed in the twilight, as cool as the water under Come Happiness Bridge. The sun had lost its heat, and a refreshing sea breeze streamed through Third Aunt's wide-open windows. I undid the top buttons on my shirt to make the most of it.

What immediately captured my attention out the window was the Guia Lighthouse, not far from Third Aunt's home on top of the small hill, majestic and upright in brilliant white. Clustered around it were tough but short pine trees. *Aha, I have my first exploration target*, I thought. From the other windows I could see down the hill to the Macau metropolis, now blinking in the evening glow. I hastened to savour all the blessings that had been granted to me so far.

'Now have some food, you must be starving,' said Third Aunt.

Eagerly I sank my teeth into a baguette with butter, while she looked on with a gentle smile and murmured her thanks to Buddha. I chewed the crisp crust and sucked the soft bread as it melted in my mouth, relishing it exactly as I'd wanted to do when dreaming of food while sitting on the levee wall.

After devouring the biggest bowl of noodles with vegetable dumplings I had ever eaten in my life, I felt a fullness in my stomach that was foreign to me – or at least long forgotten after years of starvation. Third Aunt smiled again, glowing with compassion.

I took a refreshing shower, changed into a brand-new pair of pyjamas she had ready for me, and hopped straight into bed. It was hard to resist the comfort of a mattress.

'Leave the windows open to keep cool in the night,' Third Aunt said, before switching off the light. 'You're safe here.' She must have noticed the doubt in my eyes. How did she know that we always closed the windows and doors to our room at home in Shiqi when we went to bed?

My memory of Mama's quiet image in the kitchen hit me as soon as I got myself comfortable in the cosy bed. Oh, how I missed her. She and the rest of the family were but skin and bones like me. If Third Aunt could see them now she'd cry with great sadness. What the authorities had done to Baba was so unfair, so demeaning. I prayed he would have fewer cuts to his hands mending those old pots and woks, and that Mama would take comfort knowing I'd do all the things she had told me to do and not to do. I prayed that Weng and Ying would receive no more criticism from the school or on the streets, and that my gang of friends would have more food. Like Third Aunt, I now prayed to Buddha and the Goddess of Mercy for compassion. I don't remember how late it was before I fell asleep. I do remember the tears on my pillow the first night in Macau, and on the many nights that followed.

CHAPTER 21

'Education, education, education.' Third Aunt's first words to me rang loud and clear the next morning. 'That's the priority. No doubt about it. You must have a good education, and it begins with A, B, C – English, the language that's your ticket to the world. It opens up doors for a better life and opportunities out of China.' I was glad that she sounded just like Baba and Mama.

The first thing she did that morning, after feeding me yummy butter and jam on toast, was to enrol me in an English language class, held on the third floor of a building in busy downtown Macau. There were shops at street level with residential units upstairs where all kinds of businesses were run, including the English school. Lots of signs, large and small, hung from many of the windows to attract customers, and more signs guided them up the narrow stairways. By the summer of 1962 the constant stream of people arriving in Macau, legally and illegally, had turned the once-quiet Portuguese colony into a busy hub.

'It'll be twelve dollars a month,' the kind owner-teacher said to my aunt. 'The beginners' class starts at nine in the morning and finishes at eleven each day.'

'He's only a little boy.' Third Aunt pointed at me. 'Not even a teenager. But a very good boy, and he can clean up after class to help you. Will you please give me a discount?'

I was sure the teacher knew I was a new arrival: skinny,

gaunt and dark, with a scrawny face typical of refugees from the mainland – there were thousands of them in the streets. My large staring eyes must have affected her because she lowered her head, perhaps to hide her own eyes, then nodded at my aunt. 'For him, ten will do.'

My aunt said to me, 'You'll tidy up the room before the class begins in the morning and after it finishes.' She was very good at giving instructions, and I'd become used to her as a young child when she was living in Kwong Street. We climbed down the stairs and headed to the barber shop. 'Always be polite,' she told me. 'Don't forget to say "thank you" and "please". And study hard.' To the barber, she said, 'A schoolboy's haircut, please. A really good one, and no less.'

The barber bowed and put on a welcoming smile. In less than a few minutes, I found a strange-looking bony boy with a pale shaven scalp, large haunting eyes and a suntanned face peering at me from the mirror. Third Aunt happily paid the barber. She then took me shopping for a pair of leather shoes, white socks and other essential items, and for clothes that were all at least a size or two bigger than my emaciated frame. 'You'll grow into them soon,' she said to me with her usual confidence on the way back to her bungalow.

*

At the small English language school, fifteen chairs were packed into the living room. Adults and children of all ages conscientiously attended their daily two-hour lessons. I was more than happy to sweep and clean before and after my lesson had finished, then I would hang around and stay on for the next lesson, free of charge. I'd worked out quickly that if I learnt twice the number of new words each day, I would be twice as good in half the time. After all, I'd rather have been cleaning and sweeping to earn an extra lesson than shouting slogans and feeling tired and hungry all the time. I looked forward to my classes every day the way I had longed for food in Shiqi. The opportunity to learn was too precious to miss, and I felt privileged to be able to learn English. This was exactly what my parents had wished for me.

If not for the never-ending sea breeze, walking up and down Fortaleza e Farol da Guia wouldn't have been so pleasant. There were only a few homes on that insignificant hill, and not many people liked hiking the steep incline, so rent was relatively low, according to Third Aunt. But she liked it there in her bungalow without the fuss of the town around, beside the peace of the pine trees. It was a quiet road even during peak times, and when walking to and from class I had the whole footpath to myself. I practised my pronunciation aloud as my teacher had told us to do, and, like the senior class, I turned words into sentences, feeling accomplished. I marvelled at the flexibility of the language and the many ways in which words could present themselves with different meanings in different situations.

Whenever I walked downtown, I held on firmly to my precious first-ever English textbooks for fear of losing them among the crowds. There were no loudspeakers blaring over my head on street corners, and no posters denouncing our countless enemies, real or perceived. Instead, there were the spirited sounds of free people, and a feeling of energy and vigour. Since as far back as I could remember, the Party had commanded us to reject the capitalist world, painting an ugly portrait that didn't resemble the reality I was now experiencing.

My stiff leather shoes softened until they were comfortable – if only Ah-dong had been there to see them.

After school, I would keep practising my English in the front courtyard of Third Aunt's home until late in the afternoon. By then I'd already changed into my pyjamas, as people did in Macau after work or school.

Only a few weeks after my arrival, Third Aunt was pleased with my fast transformation from a mainlander into a city schoolboy. 'Now you look just like a local,' she said. 'Your face is fuller and your complexion is fairer by the day.' She only needed to tell me once what to do or what to wear, and I would stick to her commands with strict obedience. My sisters used to say with envy that I was her pet. And I must have been.

Before I'd begun kindergarten, back in the Kwong Street house she would feed me in her living quarters every evening when my parents were struggling to provide for my immediate family. Her big round rosewood table, inlaid with shiny pieces of cool marble, had taken up nearly the entire centre of her room, which was off the third lounge room. The table was matched with four round stools, all too high for me to climb onto, so we ate together on chairs at a much smaller wooden table. My aunt kept statues of Guan Gong, Buddha and the Goddess of Mercy in her room, and prayed to them for the family's safety, and for her husband, who was still living in New York.

To share a meal with Third Aunt was an experience. The fact was, both my older sisters had loathed eating with her because of her strict etiquette – and so when we were children, she hadn't invited them to eat with her.

'How one behaves at the dining table reflects one's upbringing and personality,' Third Aunt impressed on me every time we shared a meal.

My stomach rumbled, longing for the delicious scrambled eggs and the stir-fried crisp vegetables with tofu. All vegetarian, for respect to Buddha, she'd say. My eyes grew rounder and my mouth couldn't stop watering, but I wasn't to begin eating until she had finished her lecture on dining protocol.

'Your hands must be on your lap, and you must sit a little away from the table. Look at me when I'm talking to you. Don't start until your host has begun. Take only your fair portion in front of you. Learn to share ...' Her rules rolled out of her pretty lips, and her eyes gleamed with intelligence. Baba had always said that his sister-in-law was one of the most educated and smartest people he'd ever met, as well as being kind.

One evening a few weeks after I arrived in Macau, Third Aunt read my palm to tell my future. This was because I'd told her how I'd saved Ah-ki and Hui from drowning and she was curious about what lay ahead of me. I didn't tell her of the near accident at the Dragon Boat Festival; I didn't want her to know that Yiu-hoi and I had been stupid enough to dangle ourselves under a rickety lifesaver's tower full of spectators over a swollen river, just to watch the annual dragon boat race.

As meticulously as she ran her household, she examined the lines on my palms. She then felt the flesh and every bone in my hands from one side to the other, from one finger to the next. She looked serious. Then she said, 'It's going to be a long road, and you'll only be able to get there if you work consistently. It will take time. Work hard towards whatever goal you may set for yourself. Persevere. You can do it. Buddha teaches us to be compassionate and nurture every life, no matter how insignificant, or small – even an ant's life needs to be preserved. The fourteen credit points you have earned for saving two lives have already set you on the road to enlightenment.'

In my mind I counted twenty-eight credit points, and if I became a doctor to help people one day, I might earn more blessings.

'Also,' she said, 'you have guardian angels wherever you go.'

I smiled, but didn't tell her that she was one of them already.

I appreciated so much about my life in Macau, but I missed the cool streams of the waterways that passed through Shiqi, and I missed the Come Happiness Bridge challenge after school, and most of all I missed my parents, sisters and little gang of friends. I wished that they were all there with me. We would compete with each other to be the best at learning English, and my father could help to guide us. He had tried, with the door closed so no one else could hear, to teach me and my sisters a few phrases: 'How do you do?' 'Good morning.' 'Good evening.' 'My name is …'

*

On one of those humid afternoons in the courtyard, several weeks after my arrival, I was trying to concentrate on spelling, but my mind drifted away from my English reader and my eyes wandered to the Guia Lighthouse. It reached into the gentle sky with unyielding poise; it had weathered tempests and typhoons of all magnitudes, and after nearly a hundred years was still guiding boats up and down the estuary of the vast Pearl River Delta. With all my might I wished hard that its rays would reach my family and friends, steering them away from starvation. The sun shifted and slanted to the west. I hastened to return to my reader, and spoke the words out loud to stop my mind from straying.

'This is a boy. His name is Jack.'

'This is a girl. Her name is Jill.'

'I am a good boy.'

'You are a good girl.'

I tried to read it as the teacher did, with the same accent and punctuation. I practised the sentences a few more times until they came out of my mouth like a running stream, rising and accelerating like the current of the Wonder River. Then I was happy and turned the page to prepare for the next day's lesson.

Suddenly, I thought I heard Baba's voice: 'You are a good boy.'

I looked up, thinking I must be imagining him in the courtyard.

'Oh, what a good boy you are.' The voice was loud and triumphant – Baba was walking through the front gate with Mr Lee. I had never dreamed this would happen. They had made it out of China! How?

'Baba!' I cried and rushed towards him. He roared with laughter and gathered me up in his arms. We danced all over the courtyard. We laughed. We cried. We held on tight.

Third Aunt appeared, having heard the commotion. She too was overjoyed and rushed to light three big incense sticks to thank the guardian angels. We laughed and cried some more. Before long, evening had descended, and the lighthouse began to glow in the approaching darkness. In the distance, the Ruins of St Paul's Cathedral gleamed as though with goodness and piety. My world now seemed full of good fortune, as Third Aunt had predicted.

Baba and Mr Lee looked as if they hadn't been to bed for days, but they were jubilant. They wore new grey cotton trousers, white shirts and black leather shoes, though they stank of the sea. Third Aunt reached for the deodorant spray can – a good wash and a shave would soon sort them out.

Each of them carried a UN Refugee Program parcel containing tins of food, a one-kilo bag of milk powder and a small sack of rice. They rushed to pull out their Macau ID cards to show that they were now legal residents, and they also each carried one ten-dollar bill in Macau currency. The Colonial Portuguese Government granted residency rights to refugees from China upon arrival, while the Red Cross assisted them under the banner of the UN.

Once again we laughed and cried, and weren't ashamed of it at all. It was the first time in my life that I'd seen my father express his feelings so freely and heartily. I hugged him tight and buried my head in his lap. We were all too excited to think of anyone or anything else at that moment, even Mama and my sisters.

Third Aunt hurried away to make tea and prepare food for the hungry men. When she returned, Baba began to tell us what had happened. 'Thank heavens we've made it.' He beamed, glancing at Mr Lee. Both men were now brimming with exuberance. 'For a while I thought we were doomed. The past three days in the water have been the longest of my life.'

Mr Lee straightened his muscular torso, now looking even bigger than usual, and thanked my father with heartfelt gratitude for getting them both safely out of Shiqi.

'But it is yourself you've to thank, Ding-yan,' Baba replied. 'Your leadership on board saved many people. I wouldn't even have been able to plan this if it weren't for you – being under street arrest wasn't easy.' He lit two cigarettes and offered one to Mr Lee, who made an exception that evening and took it. Third Aunt dashed around to open more windows, mumbling her objection to cigarette smoke, but she also said this was a special night. I was sure she'd tell the men not to smoke inside her house ever again.

Baba and Mr Lee sat quietly, drawing on their imported Camel cigarettes, sipping jasmine tea and eating cookies. Then Baba told his story.

'Three days ago, Ding-yan and I got on board the riverboat in the dark bend of the Nine Meanders River. The boat belonged to another commune – someone had stolen it for the trip. It was one of those flat-bottomed boats used to transport grains in the waterways. A heavy canvas covered the entire hold, and that was where we hid. At the stern, to one side, was a small cabin. The boat squeaked and screeched under its load as we made our way down the Wonder River towards the sea. Each time we reached a checkpoint manned by the People's Militia guards along the river, someone in that cabin handed a piece of paper to their leader. They then let us pass. There were curtains over the small cabin window, so we couldn't see who was inside. I got very curious, but no one else seemed to know or care.

'It took us a good two days to navigate the maze of the waterways, sometimes playing hide-and-seek with the local People's Militia. We hid among tall river reeds during the day, and sailed in the night. On those moonless nights we couldn't see any of our surroundings except a few glow-worms glimmering on the banks. They seemed to accompany us all the way, humming like phantoms. We had to stop and manoeuvre the boat out of shallow waters several times. Smells of river mud and ripe reeds hung in the warm night air, lessening our fear.' For the next few minutes, Baba drew hard on his cigarette. From time to time his eyes shifted towards the open window, as if to make sure no one was out there listening.

He continued, 'When daylight arrived the first morning, I could see how old the boat was. There were missing boards in the cargo hold where we sat. I recognised many familiar faces from town: doctors, nurses, intellectuals, disgraced teachers and landlords. Oh yes, your Comrade Teacher Wong and her husband were there too, but we didn't talk to them. We kept to ourselves. Each time someone moved, the boat moved with them. On the wall of the cabin was the name *River Pearl 13*, in faded white paint.'

Baba took a breath and sipped his tea, savouring the mouth-watering Macau cookies and the pancakes my aunt had made, in between smoking his cigarette. He seemed to appreciate the cool breeze streaming through the large windows. Then he stretched his arms and took a long breath before going on with his story. 'It was hot under the canvas. We'd had little to eat or drink for two days by the time we left the big river behind. Macau was in sight, and everyone was excited. However, we soon became worried. Would the riverboat withstand the might of the open sea? And how would we negotiate with the People's Militia gunboats? Questions rushed into my mind,' he said, looking at Third Aunt.

'Yesterday we anchored in She-kou, the Serpent's Mouth, a small bay on the northern side of the broad channel that separates Macau from the mainland. Word came from the cabin that we were to wait for the evening to make our crossing.' After another long sip of tea and a good suck on his cigarette, he carried on. 'A young child cried, and couldn't stop. The upset tore up the silence around us. I was more than surprised that there was an infant in our party. People became worried that the noise might arouse the attention of a group of People's Militia guards having lunch in their gunboat not far from us. The child's parents weren't able to soothe her, no matter how hard they tried. Some people began to get upset, and a few others were even angry, muttering that this might end their quest for freedom. The child's mother was now sobbing quietly. And the child continued to cry.

'"Shut her up, or get rid of her!" someone roared, low but authoritative, from the cabin. We all fell silent.' Baba stopped. His face twisted a little as he tried to compose himself. 'Damn it,' he murmured, before he continued his story. 'That voice was familiar but I couldn't place the person. I felt cold in the middle of the rising heat. Somehow that voice had held all of my fears over the years. It was like anticipating an executioner's swift hand to deliver silence.

'The child's father snatched her from his wife and held his hand over her face. She struggled, turning red and then blue. Her little body writhed and her legs kicked. Soon the kicking slowed to twitches and jerks. The mother tried to prise her husband's hands away. She pleaded with him, saying she would take the child and jump into the sea.

'At that point, Ding-yan charged over and pulled the child away from the father. Poor girl, she was already limp.' My father turned to his friend. 'And you cried out, "No! We are not going to let the child die."'

Third Aunt was rolling her beads in her trembling hands as she listened. Her downcast eyes now flooded with tears. 'Mercy, mercy,' she murmured. 'Please, Goddess of Mercy, please, Buddha, have mercy.'

Baba sank into his seat and held me close. After a moment or two, he went on, 'The girl drew a breath, then another. Her face turned pink, then red as she gasped for more air. Before long she lapsed into a deep sleep in her mother's arms. The rest of the passengers sighed, and remained in silence. Ding-yan and another young man helped comfort the parents. Keeping his voice soft but firm, he said to the people, "We live and die together on this boat." He then reassured us we were only a short distance from Macau, and that we should conserve our energy for the crossing. People quietly applauded, their wet eyes lifted with new hope. I pulled Ding-yan aside and told him of my concern about the person in the cabin, the one whose voice was familiar; I feared it could be the town persecutor, the one who had banished me to Heilongjiang, though I couldn't be sure. Could he be a spy among the runaways? Was this a trap? Without any hesitation, Ding-yan went around and got the young people he'd met on the expedition together, and they prepared themselves for whatever was to come.

'Near the child, on a small gap between two planks, was a thin piece of chalk. I picked it up and walked over to the cabin. In between the 1 and 3 in *River Pearl 13*, I inscribed a number 7 for luck. It brought comfort to many eyes as they followed me like glow-worms in the dark. The young mother nursed her baby close to her heart.

'Nothing else happened until early evening. We were taking off in the direction of the dim illumination of the Guia Lighthouse in the distance. Our excitement grew as the occasional faint flash got brighter by the minute. The People's Militia gunboat also took off – but promptly changed direction and steered towards us. It was slow, and then became tenacious like a leech. Soon it cut in front of us. Two young People's Militia guards, not much older than your sister Ying, called out. With their rifles at the ready, they demanded to know where we were heading. The two boats were now almost within arm's reach of each other. Ding-yan and his dozen or more young friends stood up. They looked at the guards and said nothing. The stand-off kept us all quiet under the canvas. Only the cries of seagulls and small waves hitting the rickety riverboat could be heard. Time dragged on.

'Through a small gap I could see our men on deck. They were sizing up the guards. Ding-yan spoke in our Zhongshan dialect, "Hey, young comrades, we're delivering our load of produce to Macau. Lychees, live fish and prawns ... all for foreign currency to rebuild our Motherland." He was direct and bold. "Would you like to take a look for yourselves?" Behind the young men, we were prepared to face the guards if they came aboard – there were only a few of them, and a lot of us. The young guards now stared with suspicion at *River Pearl 173*.'

Baba turned to me and explained, 'One-Seven-Three sounds like "to survive together" in Cantonese. This was to affirm our determination and unity, and to inject some much-needed faith for the last leg of the voyage.' I always loved how my father took every opportunity to teach me things. But weren't these superstitions he didn't approve of?

'To our relief, the gunboat turned, went past us and headed to the open sea.' He was nodding to himself. 'Just as we were sighing with relief, shots cracked overhead. Needless to say, we all jumped for cover – including the skipper. The riverboat floated about like a cut-off kite, adrift and lifeless, the small engine idling. We were terrified. I stood up and, without knowing what had prompted me, grabbed a piece of loose decking and began to row. Others watched for a moment or two, then got up and joined in. The skipper returned to his position, cranked up the small motor to a higher gear and turned us towards the flash in the distance. Our pursuers also turned, heading towards us again. More people pulled decking off, and we took turns to row on each side. An older man beat at the mast like a drum, and we rowed to the rhythm as in a dragon boat race. We were gathering speed. A few more shots whistled overhead. We managed to pull away from the gunboat slowly but steadily, keeping our eyes on the faint radiance from the lighthouse. It grew brighter and bigger. Thank the gods for the unusually calm sea that evening. Thank Buddha for his mercy. Before long, the gunboat faded into the evening haze.'

Baba took a long sip of his jasmine tea, his face glowing and the sparks in his eyes dancing. Nothing could stop my father when he was at the highpoint of his story.

'After that, we were exhausted, and let the surf take us ashore. The boat hit a deserted bay. I realised it was Hac Sa Bay, the only good swimming this side of Macau – I knew it very well as a young man when I began teaching there before the liberation. I could hear the bottom of the riverboat striking coarse coral and sand. Then the boat fell apart. We were in the water, all forty-something of us. We scrambled ashore and thanked our ancestors for their blessings. On the beach, I came face to face with the man who owned that dreaded voice. He'd been the Party Secretary in Zhongshan, the persecutor who sent me to Heilongjiang. I was lost for words. Strangely, I felt no anger. There was no blame. We're in the same boat, I thought to myself, and we are now equal. I turned my back on him and walked away, accepting the irony of life, the quirk of fate.'

Baba stretched his arms again, and also his back, the way he used to do at home. I buried my face in his lap and held on tight, proud of him as my father, my hero. Mr Lee wiped away tears of gratitude as my aunt continued to chant softly, 'Mercy, mercy. Thank you, Goddess of Mercy. Thank you, Buddha.'

Outside her bungalow, Macau had rolled into another busy evening, splashing itself in thousands of neon lights and colourful billboards. Many businesses, legal and illegal, some in between, now stirred to life in the easing heat. They would buzz and hum all the way to the early hours of the morning. The small colony stayed awake at the mouth of the Pearl River, which opened wide into the perilous South China Sea, like a gigantic serpent discharging the misery and sadness of an overburdened continent perched behind it in the darkness. And the sea took it all.

CHAPTER 22

Ping and Grandmother were over the moon when they heard of Baba's safe arrival. But because they were living on a tight budget and had so many people to support, they decided not to travel to Macau to meet us. Instead they transferred some much-needed funds to assist Baba and Mr Lee.

My mind raced as I planned our future together. As much as I loved living with Third Aunt, I treasured Baba's closeness. I was hoping he would be able to find a job, and we could move into our own place. The thought excited me – oh, how I dearly wanted to go to a proper school when the new school year began in September. I wasn't sure if my English was good enough for me to go to high school, but if that was the case I didn't mind repeating Sixth Class, as long as I could go to school.

'I worry about your mother and sisters at home,' Baba said to me one afternoon in the courtyard. 'I pray to the Goddess of Mercy to spare Mama from violent retribution for not reporting my escape.' He sighed. 'We didn't know anything about the expedition until the last minute. I wish our goodbyes hadn't been so rushed. Weng is too young to understand, and Ying ... I so wanted to take her with me.' He sucked on his cigarette and fell quiet for a good few minutes before he looked at me closely. 'Your opportunity is here now: grasp it. Study hard, my son. We have to look ahead and work diligently, so that one day we can bring our family together again.'

I always loved the way Baba talked. His being so positive when things around us were challenging and, at times, seemingly hopeless, was a great comfort.

*

Barely a week had passed since Baba's arrival when something rather unnerving happened. I was strolling home from class when I saw some men escorting Mr Lee and Baba down Fortaleza e Farol da Guia. Their demeanour was unfriendly.

I hurried over to greet Baba and Mr Lee. I must have looked apprehensive, because Baba told me not to worry. He appeared calm, not like the time we'd met on Come Happiness Bridge when he was arrested back home. He said he and Mr Lee were going to a yum-cha meeting with these people, and would be home soon.

It was a very long yum-cha: they did not return that night, and Third Aunt became concerned. She could tell from my description that those men were engaged in some sort of shady business on the streets of Macau. Hurrying to burn more incense sticks, she prayed to the guardian angels to fan away the ill omen descending upon her home.

Baba and Mr Lee returned the next day, accompanied by one of the men. Baba borrowed cash from Third Aunt, handed it to the man and sent him away.

Looking tired but relieved, Baba told me and my aunt that the men had taken him and Mr Lee to a small room in a cheap back-alley lodge. Third Aunt sighed and said, 'Typical gangsters.' They'd said Baba and Mr Lee still owed money to the organiser of their escape from China. When Baba said they couldn't raise the money, the men threatened to send them back. Negotiations continued through the night.

Early the next morning, the party had a yum-cha breakfast while they determined Baba's and Mr Lee's fate. All my father could do was pin his hopes on seeing someone he knew in the crowds around them. Much to his relief he spotted a Portuguese man,

Joao, who had been in a basketball team he had coached when he was a teacher in Macau. Baba rushed over to shake hands with Joao, shocking the men at the table. It turned out that Joao was now a detective, and he knew, without Baba explaining further, what these men were up to – in fact, he had got to know them well in his precinct, as they had come to know him. Joao told the men, one by one, that they were dealing with his good and respectful friend, and that he would be after them should anything unpleasant happen to Baba and Mr Lee. Before he left he gave Baba his card, saying he wanted to keep in touch.

The men's arrogance and aggression waned as fast as the steam coming out of their teacups. Without further haggling, they agreed to settle the fare at $333 per person, instead of the $3000 promised. Baba explained to me that the number three sounds like 'live' in Cantonese, so it was 'live, live, live', a good omen for all – and the number six sounds like 'fortune', so $666 for two fares sounds like 'fortune, fortune, fortune'. Being alive was a fortune itself to behold.

*

From day one, Baba hadn't felt secure in Macau, fearing it was too close to the mainland. After this incident, he was even more worried about remaining there. He decided we must head to Hong Kong as originally planned, which was not only further away but also a much bigger city with more opportunities. Baba also believed Britain was a far more powerful nation than Portugal when it came to standing up to the communists. Unfortunately, our temporary Macau IDs didn't entitle us to a visa. We would have to make our own way into Hong Kong.

According to Baba, the illegal ferrying of people into Hong Kong had been a well-known and thriving business for many decades. He explained that it had grown to such a sizeable enterprise as a consequence of rebellions against the imperial emperors, colonisation by foreign powers, two civil wars, the Japanese invasion and, finally, the Communist Revolution. 'The money earned had to be distributed along a huge network of operators to everyone's satisfaction,' Baba told me. 'So the trade prospered in visible harmony.'

By 1962 it was more blatant than ever, now an open secret among the two colonies and communities along the southern coast of China. The so-called Bamboo Curtain, along with anticommunist sanctions and embargoes set up by Western countries, had well and truly isolated China from the rest of the world, and there were few options for those who dared to risk their lives for liberty and survival. The Portuguese authorities in Macau didn't attempt to stop people trafficking; instead, their tolerance and assistance facilitated a route to freedom for those lucky few who made their way out of China.

'People die for love. People die for freedom as well.' Baba had often said this to Mama, his eyes dreamy and voice quavering. Now that he'd decided to leave Macau, he was again filled with fervour. I couldn't help but wonder if we'd always be running in search of a safe place to call home, now that our family was broken up.

Although I trusted Baba's wisdom, to me Macau was already paradise on earth. I loved the aroma of the many wonderful bakeries filled with bread, pastries, cookies and cakes, and the countless noodle shops, cafés and restaurants along narrow streets crammed with thousands of cars, trucks, buses and rickshaws. I loved the many hawkers selling fruit, dumplings and goods of all description in the streets, and the casinos large and small. All obeyed unspoken rules, going about their business in a harmonious way I couldn't understand. Then there were the never-ending cobblestone alleyways that ran in many directions with lots of colourful billboards and abundant streetlights, adding to Macau's vitality and energy. Even the smells of burnt petrol and diesel, a rarity at home, fascinated me, and I found them civilised and modern – much to my horror and distaste in the years to come.

I also liked the optimism of the Macau people. 'It'll be fine,' they said whenever they parted. I wasn't sure if they were reassuring each other or just wishfully thinking that everything would be all right. How I wished we'd had that kind of self-confidence across the border.

I wasn't keen to be smuggled into Hong Kong, with many unknowns now seeming to threaten my new-found comfort. However, as the days went by I realised that this was the logical way forward, judging from what I overheard of adult conversations. They said everyone they knew who'd attempted the crossing had made it safely to Hong Kong. Besides, I realised it would be wonderful to see Grandmother Young, Grandmother Lee, Ping, Mr and Mrs Ho, and Je Je again. So I didn't complain, and left it to Third Aunt and Baba to work it out.

The smuggling of people from Macau to Hong Kong and from the mainland to the colonies was called 'snake business' by the locals. Baba reassured me that it was very well organised by a massive number of coordinated teams operating in Macau. The so-called snake heads oversaw the team leaders, each of whom directed a number of people who ran their own networks – 'the little snakes'. Many civilians worked in the people-trafficking trade: rickshaw men, bakers, store-owners, police officers, marine patrol officers, greengrocers, butchers, schoolteachers, even public servants, and, of course, the fishermen and owners of boats and ferries. Only God knew who else was involved, or who was in charge of the snake heads.

Third Aunt said it was too risky for a father and son to be in the same boat. She and Baba decided that I would make the crossing first, then Baba would take the next run.

Before long, my aunt had found out the best fare and the safest snake team from her favourite greengrocer. He directed her to a cookie-shop owner, not far from the English language school, and he offered a half-fare discount for me as a child. A sailing date was set ahead of the typhoon season.

The mention of typhoons had me worried. Third Aunt, ever sensitive to my feelings, noticed my anxiety and offered reassurance by reminding me of my fourteen enlightenment credit points.

Nodding in a slow rhythm, she continued to count her beads. 'It'll be fine,' she said with optimism, the same way the locals did in their daily greetings. It baffled me that they didn't seem to worry about tomorrow the way I did. Maybe they didn't want to know.

Third Aunt often said that everything in life was unpredictable, so we had to grasp what was there to make the best of it. This made me think of our life in China, as volatile as the weather in the South China Sea. Maybe my family hadn't been able to make the best of it because we *hadn't* joined the mob; maybe the District Head was one of the smarter few who had. He and his family had fared a lot better than us with their more powerful jobs, better wages and higher food rations, and gifts from the people.

What an erratic world I was in: unpredictable, cruel and unfair. To drown out my worries, I imagined I could hear the drumbeats of the dragon boats.

*

In early July 1962, I set off for Hong Kong. As Baba had done before I'd left Shiqi, Third Aunt faithfully lit three incense sticks in front of a wooden plaque carved with the names of departed family members. She said her prayers and entrusted my safety to the ancestors for the trip, and she prayed the sea would be calm, the voyage smooth, and the sun would shine on the path I would take. She prayed that prosperity would follow all the hard work that lay ahead for me, and that my guardian angels and the gods would be there to guide and protect me against all kinds of demons and evil spirits. Finally, she prayed that if I didn't make it, they would take me into their fold and not let me languish in the South China Sea. Baba and I also prayed to them and asked for their blessings for the journey. I felt a bit better after that, even though I was still apprehensive about the ghosts and water spirits of the sea.

My aunt then burned incense sticks in front of the statue of General Guan Gong, and asked him for my protection. She burned paper money to the ghosts and spirits that lurked around looking for replacements, and asked them to spare me. She then assured me that everything would be fine. 'The sea will be calm and the wind will fill your sail,' she said, counting her beads as she spoke. 'You've already travelled a long way and there's a much longer way to go yet. No one's voyage in life is predictable. So go with the wind, swim with the current, and steer your own boat. My blessings are with you always.'

She promised to keep the incense sticks burning until she heard of my safe arrival.

That evening, Baba took me to the cookie shop. As he did whenever we parted, he put his big arms around me and gave me a long hug. I'd grown to like the rich smell of Camel cigarettes on him, so unlike the crude Red Flag brand – no wonder the District Head had yearned for them.

Baba now spoke with a confident tone I'd never heard back home, and I liked it. 'It'll be fine, my son,' he said, in the same manner as the locals. 'We've gone through so much to get this far. We've many blessings from our ancestors. Go with courage but keep your eyes open. Remember not to stand under an unsafe wall. I'll see you in Hong Kong next week.'

Now I felt calm. I believed everything Baba told me; I trusted him as he trusted me.

Baba then went to talk with the cookie-shop owner, a softly spoken man in his forties with a Shiqi accent. He assured my father that I should be in Hong Kong the next day, and repeated a few times that his team was the safest one operating out of Macau every week, and offered the best price. Baba seemed relieved. He shook the man's hand before disappearing into the throng of Macau, without another word to me.

The cookie-shop owner took me to the back of his shop. There I met a young apprentice mixing and kneading dough, a cigarette dangling from the corner of his mouth. 'Hello,' he said in Cantonese with a distinctive, melodious Shiqi accent. 'Going to Hong Kong?' With a grin, he glanced at me with his narrowed eyes, smoke hissing from his nose and mouth. He didn't seem to expect an answer and went back to working the dough with a big bamboo pole hinged onto the wall.

A few boring minutes passed.

'Where you from?' he asked.

'Shiqi,' I said.

His eyes widened in surprise that he hadn't been able to tell where I was from. I felt glad that I must be speaking like a Macau local.

'Ha, so we're kinsmen,' he said with interest now, a lot friendlier. He went on to tell me that he'd make the trip one day when he'd saved up enough for the fare. 'Hong Kong is a big city,' he said, as if he'd already been there and I needed to be warned.

I was more interested in the dough he was working on than the conversation. I liked the smell of blended milk, butter, sugar and flour – ah, so rich, so mouth-watering, reminding me of the New Gold Mountain biscuits I loved. I took in deep breaths of the pleasant aroma as I watched customers being served at the till and counted the many types of Chinese cookies. I admired the colourful cookie jars, tins and boxes in different shapes and sizes at the back of the shop, trying to take my mind off my trip.

*

After the shop shut for the evening, the owner took me to a small traditional Chinese lodge in a back street. The place was dim. We went upstairs to a room with old-fashioned Chinese furniture – more ancient than any I'd seen in China, where old styles had been thrown away to make way for all things communistic. A round rosewood table and four round stools occupied the middle of the room, making the atmosphere solemn. Though it had yellow stains along its edges, the inlaid marble tabletop was very much like the one in Third Aunt's room back home. It was soothing to my sweaty palms, but it didn't calm my racing heart. A bed with a mosquito net stood lonely in one corner. The cane-skin mat looked uninviting on bare boards, and a narrow tea table between two square rosewood chairs occupied the other side of the room.

Another man appeared with some small Chinese teacups and a pot of hot jasmine tea. He offered me a cup and suggested I take a nap as more people were due to arrive. Before long, a young couple turned up; like me, they carried no luggage. They sat down at the round table and helped themselves to the tea. There was no conversation. Only the intermittent arrivals of more people interrupted the stillness of the evening. I dozed off in the large rosewood chair.

It must have been after midnight when they woke me. The room was now crowded with young southerners, although I was the only child in the party.

A man with a well-weathered tan face spoke in Cantonese. He appeared fit and confident, and was as optimistic as the locals. He welcomed us, then told us to follow instructions closely and to keep quiet throughout the trip. He seemed to be looking at me as he spoke. 'Everything'll be fine,' he said, before excusing himself from the room.

His assurance couldn't stop my lips from going dry and my heart from galloping inside my thin chest.

Sometime later the man returned to the room and broke us into small groups. One group at a time, we left the lodge by taxi. I went with a man and a young couple. No one uttered a word throughout the short trip. We soon found ourselves standing by a beachfront. A cool breeze soothed me, for now, and the coarse warm sand was comforting beneath my feet. The calm surf added to my confidence. We stood quietly in the dark, staring at the black water and the silhouettes of police officers on patrol nearby. Thankfully they weren't looking our way.

CHAPTER 23

Out of the dim night, a small sampan appeared on the beach. Three at a time, we were ferried across the gentle surf to a fishing junk about fifteen metres in length. It was anchored some fifty metres from the beach in complete darkness that to me looked sinister and threatening. The crew told us to keep quiet and sit low as we clambered aboard.

The shape of the junk reminded me of those I'd seen in storybooks about the olden days. Both the bow and the stern arched upwards, but the stern was somewhat higher so it provided a good view. The sails had been lowered, and an engine was idling underdeck.

We obediently stayed quiet while the boat pulled away from the murky shore into the blackness of the South China Sea. All I could hear were the gentle waves stroking the hull as the boat sliced through the calm sea with ease. The surrounding obscurity was no different from what I'd known for a long time when sitting on the levee wall looking into the night, so I wasn't afraid of it. Other passengers kept to themselves, with occasional timid mumbles like those of a subdued audience at a sentencing meeting.

Hours later I woke to the soft light of dawn shining through the ropes and masts. Fishing nets were heaped to one side of the small deck; it was obvious no one had bothered to cast them. A half-moon appeared every now and again through the few low clouds. There must have been a dozen or so young men and women on board, all too well dressed for a fishing expedition. Some were asleep. Occasionally a shard of golden moonshine glittered on the boat's well-oiled planks. The sounds of the sea slapping against the hull and the squeaks of the vessel complemented each other.

I was pleased to see a statue of General Guan Gong standing at the stern, as if he had just leapt off the enchanting story panels under the eaves of Great-Grandmother Good Arrival's house in Shenmingting. I was relieved he was there to protect me in my endeavour. His beard was flowing and his long sword gleamed. Three incense sticks were burning in front of him. I knew I was in good hands.

*

The stretch of some fifty kilometres of unpredictable water between Hong Kong and Macau is known to locals in the Pearl River Delta as the Lonely Sea. Many people have been lost there to temperamental weather, including frequent typhoons. July was a calmer season, they said. However, there were lots of People's Militia gunboats on patrol looking out for people trying to escape China. There were also the Royal Hong Kong Marine Police boats that guarded the colony's waters from people smugglers. But Third Aunt said the snake teams were amazingly efficient in smoothing things out for these expeditions.

That morning I found myself leaning over the side of the boat watching the universe emerge around me, alive and promising. Here we were, somewhere in the middle of the Lonely Sea, hiding from the gunboats and the police as we were tossed gently in a tepid bath between two small weather-beaten islands, their ruggedness lessened by the jade-green radiance of sparse vegetation. Comforting reflections of the pearl and gold sky danced among calm swells. The water was exceptionally smooth, just as Baba and Third Aunt had wished for me. Hundreds of large jellyfish with long tentacles floated by, so free. Seagulls hovered above, searching for their first meal of the day and sending out an occasional cry as they seized their prey.

There, between the two tiny islands, we whiled away the day. The old junk blended into the seascape with ease. There was nothing for us to do on board. Whispers ebbed like the docile ripples caressing the boat, but everyone kept their head bowed in the same way the adults did back home when talking with the comrades in charge of them. I wondered if Mama knew I was on my way to Hong Kong. Perhaps Baba had sent news to her through a trusted messenger like the cousin who'd met me at the border.

I hoped the District Head would not give Mama a hard time at the evening political meetings when he found out I had gone to Hong Kong. I prayed that she wouldn't be dragged out to the town's denouncement meetings at the sportsground. And Weng and Ying ... how was Weng going to defend herself from the jeers and torments of those mean kids at school? And they might kick Ying out of the swimming team.

A soft voice interrupted my thoughts. 'You afraid of the sea? And the darkness last night?' Sitting near me was a young woman, in a bright floral blouse.

I half-nodded but didn't answer for a moment, then recited what my parents used to say to console each other: 'It'll be light when the night passes.' I wasn't sure why I said this but it made me feel grown up. 'My mother says that if you're patient enough to wait for the clouds to disperse, the bright moon will be there for you to appreciate.'

'Are you by yourself?' She looked at me with wide eyes, clearly wondering why such a young boy was all alone at sea.

'Yes, but my father will be coming over next week.'

'Where will you go in Hong Kong until then?'

'To stay with my grandmother and older sister. What about you?'

She didn't answer me, just stared at the sea.

I was glad to have someone to talk to; it made me feel at ease. So I began telling her that I had two grandmothers in Hong Kong, my Grandmother Young and her in-law Grandmother Lee, whose daughter Bertha had married my Uncle Chong Young. I wasn't sure if the young woman was listening, but to impress her I babbled on about the last time I'd been in Hong Kong.

'I'm going to stay with my mother's cousin,' the woman finally said, interrupting my chatter. 'Never met him before. He's married with a young child.' Her voice trembled a little in the warm breeze. She pushed her hair away from her eyes as she faced the endless stream of salty air. She reminded me of the young woman who'd lived at the last house in our street – and how her fairness had attracted a sojourner from the Gold Mountain. 'I hope to get a job as soon as I get to Hong Kong,' she said after a few minutes of silence. 'I can use a sewing machine, and they say there are many machinist jobs in Hong Kong. Then I'll go to evening school to learn English,' she added, before turning to me. 'So what are you going to do?'

I hadn't thought about what I was going to do except go to school. And I'd never considered how I would afford it, and who would be responsible for my board and lodging. All I knew was that I was on my way to a new life. I shrugged and stared at her. She must have been seventeen years old, maybe eighteen. She looked so grown up; somehow, she exuded a determination I hadn't noticed in others. Perhaps until now I'd never taken notice of people's willpower and what it might mean. Her stare was intense. Whenever she spoke, I could have sworn her words were coming from a much older person.

'I hope I can go to school – I want to go,' I replied, with the first thoughts that came to mind. My English classes had inspired me. My Third Aunt had inspired me. The sudden appearance of my father had boosted my yearning for more education. I'd become confident, and I believed I might just be fortunate enough to be sent to school.

'Lucky you,' said the young woman.

She turned to stare at the deck. The varnish had peeled from the edges of the long planks here and there, exposing the coarse old timber. When our eyes met again, our glance acknowledged that we were both lucky to have left China. The trip was worth the risk.

Soon after, the snake head who'd given us instructions at the old lodge addressed his stowaways with the usual local optimism. 'It'll be fine,' he said matter-of-factly, pointing to the lightening east. 'We'll be in Hong Kong for supper tonight.'

Without another word, he went to the stern and brought out our breakfast. After we'd each finished a bowl of shrimp congee and a baguette, he grouped us together and provided detailed instructions on what we should remember once we'd disembarked, depending on the district to which we were heading; the instructions included which bus to catch and what to say if stopped by a police officer. He had an intimate knowledge of the colony and seemed to know where each of us was going. He also told us titles of movies and operas that were playing, and at which theatres, so we could speak about them and appear to be locals.

The man's confidence made me feel that I could just sit back and dream of a better time ahead. I felt my ancestors' blessings, Buddha's and Third Aunt's also. Plus my twenty-eight credit points. I shouldn't be afraid, I told myself, especially now I've made a friend.

*

At dusk we set off again. The sea had turned into a vast golden blanket. A few birds cawed overhead as the red landscape of the mainland retreated into the distance.

The chugging of the diesel engine was hypnotic for the tired mind, and I soon dozed off. Suddenly the District Head's son was shouting at me, 'Capitalist, son of counter-revolutionary, black element!' Water hit my face, squirting from his green plastic water pistol: the toy Ping had brought for me on one of her trips home. I woke abruptly and remembered how the District Head had seen my precious toy and casually mentioned to my mother that his son would like to have one, as he put a tin of condensed milk into his pocket. Mama had asked me for the water pistol that night. Although I was upset, even angry, I surrendered it with little protest. I understood how important it was to keep our District Head happy.

I couldn't get back to sleep. On several occasions, Chinese gunboats steered close to us and followed our boat at a short distance. They didn't take their eyes off us. I wondered what they were thinking. Would they take us back to China? To them, we were just another boatload of deserters fleeing communism and the Motherland. We were the scum of China, and the many re-education camps were full of people like us. Thank goodness they didn't stop our boat. Maybe they too were part of the people-smuggling network; I never knew for sure. The strip of sea that divided the capitalist and the communist worlds was narrow.

It was growing darker. The little lamp high on the mast looked tiny as it flickered in the dark, holding up our hope. There was hardly any sound on board except for the hum of the engine. Some people had dozed off, relaxed by the strange peace surrounding us; they slumped on the well-scrubbed deck like sack-loads of fish. The sails, probably raised during my nap, flapped occasionally as they filled with wind. The boat picked up speed in the open sea, powering towards our expedition's end.

'Quick, everyone!' A quiet but urgent voice roused me from my somnolence.

The snake head hurried us down a small ladder to the lower level. We were now jammed onto a smaller deck, close enough to feel each other's racing heartbeats. A doorway was open into the diesel engine compartment; on either side of it the walls were covered in wooden planks. The snake head removed a few panels near the edge of the boat on each side, exposing two entrances to narrow crawl spaces between the wall of the engine room and the outer hull.

Then he sought me out, where I hid behind the grown-ups, and told me to squeeze into one of the crawl spaces first. I stared at the opening, not much bigger than a dog's kennel, then I looked at him, wondering how I would get in there.

'Go right to the end,' he ordered.

On hands and knees I scrambled over the slimy, damp floor until I could go no further, rocked by the waves underneath as I crammed myself into the pointed end. My heart skipped many beats as it raced on.

Behind, I could hear frightened people mumbling to each other.

'No, I can't,' came the voice of a young woman, my friend from the deck.

'Yes, you can.' The snake head wasn't pleased with her.

'I get sick in a small space, especially in the dark. Please—'

'Quick. Hurry up. Now.'

'No.'

'Now!'

'No.'

I could imagine her holding her head high, the young woman who'd told me she would work as a machinist during the day and go to evening school to learn English.

'All right, step aside.' An annoyed grunt from the snake head.

A few more people entered the crawl space behind me, looking apprehensive. I crouched down, squeezed against the wooden wall that kept the sea from entering the boat, and tried to stop shaking. I took deep breaths, but the air was thick with the smell of dampness, mould and diesel. Soon the stink of sweat and tears blended in.

'Everyone keep quiet ...' Hammering sounds muffled the last words of the snake head as he nailed the exit. We whimpered. Some panicked.

'Are we going to die?' someone asked softly in the dark.

'Please, Buddha, have mercy on us,' cried another, among timid sobs.

I hadn't heard the young woman's voice inside the crawl space, and I wondered if she was in the other tunnel on the opposite side of the engine compartment. I didn't know how she was coping, but it was too late now to find out.

I don't know how long we were inside that confined space. All was quiet except for the sounds of our breathing, of the sea and of the lonely motor. I tried cheering myself up with the thought that a better life was ahead, one worth the danger and distress, and I had to be patient. The occasional splash of waves against the boat helped to break the monotony in that suffocating space. My mouth was dry. Soon I had no more saliva left, and my tongue had turned into rough cardboard. I longed for a bottle of Sunkist Orange like the one given to me at the Macau border. Then I recalled the delicious fragrance of the cookie shop, trying to bring water to my mouth. When that failed, I started counting the many colourful cookie jars, tins and boxes I could picture in the shop. That made me salivate a little, so I continued counting them, floating between the shapes and colours, in and out of some mystifying contentment. If not for the chug of the motor reminding me that I was still in the land of the living, I would have believed I was buried alive in a coffin at sea, drifting off to die. At least it seemed a lot more pleasant than being eaten, or shot at Pig Head Hill.

Much later, the motor slowed to an idling mode. By then my senses had all but dissipated. Now I could hardly think, or react to the outside world. The rocking of the boat indicated we had stopped. I heard another motor approaching. Then, suddenly, came the unmistakeable sound of heavy boots hitting the deck.

Two, perhaps three strangers were now on board. I woke from my stupor. I couldn't hear their conversation, but it sounded like negotiations were taking place.

Something was about to happen, but no one inside the crawl space seemed to care. My breathing was laboured. My heart was pounding so loud that I was sure those next to me could hear it. My mouth had cracked like the clay in the drought-stricken paddies. The dread of the unknown became worse by the minute, and it kindled my curiosity, perhaps for the last time. Something was happening on deck. But I couldn't stay conscious for long enough to know what eventuated.

The crawl space had turned into an oven, and we were being baked alive, slowly. The air seemed to have disappeared. The blessings of my ancestors were all that I had. I trusted them and those on board to deliver me to safety, as I drifted off into muddled visions. I saw Mama and my sisters tremble below a concrete stage where I was kneeling next to Baba before the whole town. My friends stared at me blank-faced; their mouths opened but there was no sound. All I could hear was the District Head and his committee members shouting slogans, denouncing Baba and me.

'No,' I cried, 'we're not counter-revolutionaries!' But no one seemed to hear. I wanted to cry. But no tears came. The slogans grew louder. A ring of regimental khaki and revolutionary red had seized all of us in an inescapable grip. The might of the people's justice was descending upon us, the deserters, the nonbelievers, the unwanted.

The grip of a rope tightened around my neck. I shook in great panic as I felt the cold barrel of a gun pressed hard against the back of my skull. I raised my head to take one last look at my family and friends. I choked. The more I struggled, the more the rope tightened, until I didn't care anymore. Giving up, I found myself floating in a strange but irresistible quiet and peace, drifting towards a distant light.

*

A loud bang brought me crashing down. In front of me, a kaleidoscope of colours exploded. *Is this paradise bursting open?* Greedily I gulped in the sweet cool air before I could make sense of anything. I could hear people talking, but that meant little to me.

Only later did I find out that someone had pulled me from the crawl space, delirious and limp. The smugglers had dodged the Royal Hong Kong Marine Police by whatever means, and now we had safely reached our destination. Three new incense sticks were burning in jubilation in front of General Guan Gong. Ahead was the amazing glow of a million lights in Hong Kong's Victoria Harbour.

At the dark end of a small bay, they lowered the sampan from the junk, the one that had brought us on board in Macau. Three at a time, they ferried us to the sandy beach. By then the night breeze had restored my senses. Each cool breath I took cleared my head more. The sampan's quiet squeak from its lone oar was the only sound that mattered.

The thought of my new life ahead made me excited. Then an image flashed through my mind of the young woman I'd met. I hadn't seen her on board, and could only wish her well as I scrambled ashore.

I began to recall the snake head's instructions, in case I had to prove my authenticity. My few weeks in Macau had converted me into a local Cantonese-speaking boy without any trace of a Shiqi accent. My self-confidence returned before the last passenger got ashore.

The bus terminal was only a short walk away. I was to pretend to be the kid brother of a young woman meeting her boyfriend there – a chaperone. I walked by her side as the couple strolled along hand in hand. We passed many lovers locked in embraces on the dark slope of Lychee Point as we headed towards the bus station. A few police were on patrol but showed no interest in us; they always seemed to look the other way in Macau and Hong Kong.

It became brighter as we reached the end of the rough road cut out by bulldozers in a land reclamation project next to the bus station. Swarms of beetles danced around the streetlights, buzzing and humming as if joining us in our quiet celebration. Nearby, the amusement park was closed for the night. We parted at the bus terminal. A middle-aged woman took my hand, and murmured, 'It's time to go home,' a signal that I was to go with her. I followed like a dutiful son, and we hopped onto a red double-decker bus to town.

My clothes had dried in the warm breeze. I was happy the ordeal was now over.

The bus took off into the wide and almost deserted streets. The woman smiled at me as if saying, *Welcome to Hong Kong*. She didn't talk until it was time to get off at the Yuen Chow Street stop, and I led the way from there. I could still remember that my grandmother's apartment was just around the corner, above a tiny store. Sanitary workers were collecting garbage and cleaning the streets. I ran and skipped over little heaps of rubbish as the woman hurried behind me. The smells of diesel and the nearby bakery hadn't changed since I'd left seven years earlier, and I breathed them in with a smile.

Grandmother Young was waiting for me to arrive. She still had her hair in a neat bun behind her head. A large smile spread across her face and she looked endearing and sweet. She paid the woman who had accompanied me to her. A large hot cup of Ovaltine and a baguette with gleaming golden butter were on the table for me – she hadn't forgotten my favourites. She kept smiling as she patted my crew cut.

Ping was still up. She danced around, bubbling with excitement, and couldn't wait to show me around Hong Kong. But after my hot drink and food, I just wanted to go to bed.

Ping also had news from home. 'Ying wrote and said Mama was in big trouble with the District Head, who shouted at her for not reporting Baba's escape. He told her to attend evening self-criticism meetings every night. But Mama doesn't care; she's just so relieved that Baba made it to Macau.' I was troubled by the thought of Mama's continuing torment, but, exhausted from the trip, I soon fell asleep.

My bed was a foldaway camping cot in the foyer. Mrs Ho, the good landlady, had agreed to let me sleep there as long as the cot was packed away early each morning. Grandmother Young and Ping shared the small room, while Grandmother Lee had moved into a nearby apartment by herself after Ping's arrival.

It was wonderful to sleep in a bed again. I didn't wake up until late into the next day.

PART III

Over the Carp Gate

CHAPTER 24

I levered myself up from the camp bed in the foyer of the apartment.
I couldn't believe how long I'd been asleep. Ping was already home
from school and had changed into her bright floral skirt with a crisp,
light blue blouse. Her well-permed shoulder-length hair shone; so
did her smiling face. In fact she looked a lot like Mama in her rare
happier times. She had my mother's gentleness as well as her big
eyes and fair complexion. Each time she had brought food to us in
Shiqi, she had only stayed overnight and we had hardly had time to
get to know each other. The years she had lived with Grandmother
Young in Hong Kong had turned her into not just a smart teenager,
but also a pretty city girl. In an instant, I felt I finally knew her.

'Baba rang when I got home. He was relieved that you had made
it. He told me to get you into a school and said he would be coming
to Hong Kong soon. Are you rested? Grandmother didn't want to
wake you for lunch. You must be hungry now.' Ping chattered on
with excitement as she helped me pack away the camping bed.

'I want to talk to you about school after dinner,' Ping continued.
'The brief English course you did in Macau isn't going to be good
enough for any decent school in Hong Kong. The standard here is
a lot higher.' I was proud that I could read picture books after only
a few weeks learning English. But now Ping was stirring a little
panic inside me. So I diverted my attention elsewhere by opening
the window and looking down at the street.

The sounds and smells of the city had not changed over the years; even the odour of decaying rubbish in the street was the same. It all reassured me that I was now *really* in Hong Kong. But I still couldn't suppress my anxiety about school.

'Where will the money come from to pay for my school fees?' I asked Ping later.

'Don't you worry,' said Ping. 'I'll write to Grandfather Young in Hawaii. We'll start some lessons tomorrow. I'll find out from my school when they're having the entrance examination. Now let's see what Grandmother has cooked for you.'

I could hear Grandmother Young's loud voice echoing down the long hallway from the kitchen, where she was talking to another tenant. I still felt ashamed that I had got scared seven years earlier and made her take me home to Shiqi. Oh my poor grandmother, who loved me so much, she must have been most disappointed with me. Had I not been such a brat, I'd now be in Form I, perhaps even Form II at a high school, instead of trying to get into Sixth Class.

As much as Grandmother was always pleasant and kind to me, it was clear as the days went on that she was worried about her finances. Grandfather Young was no longer so healthy and would be under greater pressure to provide for us. And with an extra mouth to feed, Grandmother would have less money to send to Mama and the girls in China and to Aunt Wai-hung and Young-syn in Macau. One day, she muttered to me at dinner, 'You should get a job like my friends' grandchildren, pushing trolleys in restaurants as dim-sum boys and girls.'

Ping was upset by the suggestion. She knew well that, in this status-conscious city, people tended to regard dim-sum boys and girls with disdain; indeed they occupied the lowest rung of society, even lower than street-cleaners and prostitutes. And the stigma would stick: once they had done that job they would always be referred to as dim-sum boys or girls, said Ping. Grandmother Young hadn't had an education, and could be forgiven for not understanding its importance. But Ping was determined her little brother would avoid this fate.

'I'll stop going to school so my brother can go to school,' she said to Grandmother Young the next day.

'No, no, no, you can't do that,' said Grandmother Young. 'You've almost finished high school.'

'But I want Ah-mun to have an education,' Ping said without giving it a second thought. 'He needs to go to school.'

Grandmother Young frowned. 'But how will we afford it?'

Grandmother Young had come to rely on Ping to help her negotiate the complexities of everyday life in fast-paced British Hong Kong, and needed her support just to venture out of her rented room in Sham-shui-po. Ping was so clever and able, and her impeccable Cantonese was the envy of Grandmother's many friends from home who were also in Hong Kong to receive foreign living allowances from their sojourner husbands. Resourceful Ping had helped many relatives settle in the colony.

So, after some discussion, Grandmother agreed to let Ping write to Grandfather Young again, as well as our uncles in Hawaii, to ask for more financial assistance.

*

Two weeks after my arrival, early one morning, my father made it to Hong Kong, in the same fishing junk, captained by the same snake head who had brought me.

On hearing his voice in the apartment, I was at once stirred from my slumber and rushed to hug him. I was ecstatic to see him. His arrival boosted my sagging confidence: I always felt secure with Baba around, and now I might have a better chance of going to school.

It was wonderful to be reunited with him, but I immediately felt worried for Mama and my sisters who were still in Shiqi. How were they, I asked.

'Ying wrote and told me Mama has been sent to a re-education camp just out of town for not reporting me or stopping me from escaping Shiqi,' Baba said after some food and drink. I could sense his restrained agitation, if not embarrassment, in front of Grandmother, who was silent in her own thoughts. She was so worried about her younger daughter and granddaughters left behind, and she well knew the torments the Party could put you through, having suffered herself after being condemned as a landlord.

'And Ying now has to attend evening political meetings for families of "black elements".' He looked worried. He couldn't smoke, as Grandmother would not allow it, so he sat sipping tea instead.

'How cruel and unfair,' Grandmother said. 'Why do they hurt us so much? They took our land, our home, every valuable thing we had. And now they've put my dear daughter Wai-syn in prison. And Wai-hung's two boys are still in Shenmingting, starving, with no hope. Oh please, Goddess of Mercy, take pity on us.'

'I'll find a job tomorrow,' Baba said, 'any job. We'll be all right. Our new life has begun. It can't be any worse than Shiqi.'

Judging from the huge number of healthy-looking people in Hong Kong, no one seemed to be starving. So it seemed likely we'd be able to get by now that Baba was with us. But the worry and sadness I felt about Mama and my other sisters weighed heavily on my mind. Fearful of retribution, Ping and Grandmother felt they could no longer make the trip to Shiqi, though Grandmother continued to send as much money as she could. We'd just have to hope Mama and the girls would survive by using it to buy extra food on the burgeoning black market.

*

Baba was up early the next day, ready to go job-seeking.

'Hong Kong is a very different place from Shiqi,' he said to me. 'Everything depends on your credentials or experiences. Good references also help, but I've none of those now. So I'll just have to see how I go.'

'What's a credential?' I asked. It sounded a bit alarming, like the constant noises of the city, buzzing non-stop, droning all day long, and into the night.

'A certificate from a reputable organisation like a school, university or business, saying that you are a hard worker and qualified to do particular jobs.' He paused on his way out of the apartment. 'From today, we've got to start all over again to build ourselves a new place to call home. So let's work hard together. You learn your English well so that you can get into a good school in September. And I'll go and visit my cousin to see if he can give me a job. I'll also go to the Education Department to see if they still have my teaching record there. Our education is our best hope for a bright future.' And with that he opened the door and walked out into the busy city.

Yes, the door is now open to us, I thought for a brief moment. Then I picked up my English reader and began preparing for the entrance examination to the Tsung Tsin Grammar School in Sham-shui-po. It was the obvious choice given its modest fees and a good academic reputation; it was also where Ping went and was only a few blocks away from home.

After six weeks, I sat the entrance examination, which involved questions on Maths, English and Chinese. My schooling in China had consisted mainly of brainwashing political studies, slogan-shouting and propaganda, collecting firewood and waste metal, and killing pests, so it was no surprise when I was told I had been accepted into the school but would have to repeat Sixth Class.

I wrote to Mama, Ying and Weng often to try to brighten their days. I imagined Mama's happy face when she opened my letters and read about the things I was doing at school and at home with Grandmother and Ping. I was careful not to mention anything the District Head might consider inappropriate.

From their replies, we were very glad to learn that food rationing was being eased and that once a month people were permitted to sell their goods in one designated street in Shiqi. All kinds of farm produce was on sale there, as well as clothing, second-hand furniture, antiques, puppies, chickens and ducklings – even single imported cigarettes could be bought! And bartering was allowed.

For us, knowing the family was no longer at risk of starving in Shiqi was a great relief.

Baba settled for a job as a bookkeeper at his cousin's poultry store in Hong Kong's Central Market. He and a few workers slept in the store, as renting an apartment was beyond their means. Baba didn't mind. On his day off, once a week, he would come to visit us in Sham-shui-po. He was fairly happy with his progress in re-establishing his life in the capitalist world. He was undertaking a postgraduate course at night school in teaching. In the meantime he was biding his time at the Central Market while patiently waiting for a teaching job to come up.

It was a wonderful feeling to go to school every day. I didn't have to smash rocks, break up tiles and bricks to make gravel, search for waste metal, stamp out pests, or hunt for food to ease my hunger. There were no political studies to attend, no slogans to shout, no comrades to impress. I wasn't made to suffer the indignity of being regularly criticised as the son of a counter-revolutionary and grandson of a bankrupted capitalist. And I wasn't forced to watch public sentencings and horrifying executions. At last, I could leave all my nightmares behind and concentrate on my studies and my future. Now that my dream was coming true, I vowed to work hard. Fortunately, Grandfather Young and my uncles in Hawaii had agreed to pay for my schooling. I was overjoyed. But I still couldn't forget my desperate family back in Shiqi, and their struggles.

Learning in Hong Kong wasn't easy for me. I struggled with English from the first day, and through the first semester failed nearly every weekly dictation test. Comprehension was difficult and I often failed that too. In fact, despite spending all my after-school hours studying, I regularly scored zero in tests. Miss Miu, my Sixth Class teacher – a slim young woman with permed hair who dressed smartly in the Western style – was particularly hard on me. She didn't think I was up to the standard required for Sixth Class.

'Mainlanders have been so badly brainwashed that they've no capacity left for learning,' Miss Miu told the class one day as she handed me my dictation result – a big zero in red ink. My enthusiasm for school started to evaporate. It appeared that, like many in Hong Kong, Miss Miu had little time for mainlanders and considered them a threat to the economy and security of the colony.

To some extent it was understandable, given that the numbers of mainlanders swarming into Hong Kong had increased dramatically. In China, the border guards could not stop the exodus and eventually just started showing people the way to leave; some even abandoned their weapons and joined the rush. Kind people in nearby villages and small towns on the Hong Kong mainland fed and assisted the hungry refugees. Many were smuggled to Hong Kong in boats, as I was; some even swam across to the colony. At the height of the flight in 1961 to 1962, over a hundred thousand refugees a month were flocking into Hong Kong. Everywhere you turned there were groups of new arrivals. City residents became deeply worried about whether Hong Kong could cope with this sudden increase in population.

Up to 1962 the Colonial Hong Kong Government had granted residential rights to mainlanders on their arrival if they presented themselves to the Immigration Department, as Baba had done. But it became clear that it was impossible to accept all the refugees, and in 1963 the government began actively sending incomers back to China. Many, driven by desperation, made several attempts to return.

All the talk of refugees made us hopeful that Mama and my sisters might eventually make it out of China and join us. But while the authorities were still watching and punishing Mama, it wasn't likely to happen in the short term.

*

As I walked up the rise to the school gate on Castle Peak Road one day in early 1963, I had a vision of being snarled at by Miss Miu. I'd been immediately attracted to her beautiful-sounding English, and wished that one day I would be able to speak English like her. She was obviously a keen teacher, diligent at helping students, and maybe she cared about me, but I sensed that her patience was running thinner as the weeks went by and I had shown no improvement.

As usual, Ping was quick to come up with an idea. She asked one of her classmates to help me. Deng was a mainlander but he was also a high achiever, apart from being a handsome young man who made the girls at school blush with admiration.

'What do you think is the problem with English?' he asked me when we met on the grassy slope beside the playground. I told him the difficulty I had with dictation and comprehension: I was too slow in writing, and missed most of the paragraph during a dictation.

'Well, every problem has a solution,' Deng said. 'So what are you going to do about it?'

What a smartie, I thought to myself. I was rather displeased with his challenge. But then I reflected further on my situation. The idea of becoming a dim-sum boy if I couldn't master English drove me to come up with a response: 'What if I learn the whole paragraph by heart, and write it out at my own speed?' That was how I had learnt Chairman Mao's quotations and slogans, and then regurgitated them at political studies classes. Deng said it was a good idea and to give it a go.

Miss Miu was stern-faced when she gave out the dictation results the following week. After I'd spent nearly a whole semester scoring zero in every dictation and comprehension test, she was more than surprised to find only three mistakes in my paper. That meant I should have scored 85 per cent.

But Miss Miu was not convinced. 'This is not your work,' she announced without looking at me. 'It's impossible for you to achieve these marks. I can only give you 50 per cent, as a warning.'

'Unfair, but that's life,' Deng said to me later. 'Keep up your diligence and don't get angry with her. Anger eats away your energy and wears down your fighting spirit. You need both for the long journey.' He then told me how important it was to pay attention to the 'bigger picture'.

But what was the bigger picture? My world had expanded so much in Hong Kong, with all its freedoms, that at times it was scary. Where should I begin? How was I to steer my own boat when I didn't have one? I lay awake in my camp bed for many nights, wondering how to see this bigger picture. Then I realised what Deng was saying, that English might be the key, as my parents and Third Aunt had often said. It could open doors for me, even to a bigger world beyond the colony, so that I would be free to sail even further afield and experience and feel so much more. Aha, I thought, I've got it. From now on I will devote all my energy to mastering English. No wonder schoolmates looked up to Deng.

Miss Miu made me sit at the teacher's desk for my weekly tests for the rest of the semester. When she dictated the paragraphs to us, she stood behind me to watch me write my answers in my slow scrawl. Letter by letter, word by word, sentence by sentence, I reproduced the memorised page at my own speed. Sometimes she would deliberately slow down her dictation so that I could catch up. Soon I was consistently scoring 90 to 100 per cent in the tests. Miss Miu was delighted. I was awarded second place in the class at the end of my first year, and English became my favourite subject.

CHAPTER 25

In early 1964, Baba got a job as a physical education and Chinese literature teacher at a small mission school in Diamond Hill. He was delighted.

'I know that area well,' he told us at a celebratory yum-cha lunch. 'Once upon a time, my oldest brother, with your Grandfather Woon-duk's financial support, operated a school for the poor in a nearby district. Unfortunately it had to close during World War II. Now's my chance to do something for those people.'

I always admired Baba's desire to help the less fortunate.

Baba rented a back room in a bungalow in Diamond Hill. However, his remuneration was meagre at the mission school, so he continued to look after the account books for his cousin on weekends.

Even though I was making good progress at school, which made me happy, I found it hard to recover from the traumatic experience of the trip to Hong Kong. Memories of it intertwined with long night terrors about the revolution, as well as worries about Mama and my sisters. Often I woke with my pyjamas saturated in sweat, feeling suffocated, and couldn't stop shaking. Everything in my nightmares was so vivid I could sense it on my skin, taste it in my mouth and feel it in my heart. My foldaway bed squeaked like the boat I'd travelled in.

The slightest upset or worry would trigger a feeling of suffocation. Sometimes, even a casual conversation could bring it on. It was hard to believe that I was living in Hong Kong now, and I no longer needed to sit on the levee wall every morning feeling hungry, dreaming of food or trying to shake off the desperation of starvation. Better still, I no longer had to steal food. I pinched myself and pulled my hair from time to time, just to be assured of this new, miraculous reality. Then I thanked my ancestors for their blessings and General Guan Gong for his protection, and all my guardian angels around me.

According to relatives who still visited Shiqi, despite the denouncements and public criticism inflicted on Mama, Ying and even Weng for their failure to report Baba's escape, they continued to apply to the District Head to leave China, and to look for other ways to free themselves. 'Your mother lost her wedding ring when she gave it to a trafficker as a deposit,' the cousin who had met me at the border wrote to us from Macau.

I remember how concerned Baba was when he heard that. He rang the cousin that evening. 'Just like that?' he asked over the phone to the cousin as he drew on his cigarette. 'And Wai-syn couldn't find the man again after giving him the rest of her remaining jewellery? For a deposit for the three of them?'

The cousin also told us how Mama had given away anything that the Street Committee Member or the District Head fancied, in the hope that her application to leave would be treated favourably. But this hadn't worked either. Baba later tried to explain to Ping and me that life was hard and starvation had eroded the spirit of the people, even the comrades. Those in charge needed essential materials and food for themselves and their families. They couldn't afford to let people like Mama go.

The worst news came in the early summer of 1964, after Mama and the girls made another unsuccessful attempt to escape, this time by boat. Mama and Ying were both sent to re-education camps for three months; Weng was spared because of her young age – she was not even thirteen at the time. After their release Mama and Ying were kept under surveillance by neighbours and tenants like Choi-lin. It was not until after months and many gifts that Mama was allowed to apply again to leave China. She later pinned her hopes on the District Head's wife, who kept promising favourable consideration in return for food items and goods that my mother could purchase from the Overseas Chinese Friendship Store with her foreign currency vouchers, or from the black market. But this would go on for years.

I longed for Mama's letter every month, and I pictured her likewise waiting anxiously at the street entrance for mine. I wrote to her about how I was getting on at school, even describing the challenges with a strict teacher like Miss Miu. I knew Mama would be glad that I had finally got to grips with English, and I hoped that might help ease some of the sorrow of our separation.

In their letters to us, Mama and Ying said nothing about the re-education camp, or the evening political meetings they had to attend after their release. We learnt about these things only through those relatives or friends who visited Shiqi. 'They inspect all the letters you send to your Mama and sisters,' said to us, 'so be careful and don't say anything political or anti-communist, or your family will suffer.' One piece of positive news was that Ho-bun was now dropping by our home regularly to help out with household chores. He was frustrated because he hadn't been allocated a job and his family in Hong Kong had to continue to send him a living allowance.

At our now weekly yum-cha lunch, we passed on news of Mama, Ying and Weng to Baba, and he would give us messages to include in our letters. 'This way,' Baba said, 'we are less likely to aggravate the District Head.' Baba's usual message was 'Seize the day', which I believed was meant to encourage Mama to continue working hard towards our goal of reuniting the family.

'It will be hard, but not impossible, for the family to be together again one day,' Baba would say whenever he noticed that I was ruminating on our situation, 'though the odds are not good, and no one knows when it will happen.' All we could do, he said, was to be patient and hopeful. He was also glad that Ho-bun was helping the family.

*

Grandmother Young decided to leave Hong Kong and join her husband in Hawaii. Having left in 1921 when Mama was only six months old, Grandfather had only ever returned to Zhongshan twice: in 1934 after the Great Depression, and in 1948 after World War II, so he and Grandmother had spent little time together. During the McCarthy era of the early 1950s, he was so frightened of being persecuted for having Chinese contacts that he reported his children had been lost during the war. When, in 1961, he had visited Hong Kong to recuperate from illness, he had remarried Grandmother in order to obtain a marriage certificate that would be valid in America and allow them to be reunited in Hawaii one day. In 1964, that day finally arrived.

From my foldaway bed, I could hear her brewing her coffee as she usually did just before dawn every day. The gentle aroma wafted from the hallway through the whole apartment. Ping was already up. She couldn't stop blowing her nose, and her eyes were red from crying. Three incense sticks were burning in front of General Guan Gong and the other gods. Grandmother was dressed in her silk cheongsam, her hair well lacquered into a bun at the back of her scalp, her face powdered and her brows painted. She looked nearly young enough to be my mother. She was sad too.

'I worry about the two of you,' she said to Ping and me at breakfast. 'I'll miss you. I hope I can find someone in Hawaii who can write letters for me. I'll miss my girls too. I just hope the food rationing goes up and they are not going to starve.' She sighed and continued, 'Honestly, I don't want to be so far away from my girls, in the Gold Mountain of Hawaii. But I feel this may be my only chance to be with your grandfather and his family.'

Grandmother looked at Ping and said, 'You've been such lovely company all these years and helped me with so many things here in Hong Kong; for this I thank you. Take good care and no more tears. One day I would like you to come and live with me again. Take good care of Ah-mun too, and make sure he does well at school. I didn't have the opportunity to go to school and I can't even write my own name. Now the long trip ahead, and the aeroplane ...'

A tough woman in many ways, Grandmother softened up that morning. I put my arms around her and promised to be a good student. 'I love you Grandmother,' I said. 'We shall meet again. Please give my best regards to Grandfather, and our uncles and aunties too.'

On hearing that Grandmother was leaving, Mama had written us a letter. We could feel the desperation and sadness in her words: 'Tell my mother how much I wish I could be there to see her off. And how bad I feel for letting her down over the years, for being such a burden to her and my father.' In another letter she wrote: 'I owe your grandparents everything and I feel terrible that I've not been able to repay them.'

Some relatives and friends came to Kai Tak Airport to see Grandmother off. She broke into her Shenmingting dialect to hide her trepidation. She was going on her first ever plane trip by herself, not knowing a word of English. I sensed her quiet courage, which I knew she had passed on to Mama and Aunt Wai-hung, perhaps even to me.

*

After Grandmother left, we could not afford to stay in Sham-shui-po, so we moved into Baba's place in Diamond Hill. It was an audacious name for what was well known in Hong Kong as a slum area. And, I soon realised, little more than wishful thinking. Essentially a shantytown, Diamond Hill was situated on the far slope of Lion's Rock in Kowloon, where the poorest of the colony, including hordes of new arrivals from the mainland, flocked for the cheap rent. Sanitation was almost non-existent. Heaps of rotting rubbish lay at the sides of the streets, smelly liquid oozing, trickling and seeping out onto the pavement, making it wet and slippery everywhere most of the time. It was even worse on humid days. Sanitation workers wore thick masks when collecting garbage in Diamond Hill.

Illegally erected shacks and shelters housed the growing number of residents, making the already narrow and convoluted streets and alleys hard to pass through. Fires often broke out from the portable kerosene stoves people cooked on. The fire engines found it difficult to navigate their way through the chaotic streets, and many homes could be lost in a single blaze. The homeless were then given priority for public housing in the new residential estates nearby, such as the Rainbow Estate. Baba suspected some of the fires were set deliberately.

We didn't have visitors. We were embarrassed to tell friends and acquaintances where we lived. Instead, we told people we lived near the Rainbow Estate. Ping disliked the area with a passion. For her, it was too rough and dirty a neighbourhood, much worse than Sham-shui-po. She had just begun to work at Cathay Pacific Airways. In her smart red uniform, she really stood out in Diamond Hill, but she hated the stares.

'We mustn't complain,' Baba often said. 'At least we've a place to call home, away from starvation and persecution, and the unpredictable typhoons and seasonal floods that the family back home still have to endure.'

Things improved further when Baba took on an extra job teaching in the afternoons at a private school in Kowloon City, a suburb close to Kai Tak Airport. This helped with our expenses and ensured adequate funds could be transferred to Mama and my sisters in Shiqi. But the challenge remained: how to get them out of China?

With Baba and Ping both at work, I was responsible for cooking the evening meals. On the way home from school I stopped by the fishmonger's to check out the good variety of freshwater fish, eels, crabs and different types of shellfish displayed in wooden buckets. Some fish had already been filleted and parts were sold as requested by customers – some liked the tail, others the stomach, and even the head of the fish was favoured by a few shoppers. The fishmonger always left the beating heart on the cut-up fish to show how fresh it was. From time to time he splashed water on it to keep it moist.

Helpless, the fish opened its mouth to take in irregular gasps of air and savoured the water that fell on its motionless body. Then it slowly succumbed to its fate, its eyes clear to the end.

Sometimes I bought half a freshwater trout. It was the same kind of fish the commune kept in the fishponds near our home in Shiqi. It reminded me of how Ah-dong thought he was a trout when he was delirious from hunger. He'd mumbled something about jumping out of the fisherman's tank on the way to the market and swimming to Hong Kong to free himself from starvation. He'd never have wanted to be a fish if he'd known what happened at the fishmonger's in Diamond Hill. Since leaving Shiqi, I'd had no news of my good friends like Ah-dong and Big Eye, and I often thought of our times together, sitting on the levee wall dreaming about food, or planning the next fishing trip or just how to find something to eat.

CHAPTER 26

In September 1965 I began Form III, or Year 9. Despite my position as a top student at Tsung Tsin Grammar School, I felt the need for bigger challenges. The influx of a million or more refugees from China had inflated the population by more than a quarter over a short span of time. Every schoolboy in the colony aspired to study at exclusive schools like La Salle College in Kowloon and the King's College in Hong Kong. These schools were well known for both their academic excellence and sporting prowess, and the old school tie guaranteed good job prospects and career advancement. Competition was intense at all levels of society, entry to schools of excellence included. The pressure to succeed academically now gnawed at me with increasing urgency.

Every day my school bus went along Boundary Street past La Salle College, which was run by the De La Salle Brothers, and I watched the La Salle boys in their smart black school jackets. They attracted admiring looks from many people, especially schoolgirls. I began imagining myself attending La Salle College. One day I mentioned my ambition to Ping, aware that she knew a La Salle old boy who might be able to advise me. From him I soon found out the school had six classes in each Form, and Form I had two classes that were reserved for boys from their own La Salle Primary School, while the rest were filled by boys who'd sat an annual public entry examination – several thousand boys battled it out for the

160 places available. Transferring from other schools to prestigious ones like La Salle was rare. The information was like a predawn star, twinkling.

I could see the big dome of the majestic La Salle College sandstone building through the window of the double-decker bus I travelled on. It stood there on top of a diminutive hill, gleaming in the island sun, a distinctive local landmark among the growing number of apartment blocks that surrounded it.

My aspiration to be a La Salle boy soon became something of an obsession. One afternoon I rang and made an appointment to see the principal, Brother Casimir. I presented myself at his office in my navy school jacket and neatly pressed grey trousers at four o'clock that same day. He soon appeared through the large door to his office, a robust middle-aged man with a big waist and a crop of thinning hair that swung across his prominent forehead. He wore a long white robe and a bright green cloth sash whose square ends hung down to his knees. My first impression was that he appeared saintly.

He cupped his large hands together in front of him and looked at me with deep-set eyes. Then he spoke in a gentle voice: 'What can I do for you, young man?'

Young man? He calls me a young man. I didn't think I was big and strong like a man yet, for I was still small for my age despite my recently improved diet. My confidence was boosted by his friendliness. I felt his blue eyes piercing me, but that impression was softened by the delicate scent of sandalwood eau de cologne that religious ministers wore in subtropical Hong Kong. For reasons I still don't understand he stirred up an unusual sense of reassurance, or courage, inside me and I felt at ease in that moment. I turned away from his gaze, bowed and mumbled the English lines I had rehearsed for weeks: 'Brother, I sincerely want to be a student here. I have done very well in my studies, and here are my report cards ...'

I dug into my schoolbag to fetch the reports. But he didn't seem interested and turned to look at his large desk covered in piles of files and began to fiddle with some papers. A large portrait of Saint Jean-Baptiste de La Salle looked down from one wall. Not a trace of island breeze came through the two large windows facing Boundary Street below and I grew increasingly nervous.

'Sorry, young man, we don't have a vacancy,' he said. Then, without another word, he ushered me out of his office and down the vast long hallway to the front door of the school building.

I tried to suppress the hot lump expanding and rising into my throat, something I hadn't experienced since leaving home on the small bus, not even when I was being smuggled into Hong Kong. It grew, but I was able to keep it down by taking deep breaths.

I dragged myself towards the steps leading down to Boundary Street. The lump was now heavy under my ribs, churning like those whitecaps on the Wonder River that morning when I refused to dive in. How I wished that it would just burst and let me cry.

I didn't want to leave. At the top of the steps I sat down, oblivious to the fact that evening was arriving. I looked back at the school building with its huge round columns, its large dome and its grand sandstone façade with big windows. The pillars were losing their sheen as the sun set behind the cityscape. I watched the sunlight wane on the dome.

Maybe I was wasting my time and being too ambitious, I thought. Maybe I was overconfident. Perhaps I should be content with what I had and grateful for what I had achieved so far. Suddenly I felt drained of the enthusiasm that I had nurtured for weeks before coming to see the principal.

I didn't care how long I sat there. I didn't care that night was falling and Baba and Ping would begin to worry. Although I had experienced many rejections, this one was hard to accept.

The humidity had not subsided as it normally did. I sweated in my school blazer and felt lonely. I thought of my friends back in China who struggled to find food and stay alive. I should be thankful. *Perhaps I'm not meant to attend this famous school. Perhaps I need to accept my situation as it is, and just be grateful for what I've achieved so far ...*

But then I remembered what Baba had often said: 'Our destiny is in our hands ... and we don't give up ... We must steer our own boat.'

The lights were all out now at the school, except the one in Brother Casimir's office. He was clearly working on into the night, and he had left his curtains open, as if he knew I was still outside and wanted to lend me some light. I suddenly became aware that if it hadn't been for that light from the headmaster's office, I would have been in complete darkness.

Then I thought of the many stories Baba used to tell us. One that stood out for me was how a young monkey from *Journey to the West* kept returning to the Master to beg to be accepted as his student, so that he could become as wise as a human. The Master would say to him, 'You are only a monkey, how can you ever be as clever as a man?' Many days went by and the Master kept saying the same thing. The young monkey went away each time disappointed. One day the Master told him exactly the same thing again, but this time before he finished, he tapped on the monkey's head three times, turned his back on the monkey and walked towards his house with his hands clasped behind him. At exactly three o'clock the next morning, the young monkey was at the back door of the Master's house, where the wise man was waiting to admit him as his student. Later, the young monkey would master the power of magic, and he became so wise and intelligent that his peers made him the Monkey King.

That's what I will do. I will be persistent like the young monkey until I've got myself into La Salle College. I stood up and headed down the steps to Boundary Street to catch a bus home. I couldn't take my eyes off the school until it disappeared into the darkening night. *I'll come back tomorrow,* I promised myself, and headed home.

Baba knew that I was upset. He took me out for a walk.

'There is a champion in every field. Champions come from anywhere,' he reminded me. 'As long as you can make a success of your life one day, does it matter if you don't graduate from La Salle College?'

For the first time in my life I disagreed with Baba, but I didn't reply.

The next day after school, I made another appointment to see Brother Casimir. In two subsequent interviews, he confirmed that there was not a single vacancy available. But he didn't say it was impossible, and he didn't try to quell my enthusiasm. Although he didn't tap me on my head like the Master did to the young monkey, a faint hope rose inside me. It was like the tiny flicker I saw in Mama's eyes each time she handed in her visa application to the District Head; like the quiet rumble of distant drumbeats across the Wonder River that kept returning, year after year, to remind us to stay positive. It was the feeling I sensed from Baba at the bus stop when I was leaving Shiqi for the last time, and felt myself when I was being smuggled into Hong Kong. Hope was always there, and now it was churning inside me, refusing to settle.

For the ensuing three weeks I sat outside Brother Casimir's office every day after school. While I waited, I read Shakespeare's *Hamlet*. Teachers, staff and students walked past, and much to my surprise, as the days went by, some of them even smiled at me. Initially I was embarrassed, not knowing if they were laughing at me, and I suspected that everyone would be talking about the strange boy sitting outside the headmaster's office. But, little by little, I became more confident, and soon I started to smile back at them and even chatted with some of them.

Some days Brother Casimir was not around; other days he would walk past me as if I wasn't there. Later I found out he had instructed the front desk not to offer me any more appointments.

Four weeks had now gone by. I continued to return to La Salle College every day after school, sitting outside Brother Casimir's office and reading *Hamlet* for the umpteenth time. I kept reminding myself to be patient and focused, and not to give up. Anger consumes energy, as Deng had said; and now it could smother inspiration. I had to guard against that while accepting that maybe there isn't always a solution to everything in life.

Finally, on a Friday afternoon, five weeks after I had first met Brother Casimir, his door swung open. He invited me into his office.

'What do you want young man?' he asked in the same gentle voice. This time, however, with his hands resting on his hips, he stared straight into my eyes. I looked back and saw his blue eyes glint. I felt comfortable. I felt like reaching out to hug him as if he were one of my uncles.

'Brother Casimir,' I said, loud and clear, 'I would like to be one of the students at La Salle College. I need more challenges.'

'Our standard is very high here, son,' Brother Casimir said as he removed his glasses from his prominent nose. 'You may not be able to keep up.' He then turned, placed his hands behind his back, and walked over to the large window that looked out over the steps where I had often sat during the past weeks. He stood there for many minutes. I kept thinking of the Monkey King and the Master.

All of a sudden Brother Casimir spun to face me, hands clasped in front of him now, and said, 'You are a pain. I'll put you in Form II, but for one semester's trial only. You'll have to leave if you can't keep up. This makes you the forty-first student in the class.'

'Oh, thank you so much! Thank you, thank you, Brother Casimir.' I grabbed his large hand with both of mine, and couldn't stop shaking it. I accepted the deal without hesitation, even though it meant repeating a year and being older than my classmates, maybe even the whole form. Behind those blue eyes, something glinted and my own vision blurred.

It was the best Friday afternoon of my life since leaving Shiqi. I could hardly wait for Baba and Ping to come home from work. For the first time since the three of us had moved in together, we went out to celebrate in a local Shanghai restaurant.

*

Ping thought I looked superb in my black school blazer the following Monday, and it was a very proud moment going to school on the bus with students from other schools staring at me and admiring my distinctive uniform.

I had hardly any problem adapting to the new school, for I was already familiar with many faces there. I promptly became involved in many sporting clubs and societies. They included geography, photography and stamp collecting clubs, but my favourite was the fencing club. I even joined the catechism study group and was soon baptised as Andrew, a name that made me feel more at home at La Salle College, where nearly all the boys had English names.

However, I was soon brought down to earth. In my first monthly tests, I was shocked to find myself close to the bottom of my class, Form IIF. Brother Casimir came into the classroom to give out the results, as he did with all other classes. One by one, we went up to him when called. He looked at my report card and was clearly less than impressed, but he was kind enough not to mention the deal we had made.

'You'll have to work harder, son,' he muttered as he took off his glasses and stared at me.

I immediately reassessed my many extra-curricular activities and resigned from all societies except the fencing club. Serious study was needed.

Three months later I made it to twenty-third in the class of forty-one. Brother Casimir was still not happy with my result. It was not until after the annual examination, when I got to seventh place, that he actually smiled at me. He even stopped in the middle of giving out the report cards to say a few words to me, a rare honour.

'Have you heard of the race between the hare and the tortoise?' he asked.

'No, Brother,' I said in front of the class. Everyone burst out laughing. All the children in Hong Kong knew the hare and the tortoise story from their kindergarten years.

Brother Casimir told me the story that day, then said to the entire class, 'Work consistently with diligence and you'll get to where you want to be.'

With much gratitude and respect, I began to consider Brother Casimir one of my guardian angels.

CHAPTER 27

From Ying and Mama's regular mail, we learnt with great interest that Ying's friendship with Ho-bun had blossomed over time and the two of them were now engaged. Most of Ho-bun's family lived in Hong Kong, but the authorities had rejected his many applications for an exit visa. Baba said that the money his relatives sent regularly to support him was the real reason for the refusal: China didn't want to lose any foreign funds.

In early 1966, a trusted friend brought us news that Ying and Ho-bun were planning to make their own way out of China together. We worried for their safety as we waited with excitement and patience for their arrival.

When the news of Ho-bun's appearance in Hong Kong reached Baba, he was joyous. It was a memorable day for us and we met up in a café as soon as we could.

A fit young man, standing head and shoulders above most southern Chinese in Hong Kong, Ho-bun looked fresh in his new white shirt. His suntan marked him out as a newly arrived mainlander. But there was no sign of Ying.

'Why isn't she with you? What has happened to my daughter?' Baba quizzed Ho-bun before we'd even sat down.

Ho-bun kept his head bowed. He couldn't look Baba in the eye. Instead, he fiddled with his glass of water, stirring the ice cubes with a straw, as if looking for a place to hide. I couldn't help but feel sorry for him, while fending off the terrifying image of my sister's body floating in the South China Sea.

Ho-bun was flushed from the base of his neck all the way to his forehead. Sweat trickled down his handsome face. It was quite a while before he was able to recount his daring getaway. His unease made him almost incoherent as, talking to us in our Zhongshan dialect, he tried to find the right words to piece together his story.

'Ying and I met our guide outside the last town before the prohibited border territory,' Ho-bun said, voice trembling. 'The guide was nervous, yet he was supposed to be experienced. There was something strange about him. Ying pulled me aside and said we should be careful.

'The guide refused to take both of us, and said he would only take us separately. This was not what we had agreed. We were shocked, but decided that your sister Ying should go first.' Ho-bun raised his heavy eyes and glanced at me, avoiding Baba's gaze.

'I was to follow a few days later before the moon became too bright,' Ho-bun continued. He was now holding his empty glass in both hands. 'But for reasons I still don't understand, at the very last moment, Ying refused to leave. She wanted me to take the first opportunity, which had taken a long time to arrange. You know how determined your sister can be. I couldn't persuade her to do otherwise. The guide was getting restless. He pushed half the agreed fee into Ying's hand and started to walk away.'

Yes, that's my sister Ying, I thought to myself.

'Ying insisted I should go first. Then she turned and walked towards Shiqi. She didn't look back. I knew she was crying. She didn't even say goodbye,' Ho-bun mumbled. 'The guide and I walked for hours, dodging militia posts on the way. There was a new moon. No stars.'

The small café was crowded. Baba and I leant closer to hear Ho-bun. 'Insects hummed on, but stopped as we approached. It felt like we were walking in a bubble. The world had shrunk into a sphere that wrapped around us, keeping us safe. I stayed two steps behind the guide. My mouth was dry, but my palms were wet. I clutched two deflated football bladders – my swimming floats – under my worker's jacket. These were the most important things I had for the journey and I couldn't afford to lose them.'

Then there was silence. Other customers in the café seemed to be quiet also. But we were in a bubble of our own.

'Life is so unfair,' Ho-bun carried on, after what seemed to be a long pause. Tears now pooled in his eyes. He rubbed the fresh scars on his hands, probably cut by rocks and seashells.

Baba sighed. He lit another cigarette, drawing deep and hard on it – the way he used to do at home when he was in a funny mood. This was the worst I'd ever seen Baba since leaving Shiqi. He tapped the ash into an ashtray, keeping his gaze on the young man.

Ho-bun emptied another glass of iced water in one gulp.

Baba ordered him a 7 Up lemonade with ice.

Ho-bun then told us how the guide had instructed him to swim to the mouth of the river to catch the current. Ten metres before the searchlights hit, he was to dive underwater and not resurface until the lights swung back towards the shore. He was not to use the bladders until then either. The guide also told him to ignore the first light on the horizon immediately to his right, a decoy set up by the authorities, and float in the current until the water became very salty. Then he would notice a brighter and bigger radiance at the two o'clock position along the shoreline. 'Aim for that one,' said the guide, 'and you'll reach Macau. The tide has now turned – for you too, I hope.'

Looking somewhat relieved now, Ho-bun took a deep breath before finishing his story, 'I was alone. The tide was going out. Some five hundred metres away the searchlights from both banks had turned the water into a big white sheet. The beams spanned seawards in an arc with decreasing intensity before swinging back to shore. I counted forty or more seconds for each cycle. Crouching there without making a sound, I held my breath as if I were underwater as the lights moved out to the sea, and added ten more seconds. The humming of insects and beetles resumed, only to be silenced as I gasped for breath. I practised several times before I felt confident enough to make the crossing.'

He took a long sip of his drink, raised his head, and looked at Baba, the way he used to when he was training. But his eyes were filled with sadness that day, seeking forgiveness.

Baba nodded.

Ho-bun broke down and wept. His muscular body convulsed.

Baba reached across the table and put his hand on Ho-bun's shoulder, saying nothing. He looked away from his distressed student and stared at his cigarette again. A few patrons looked our way. I stared back at them. The café was suffocating.

More tears. More sighs. More cigarettes. I was not embarrassed. I was sad for Ying and Ho-bun. How could life be so unfair?

'Yes, the tide has turned,' Baba finally said. 'For all of us.'

CHAPTER 28

Just days after Ho-bun's arrival in Hong Kong in May 1966, I was preparing dinner in Diamond Hill, sizzling up the garlic for a stir-fried vegetable dish that we all loved, and of course, grilling the fish and browning its skin and edges to send out a welcome-home aroma that Baba and Ping would notice as they walked through the front gate of the bungalow after a long day at work. The automatic rice cooker gave off the distinctive sweet fragrance of cooked rice – a comforting smell I'd always loved and a symbol of food and survival during the famine; it still makes my mouth water and my stomach rumble.

'The world belongs to you. China's future belongs to you.' Chairman Mao's voice burst into the kitchen through the Radio Hong Kong news I was listening to as I cooked.

I shook.

'It is your right to rebel!' he went on, inciting the youth of China to wipe out the decaying Chinese culture and rebel against the authorities and administration. 'In every organisation, village, town and city, province … all over China.'

The latest slogans were much more ominous than the revolutionary ones I had shouted. They were also confusing. *Haven't we already been successful in our revolution? Haven't we already beaten the capitalists and cleansed the people? Why another revolution?* I stopped stirring the vegetables. I sensed terror ahead. Fear for the safety of Mama, my sisters, Ah-dong, Yiu-hoi, Ah-ki and my other cousins and friends seized me the way it had done when Baba was arrested by the People's Militia.

The vegetables and fish burned.

'Sorry I forgot to add soy sauce to the fish,' I said during dinner. 'I was thinking of the family and friends at home in Shiqi, and worrying about their safety. Those ferocious slogans, I'm not sure what they mean.'

Baba didn't reply.

'I saw several communist posters near our office in Victoria,' said Ping. 'There were loudspeakers blaring from the Bank of China building, calling for the dismissal of the British colonial government.' She looked to Baba for an explanation.

'The world is dangerous,' Baba finally said and sighed. 'Communist factions have emerged on the mainland and are fighting for control. It'll affect us here in Hong Kong.' He frowned.

'But Chairman Liu is in charge now,' I said.

'My son, don't ever believe what they say. For the communists, power comes from the gun barrel. All revolutions are bloody and violent, infused with ruthlessness and terror.'

In the weeks that followed, more and more slogans and news flooded the local media. After dinner, we crowded in front of the landlady's black and white TV watching news clips of the Red Guards marching and masses of people moving about in China. Most of them were my age, young teenagers. They wore red armbands and waved Chairman Mao's Little Red Book (a famous collection of his sayings) in the air while chanting slogans and declaring their allegiance to the Great Leader. I looked hard at the screen to see if any of my friends and cousins were in the mobs, and felt relieved when I didn't recognise anyone.

Launched in 1966, Mao's Cultural Revolution, a campaign to purge capitalist elements from Chinese society and thereby preserve communism, had erupted and swept through China and even Hong Kong like the biggest typhoon ever. Hordes of Red Guards began to demonstrate in the Chinese border town of Shenzhen; on several occasions they tried to march across the border into Hong Kong. The Chinese border guards, the Hong Kong Border Police and the Royal Ghurkha Guards were able to stop them initially, but then the Chinese guards refrained from interfering, and there were even exchanges of gunfire between the Chinese border guards and the Hong Kong authorities. Both sides suffered casualties. In 1967, left-wing protesters in Hong Kong began striking, marching around and waving their Little Red Books to imitate the mainland Red Guards. Riots broke out in Kowloon. Violence and terror began. Bomb hoaxes and unrest escalated in many parts of the colony.

'I had to come home early today,' I said to Baba and Ping at dinner one evening near the end of the school year. 'There was a bomb planted at the school. They said it was because La Salle College is foreign and has many gweilo teachers and students.'

'Keep your eyes peeled. Be alert and don't touch any parcels lying around on buses or in the streets,' Baba warned us. 'They are saying in the papers that the communists infiltrated Hong Kong during the refugee influx a few years ago and are now trying to get rid of the British. The police found out they are making bombs in leftist schools and factories. Eight thousand homemade bombs have been detonated. Unbelievable. Barbaric. Senseless,' Baba said, his eyebrows locked together and pain showing on his face. He was smoking more again; his night terrors had returned.

When an eight-year-old girl and her two-year-old brother were killed by a bomb outside their home, it brought a stronger reaction from the people of Hong Kong. Lam Bun, a popular radio commentator, fiercely attacked the terrorist leftists. Soon after, he was burned alive in his car, together with his cousin. This cruel act aroused even more unforgiving condemnation from many people in the colony, and soon they too were on the assassins' list.

Hong Kong plunged into turmoil. Strikes organised by leftist unions broke out amid more terror and violence. Many businesses were affected, and within months many had abruptly shut down. The Hang Seng Stock Exchange Index dropped 90 per cent during the period of riot and terror, according to the adults. We, and all the people in Hong Kong, were worried.

Looking out of the packed double-decker bus on my way to and from school, I often saw protesters being chased by squads of policemen in riot gear. *Why the terror and violence? Why can't we live in peace? Why is life so challenging?* More questions swamped my head. Even Baba had no answers for them. I felt powerless to avoid a bomb in a crowded bus, and called on God and General Guan Gong to protect me. I dreamed that the District Head was in the crowds looking for Baba and me, and woke up in a pond of sweat. The image of Pig Head Hill loomed large. The sanctuary we'd found in Diamond Hill was clearly fragile. But where else could we go?

Baba talked little while watching the unrest going on. I could sense his anxiety. 'We need to look beyond Hong Kong, far away from here,' Baba said one evening when things seemed less chaotic in the streets. 'The quiet out there won't last, and we'd better be prepared. But the family in China is the biggest worry.'

'We can go to Hawaii,' Ping said. 'We've family there.'

'We are already indebted to the Young family,' said Baba, 'and I wouldn't like to burden them further. Besides, the grandparents are getting older, and the uncles have their own families to look after and worries of their own. Also, since Grandfather declared his children had been lost during the war, we have no official status as family members. No, we'll have to figure it out ourselves.

'No countries accept immigrants these days unless they are immediate family,' Baba said, directing his gaze towards me. 'But that doesn't mean we can't try. We have to come up with a long-term plan, which might demand a lot of resources we don't have.'

A warm glow flashed across his face. 'Ah-mun,' he said to me. 'How would you feel about studying overseas? Anywhere, any country. I don't mind if I have to take on more work to support you.'

Ping nodded and said without hesitation, 'I'd do my best to help you out too. Hong Kong is no longer safe for us, and we have to leave. I heard from friends that some students work to support themselves while studying abroad. It's hard, but possible.'

Education, education, education. Third Aunt's words rang loud in our rented room in Diamond Hill that evening.

Some people who could afford to leave Hong Kong had already left. I later read that special British envoys were dispatched to Beijing to make deals to end the troubles. That probably explained why towards the end of December 1967, much to everyone's surprise, the riots abruptly ended in Hong Kong.

By 1968 the Vietnam War was in full swing too, and once the riots in Hong Kong had ceased, many American soldiers spent their leave in the colony. It was clearly one of their favourite destinations, judging from the number of them coming and going. I couldn't stop wondering how much rice, vegetables and fish from home in Shiqi were being consumed by the visiting Americans, the arch-enemy of China, and how many American dollars were flowing to the mainland. That made my world seem even more perplexing and dangerous – as befuddling as Hamlet's.

On the Star Ferry, I often saw American soldiers and sailors in their smart, well-laundered uniforms – there were no holes or patches like those in the PLA uniforms. Some of these young men and women were Ying's age. They looked and acted like the other gweilo people in Hong Kong, chatting, laughing and marvelling at the beauty of Victoria Harbour. I was curious about them and tried to sit close to them. They smelled fresh, and stood up to offer their seats to women and older people. I liked the way they said, 'Yes, sir', 'No, ma'am', 'Thank you' and 'Please'. I was surprised to hear they also listened to The Beatles, The Rolling Stones, Cliff Richard and Elvis Presley, and talked about the Top 40 hit songs, just as we did at La Salle College. It was so different from what I had been told in Shiqi: that they were nasty and ugly with big crooked noses and evil eyes. Sometimes I said hello, seizing an opportunity to practise my English. And they would say 'Hi', and smile. Then I'd not know what to say and just giggle at my inadequate conversational English.

Baba said thank goodness when the riots settled, and told us Hong Kong would begin to prosper again with the big influx of American tourists, as long as the Vietnam War continued. It sounded awful to Ping and me, but it was something for which to be grateful, for now. But at whose expense? My teenage brain found it hard to comprehend such a crazy world as the one in the 1960s, with those endless wars, conflicts, revolutions, invasions, starvations, killings, persecutions, imprisonments, murders, illicit drugs, prostitution … It was more complex than I'd ever imagined it could be, making the thought of going overseas quite terrifying. It was a relief to listen to those rock-and-roll hits, that sometimes angry music, which raised a voice of protest only we, the young ones, could understand.

By the summer of 1968, the fury of the Cultural Revolution was intensifying across the border. Every day, large numbers of corpses began floating down the Pearl River into the waters of Hong Kong and the surrounding islands. The bodies were different from those that had appeared during the mass exodus to escape starvation a few years earlier; they were not starved and emaciated like the refugees of earlier years.

Graphic photographs of atrocities appeared in the local newspapers, including images of victims who had been bound and gagged, and had multiple wounds. In some cases, several people appeared to have been chained together and drowned. The dead were mostly young people, and many were wearing Red Guard armbands. Some had been partly eaten by sea life as they'd floated to the South China Sea. Baba wouldn't watch the evening TV news; instead he sat in our room and grieved over the loss of human lives. I often sat with him in silence, wishing the rumbles of dragon boats were there to revive us, to rekindle our hope for humanity.

'Another one hundred and fifteen bodies from the harbour.' Baba shook his head as he mumbled to himself after checking the morning newspaper. Every day he started at the top left-hand corner of the front page, where the number of bodies retrieved around the colony's waters was inscribed in a black box like the outline of a coffin – this daily official count appeared on every newspaper in the colony. Before he left for work, he read every bit of news about China, the scar in the middle of his forehead twitching as he frowned and grimaced in sorrow. He talked little but drew hard on his cigarettes. There was nothing we could do but keep hoping that one day the family would be together again.

For months, the daily count ran into the hundreds. The Royal Hong Kong Marine Police were no longer able to cope and the Colonial Government began hiring local fishermen to recover the bodies to stop them from floating into busy Victoria Harbour. A bounty of ten Hong Kong dollars was paid for each body recovered. It was more profitable than fishing.

Hong Kong was now as bleak as a gloomy, never-ending winter, even though it seemed to be booming with trade and commerce. People were subdued. Everyone was fearful for their families and friends back in China, as well as their own future. A glut of ghost stories circulated, each more horrible than the last, and we stayed away from the beaches for fear of vengeful spirits looking for replacements. Even during the day, I often looked behind me when walking along shadowy streets to make sure I was not being followed by wandering spirits. I'd hold my breath as I hurried to a brighter part of the street, then gasp for air to calm my pounding heart. I often felt chilled and couldn't keep my face and hands warm; I rubbed hard to ease the tingling sensation around my lips and in my fingertips. Religious organisations held regular services by the waterside to pray for the lost souls and angry spirits, while the residents of the colony continued to count on their luck, and whatever blessings they had.

At home in Diamond Hill, the three of us asked for blessings from our ancestors. Ping and I also prayed to God for the safety of our family in China. We began attending St Teresa's Church regularly, and there we found comfort, and gained a sense of security and peace at mass. Hoping and praying were all we could do for our family and friends. We also prayed for others who were a lot worse off than us. And we prayed for a miracle.

Every day I ploughed through the newspapers trying to understand what was going on across the border, as well as how it might affect us in Hong Kong. I shivered when I read about the vicious acts perpetrated by the Red Guards against comrades in charge of towns, cities, villages and even local enterprises like factories, schools and communes. Disputes between factions led to even more bloodshed, misery and grief. I was worried sick about our family and friends back home, and felt as helpless as Baba and Ping.

How safe were Mama, Ying and Weng, and the rest of the family and friends in Shiqi? No one knew. They sent fewer letters and they were short, often saying little more than that they were okay. There was so much confusion over there; I imagined they all must have stopped criticising the Russians and Americans as arch-enemies for now, and focused on pledging their loyalty to Chairman Mao to ensure their survival. It was a confronting world.

Then we heard some terrible news about Uncle Beng'e and his family. The Red Guards had arrested him for refusing to surrender his much-treasured copies of Chinese classics to be burned. Then he disappeared. His bound, gagged and mutilated body was later found in a nearby shallow stream. The authorities told Aunt Wai-hung that he had committed suicide, and when she and her son Young-syn, visited Shiqi for the funeral, they were not permitted to return to Macau. To return to Shiqi was to flirt with fate.

I prayed more and wished harder. My prayers often brought me to tears as I struggled to grasp the magnitude of the suffering in China, a place I could no longer call home.

We heard more snippets about the family in Shiqi from friends who were allowed to visit. Little sister Weng had lost her dimples and no longer smiled, and both she and Ying had been having a hard time. Ying had ended up unemployed after finishing high school. That she'd been allowed to complete high school was a miracle in itself, my father said; it probably had something to do with her having been a national swimmer as well as a member of the Red Scarf. As for Weng, she had been prevented from continuing to high school as retribution for Baba's escape. I later found out that the same punishment had been inflicted on my cousins Yiu-hoi and Ah-ki after their father, my tall Eighth Uncle, was denounced by the Red Guards at public meetings. The guards also ransacked his home, as they did many others in Shiqi. Without education, the future was bleak for them.

During the so-called Up to the Mountains and Down to the Countryside Movement, a campaign launched in 1968 at the peak of the Cultural Revolution, Weng was among the first thousand or more young people of Shiqi to be sent to live in rural areas, 'to learn from the peasants'. She was barely sixteen years old. Baba said it was the Party's way of controlling the tens of millions of young people who had found themselves without work and were left to roam the streets, often terrorising people.

In one of her few letters, Mama told us that Weng and many of her unfortunate schoolmates had been dispatched to remote, impoverished locations where the peasants hated them because they had to share their already meagre produce and food supplies. Some of those young people were the children of disgraced Party members who had lost their former privileges as a result of the Cultural Revolution, and they had to endure what many children of people who had fallen out of favour, like my family, had been suffering all along. It particularly worried us when we heard that Weng had been sent to a low-lying area in the Pearl River Delta that was prone to typhoons and frequent flash floods, and the scene of many drownings. No doubt many disgruntled ghosts roamed the delta.

Mama said in one of her letters that Weng was miserable and could not wait for her monthly three-day leave to arrive; after each break there was another long month of peasant life to endure before the next leave. Weng became sunburned working outdoors. On her days off she spent most of the time in bed sleeping. She seldom talked and did not laugh or smile as she used to do ever so readily.

Mama wrote about how she had tried to cheer Weng up with a small parcel of food to take on her trip back to the country outpost. 'Here you are, my dearest,' she said to Weng, 'I've saved these three sweet potatoes just for you, and an extra bowl of brown rice – see, all cooked and ready for you to take.'

'Why worry?' Weng had replied. 'It'll only last a day or two, and I have nowhere to store it.' Then she jumped on her rattling bicycle and pedalled away from home without taking the food.

I couldn't imagine how heartbroken Mama must have been as she waved Weng goodbye for another month. As I travelled to school on the crowded bus, how I wished that Weng could be there with me. I would show her how to estimate where the bus would stop as the impatient driver tried to dodge the crowds waiting at the bus stop and keep his usually full load of passengers moving along. One day I caught my reflection in the dusty window. I realised I was now frowning just like my parents.

CHAPTER 29

'This time we must go as far away from China as we can, even if it means the South Pole,' Baba declared one morning, after a night of bad dreams. Many people we knew had already left Hong Kong. I'd got used to waving goodbye at Kai Tak Airport to classmates who were going to continue their studies overseas. I couldn't help being envious.

However, for the many millions of people in Hong Kong like us with little or no wealth or connections, the way out was difficult, if not impossible. International sanctions against China continued, and the Cold War was threatening the world with nuclear war. No one wanted anything to do with a communist state like China that was wretchedly poor, and all Chinese were regarded as possible communists. Our grandparents and uncles in Hawaii didn't even acknowledge that they still had family in China for fear of arousing suspicion; anti-communist sentiment was entrenched in America and allied countries. For us to apply to emigrate to the United States was definitely out of the question.

My desire to leave the colony became a constant thought that soon turned into an obsession, so much so that later I felt ashamed of myself for trying to escape my past and lunge ahead to secure my own future. But I needed to break free, to breathe, to shout, to jump. I didn't care how far away I had to go, and Australia started to seem like the logical destination – partly because it was close to the South Pole.

One of the brothers at La Salle College was Australian. He often told us fascinating stories of the country's outback, its Aboriginal people, bushfires, kangaroos, and its many beautiful beaches. He showed us pictures of Sydney Harbour Bridge, Ayers Rock (now Uluru), and sports such as cricket and rugby. We even had a rugby team at La Salle.

Several classmates had already gone to, or were planning to leave for, Australia. It looked like the ideal country, a place where I could work and study at the same time.

Encouraged by Ping, I brought up the topic with Baba one evening. He asked many questions and nodded as Ping and I tried our best to answer them. I could see he was deep in thought, his eyes half-shut while he smoked. He wanted to know where I'd stay, what school I would attend, how much it would cost a year, and how we would afford it. Were students even allowed to work part-time? We talked late into the night, identifying and solving many potential problems, and noting down the ones that we didn't have the answers for. By the time I went to bed, I was starting to feel hopeful. I lay thinking about Australia and imagining all the possibilities, and my excitement kept me awake for many nights that followed.

'You were restless in your sleep again last night,' Baba said to me at breakfast one morning.

'I'm excited about Australia. I really want to go there to continue my schooling,' I replied. 'I can see the Harbour Bridge and kangaroos whenever I close my eyes.'

'I worry about how you will get on without any friends or family.'

'I'll be fine, I can make friends,' I replied. My successful passage from Macau, my increased confidence in learning a new language, the wonderful school I was attending, and my good friends – all seemed to have increased my self-assurance. The previous six years living in Hong Kong had opened my eyes to the world, and I was ready to explore it.

'I am happy for you to try to get there, my son.' Baba put his arms on my shoulders and looked at me closely. 'Perhaps it's the final proof that you are now a man who is able to fend for himself away from home.'

'Here's the deal then,' Baba continued. He told me he would agree to me leaving for Australia, provided I took full responsibility for arranging all the necessary paperwork, including my applications for a passport and an Australian student visa, passing the English test, organising accommodation, finding a school to accept me, and even purchasing the airfare.

Through my classmates I found out how to apply for a visa to Australia. I then visited the Australian High Commission in Victoria to seek further information and obtained all the necessary documents, including forms to be signed by a financial guarantor, an Australian guarantor and a guardian.

Baba's meagre bank account did not allow him to guarantee my expenses in Australia, but a cousin of his was happy to help us out on that front and sign the paperwork; he trusted my father to take care of the costs. A friend of a friend of Ping's in Sydney, Dr Mabel Lee, gladly accepted the job as my guardian.

Ping was delighted. 'Now you only need to find a school and pass the English test.' Ping was still working for Cathay Pacific and had got to know many people there. Based on a suggestion from one of her colleagues, I applied to Holy Cross College in Ryde to be a boarder. I'd read up on the school and had even worked out on the map how far it was from Sydney. St Joseph's College in Hunters Hill was far too expensive for us.

In the autumn of 1968, I successfully passed the English test and was accepted into Holy Cross College. Other necessary travel documents were approved by the Colonial Hong Kong Government for the journey, and the Australian High Commission then issued my student visa without any hitch.

I wrote to my uncles and grandfather in Hawaii, explaining how I planned to further my studies in Australia, and asking them for financial assistance. They promptly sent my airfare, along with their encouragement, and Ping found a great deal with Pan American Airways.

I was ready to go.

CHAPTER 30

The District Head in Shiqi continued to deny permission for Mama and my sisters to join us, while the Hong Kong newspapers and radio stations kept up their reports on the upheavals on the mainland, including stories of atrocities inflicted on many. Mama's letters told us they were safe for the time being, but never offered much hope for the future. She could not tell us anything about the chaos at home for fear of repercussions. I missed them all so much, especially now that I was heading overseas. All we could do was keep our optimism and hope alive and try not to give in to anger and hatred for China, which was commonly expressed in the news at the time. We made sure there was nothing in our letters that could jeopardise Mama's and my sisters' safety.

When they heard I was applying to go overseas for further education, they wrote more often. Mama's repeated message to me was, 'Don't look back.'

Don't look back. Mama finished every letter with the same words. I sensed that she was cutting the strings and letting me fly. I absorbed her letters with sorrow, feeling her pain as I read between the lines, treasuring the unspoken meaning behind each word. With so much encouragement and support from Mama, I could not let myself be afraid or let anything hold me back.

On the eve of my departure from Hong Kong, Mama, Ying and Weng wrote to offer their best wishes. Their hope and excitement seemed to jump off the paper and envelop me in a warm hug. But I also sensed their intense disappointment at not being able to see me off, and their sad acceptance of the fact that we could not be together as one family. It was now nearly seven years since I had last seen them.

On 29 January 1969, Baba, Ping and I thanked our ancestors in our small living quarters in Diamond Hill before heading to the airport. Ping and I prayed to God for a safe journey as we remembered all the good people in our lives, and asked for blessings from them all. Without their generosity, we would not have been able to get to where we were at the time.

My flight was due to take off at midnight. Our landlady insisted that I must leave the house by the front door for good luck. The afternoon rush had long died down. The air was chilly up where we were. A few pedestrians were still about, huddling in their bulky overcoats to keep warm against the north wind that howled across the sky.

In front of the bungalow in Diamond Hill, the old banyan trees on Grand View Road rustled in the cold wind and the sparrows were subdued, offering only occasional dull twitters. I would miss the concerto they so eagerly performed every evening in the warmer months. I looked out from the gate, past the undulating landscape of huts and makeshift shelters dotted with occasional bungalows like ours, to the main road that led towards Kowloon Bay and on to Kai Tak Airport where a jet plane was waiting to take me far away to another country. I was fearful. I braced myself and tried not to think about what might happen out there in the unknown world. I had to trust my guardian angels, and the blessings of home, and remember my enlightenment credit points, which would surely offer me some protection.

I thought about Lei-yue-mun, the Carp Gate, at the northern end of Hong Kong Harbour, the mythical exit to the ocean and beyond, and I remembered my favourite legend about the carp that kept trying to jump over the gate in order to transform themselves into dragons – supreme beings among all. Now I, too, had to fly over the Carp Gate.

Feeling better, more eager for the adventure ahead, I quickened my pace to catch up with Baba and Ping. I was wearing my navy blue tailor-made suit, with a contrasting light blue shirt. The good Shanghai tailor in Diamond Hill had assured Baba that it would look smart on me, as well as keeping me warm without being bulky and cumbersome. Baba had bargained hard, so much so that the tailor was begging and almost crying at the end, saying what a privilege it was to sew a suit for someone from Diamond Hill going overseas to study. As he ran his well-worn tape over me, he promised to make me look like a millionaire's son. I think that broke Baba's fortitude in the bargaining tussle. Unable to resist such flattery, Baba parted happily with his hard-earned money for my first suit. He was proud as I slipped into my suit with a tie to match, and the tailor was right: I felt warm and comfortable in the cosy pure wool. I straightened my back and looked taller. My frown disappeared. My eyes opened wide and twinkled a lot that day.

The unpleasant odour of the narrow streets in Diamond Hill didn't dampen our excitement as we marched towards the main road to catch the bus to the airport. I dropped by our favourite noodle stall to say goodbye to the owners and their children. They wished me well, and then turned to their children who were helping in the family business and said, 'You all have to work hard like Ah-mun, and one day you'll study overseas and be successful.' The children nodded, and stared at me with envy.

I smiled back and felt very grown up. Under the streetlight, the Pan Am logo on my cabin bag on my shoulder stood out: a bold white globe, a rare sight in Diamond Hill. With the brand-new Olympia typewriter Ping had bought me as a farewell gift in the other hand, I felt like a real scholar. Now I had the world within my reach. Customers turned to offer their best wishes to their lucky neighbour. A few were jealous, but all were happy that one of theirs was breaking out of the slum. The battle was worth fighting. There were opportunities in the colony for everyone.

Baba carried my suitcase and Ping walked beside me. We said little to each other as we walked down Grand View Road, but I could feel a spring in my feet as we approached the bus stop.

Below Diamond Hill, near the main road, several restaurants offered northern-style cuisines. The rich array of dishes, with their exotic aromas and spices, was a stark contrast to the plain noodles we'd eaten before I departed from Shiqi. I was able to laugh at the contradiction, and Baba read my thoughts, as he often did without even trying.

'Let's have some delicious Shanghai noodles,' he said with the air of a rich man wanting to celebrate. 'It's a lot cheaper here than at the airport.'

The waiter brought us a thick menu, and Baba laughed. It was a laugh of triumph and pride. His face glowed under the gaudy chandeliers of the cheap restaurant and his eyes shone with confidence.

I ordered a bowl of plain noodles, conscious of the price and our meagre financial state. In my mind, every dollar not spent was a dollar saved for my education.

'We can afford more than that today, son,' Baba said to me with a broad smile, looking younger than ever.

'Yes, we should celebrate!' Ping was elated, and also very proud of me. Her job as a receptionist at the Cathay Pacific Airways Head Office had boosted her poise, and she was as beautiful as any movie star gracing the front cover of a magazine. No wonder so many people looked her way wherever she went.

The heater in the restaurant hummed as it warmed the cold air coming through the swinging doors. My steaming hot noodles arrived, along with a plate of smoked fish and hot tofu. The waiter brought us hot jasmine tea.

I thought of my little gang of friends back home and wondered if they knew I was leaving for a foreign land. I thought Ah-dong would die with envy if he knew I was going abroad to study, rather than as a sojourner.

'Please ask Mama to tell Ah-dong that I have gone to Sydney, and I hope one day he'll come to visit me.'

Baba nodded, but said nothing.

I knew it was impossible. There was not a chance, not a hope, that Ah-dong would ever make it out of China. Sadness struck. I turned to my bowl of noodles.

The eight o'clock bus was quiet. Even with all the windows shut, it was cold sitting on the plastic seats. Neon billboards trembled outside. It was only a few stops to the airport. I didn't know what to think as we got off. In a way, I was just as ready to leave as I had been on that May morning in Shiqi. But then I had left without any desire to return – even though it was my home and birthplace, and the home of Baba, his father and our ancestors – whereas I was leaving Hong Kong with a plan to return one day, after successfully completing my academic studies.

Many classmates and friends came to the airport to see me off. I lingered on to say goodbye to each one of them. We took many photographs. Both Baba and Ping were as proud as could be.

'Your opportunity has arrived,' Baba said to me. 'Grasp it. Take great care when making friends. True friends are hard to come by, so treasure them. Don't fall into bad company. It rubs off on you as a person.'

I didn't enter the gate until the final call. I had already made up my mind not to look back – just as I'd done when leaving Shiqi. It was not a time for sadness and tears.

As I stepped into the cabin, a poem that had been Ying's farewell gift in her last letter to me rang in my ears:

Fly my young eagle, fly.
Let the sky be the limit,
Far away you must roam.
With no fear but much courage,
Far away you must go.
Fly my young eagle, fly!

With the assistance of an air steward, I fastened my seatbelt and sat back. Clutching the armrests in anticipation, I looked around from my lonely seat at the very rear of the Pan Am 707 jet plane as it began to taxi towards the runway. It was my first-ever plane trip and I couldn't help but feel uneasy, even though it was a lot more comfortable than my frightening journey inside the crawl space at the pointy end of the fishing junk that had smuggled me into Hong Kong a mere seven years earlier.

The 'Seven-O-Seven', as this model of Boeing jet was known, took off from Kai Tak Airport with a thunderous roar, like ten thousand dragon boats fervently beating their drums. It was like travelling in a perpetual thunderbolt, booming and shaking the entire continent and my whole universe.

I stretched my shoulders to feel the strength of my wings. Everything smelled fresh inside the plane, thanks to a constant stream of cool air coming from the roof of the giant roaring eagle. I didn't mind in the least that immediately behind me were the plane's toilet and small working area for the staff. Leaning forward hard, I peeped through a small round window. The glimpse of Hong Kong Harbour with its million lights was reassuring, and reminded me of the relief I'd felt when I saw those same lights as my fishing junk successfully reached the island.

Already exhausted by everything I'd experienced in my young life, I didn't care. I slumped deep into my seat, seeking to relieve my fatigued mind and body, and before long I lapsed into sleep. I felt liberated, ready to move on, roam and explore.

Fly, young eagle, fly!

CHAPTER 31

A very deep sleep it was. I don't recall taking any of the refreshments offered to me, nor did I dream. The constant roar of the powerful engines and the incessant rocking and vibrations at the tail end of the jet are all I remember. But then a bump and sudden change of engine noise shook me from my slumber. There was hardly any light inside the cabin and the passengers stirred, mumbling to their companions. A few shrieked in alarm. Suddenly we were on the ground, taxiing.

Didn't we just take off from Hong Kong? Where are the harbour lights? What's going on? Ah, maybe we have arrived in Australia! But why is it so dark? A flood of different thoughts rushed at me.

The captain's voice came over the speaker: 'Ladies and gentlemen, we've just arrived in Manila to refuel as scheduled. It shouldn't take too long ...'

Manila? The Philippines? Oh yes, we need to refuel. We've a long way to go yet. No worries.

I sat up in my seat, and stretched towards the window by the seat in front of me. Outside it was blacker than the predawn darkness with which I'd grown so familiar while sitting on the levee wall. *Where are the lights?*

Pop, pop, pop. Da-da-da-da-da ... As the Seven-O-Seven proceeded in the dark, I heard rapid repeating noises like gunshots in movies, interspersed with explosions like thunder. The commotion gradually became louder. It was obvious that something wasn't right outside.

The plane slowed to make a left-hand turn. But then it moved off faster than when taxiing, as if trying to get away from something dangerous. The glow beyond the window came into view. The main airport building was in ruins, and on fire. Explosions sent fireballs in all directions. A burning smell permeated the cabin. Some passengers screamed, others cried; all were in shock. In the background, the silhouette of the city of Manila was repeatedly lit up by projectiles flying back and forth. The blasts and bangs were getting louder. Inside the plane everyone was petrified.

'This is the captain speaking.' The calm voice came at just the right moment. 'Please leave all hand luggage on board and follow the instructions of the staff. Don't be afraid: the soldiers are here to protect us and will take us into a hangar ahead. As soon as we have refuelled, we will take off again for Sydney. God bless.'

The pungent smell of smoke and explosives seemed to suck air from our lungs. The deafening blasts and volleys of shots continued to ring out in the pitch-black night, their bright flashes lighting our way towards waiting buses.

Once on board, we were instructed to sit in seats just vacated by soldiers, who now stood with their rifles pointing at the darkness outside. Other soldiers occupied every second window seat. 'Keep your heads down,' they said to us.

Our small convoy of buses then set off. I could hear other vehicles around us as we moved forward and away from the sounds of calamity behind us. I raised my head cautiously to peep through the window.

'Yukon!' *Head down.* A rough Filipino hand pressed my head so hard from behind I nearly dislocated my neck. The quick glance I'd stolen revealed that other vehicles were moving alongside us, wrapping around us like the layers of a lotus blossom to protect us. They were lit up only by occasional distant explosions, which were bright enough for me to see trucks and jeeps with big machine guns around us.

271

I prayed to General Guan Gong, Buddha and my ancestors, as well as my new-found Christian God and all the saints I had learnt about at La Salle College.

At last the bus stopped and we were ushered into not a hangar, as the captain had said, but the foyer of the Miramar Hotel. The staff served us cool drinks and refreshments. Soldiers were everywhere, both inside and out, weapons at the ready. After an hour or so, the soldiers guided us back to the waiting plane. It took off into the darkness without delay, and soon rose to a safe altitude, far away from the guns and explosions in Manila. I sat back, closed my eyes and fell into a deep sleep again. I later learnt that we had arrived in the middle of a communist rebellion that had nearly toppled the Marcos government.

I wasn't sure how long it was before I was woken by the soothing voice of the captain announcing that we had reached our destination.

My heart leapt with a peculiar joy. When I leant forward to peep through the window, the expansive grounds of the airport came into view. Beyond lay a large, tranquil bay, glinting in the early morning sun.

Relief spread across the faces around me. We even smiled at each other.

*

Stopping at the open rear door, I took in a greedy gulp of sweet, cool morning air. Fresh and relaxing, it instantly relieved my exhausted mind.

'So, are you going to Holy Cross College?'

I turned to the person behind me: the young man who had been sitting in front of me next to the little window.

'Yes,' I said, half-curious. 'How do you know?'

'Your navy blue suit and light blue shirt,' he replied, laughing. 'I was there for a few years, but now I'm going to Waverley College for Form VI. You'll be fine at Holy Cross. There are quite a number of Hong Kong boys there.' As we headed towards Immigration and

Customs, he turned to me again and said, 'I'm Richard. Were you scared last night?'

'A bit, but I was too tired to worry much about it,' I said, trying to downplay my fears. 'My name is Andrew.' I'd found out that my new name meant 'strong and fearless', which seemed appropriate for a new beginning in a new country.

I was glad to make a friend on arrival. With the Pan Am bag on my shoulder and my Olympia typewriter in one hand, I followed Richard to the baggage claim area and we chatted while waiting to be picked up.

He told me a lot about Holy Cross College, the Patrician Brothers who ran it, and some of the students from Hong Kong and Asia. It was all reassuring.

As we chatted and the sun got hotter, we kept retreating into the receding shade on the footpath outside the Kingsford Smith International Airport terminal. Richard was tall, handsome and solidly built, partly, he told me, the result of playing Rugby League football at school. 'Holy Cross has won the New South Wales Schoolboys Rugby League several times,' he proudly informed me, 'but Waverley offered me a part scholarship, which is why I'm moving there now.'

It was almost midday by then and there were only a few people about at the airport. A big car pulled up. Out jumped a thin young man in white riding gear like the clothes worn by Hong Kong jockeys. He greeted Richard like a brother and apologised for being late. He then turned to me. 'I'm Victor. Welcome to Sydney.' He was friendly and cheerful.

'Nice to meet you,' I said as I shook his sweaty hand.

'Are you being picked up?' Victor looked at me, then his watch. 'It's well past noon. Oh no, it's more than four hours since you guys arrived!'

'My friends Mr and Mrs Lee will be picking me up,' I said to him. 'I sent them a telegram a few days ago.'

'They may not have received it. Telegrams are often late here,' Victor said as he turned to Richard, who nodded.

'Come to my place and take a rest before ringing them. Have you got their phone number?'

'Yes,' I said without a second thought. These young men seemed genuine and friendly enough. Besides, my stomach had begun to ache with a hunger I hadn't felt for several years – not since I was in Shiqi.

Richard had already thrown my bag into the boot of the car, which was as roomy as the back seat I hopped into. My head was still spinning and my eyes were heavy. I couldn't keep up with the conversation, but I remember there was a discussion about how, if you couldn't make it academically, you had to become an Australian-trained jockey and go back to Hong Kong, where fortunes awaited at the weekly horse races.

Before long we arrived in a place they said was called Edgecliff. Victor got out and I watched him as he held a lit cigarette between his fingers. He looked about nineteen or twenty, and wore John Lennon–style glasses, and his body seemed to be constantly jerking to inaudible music, perhaps Beatles beats, or maybe the songs of Elvis Presley.

'Come up and ring your friend,' he said to me, pointing to a three-storey terrace house towards which Richard was already heading with his luggage. The coin-operated phone at the boarding house worked beautifully. I called Mabel Lee and she told me her husband, Howard, and her father, Mr Hunt (originally Chan Hun), would come and get me in the evening. Fortunately, Victor and Richard didn't have much planned for the day other than relaxing and chatting, and they were happy for me to stay with them as long as I needed to. It was just as well, as it was nearly midnight when Howard and Mr Hunt picked me up and took me to Hunts' Motel in Liverpool.

Mabel Lee was a softly spoken, petite woman of around thirty years of age. (I later found out that she was a lecturer at Sydney University and that she was on summer vacation at the time and helping her brother run the family-owned motel.) On our arrival, she cooked me a big T-bone steak that hung over the edge of the plate, glistening under hot potato chips. By then it was well past two in the morning, and I devoured the first proper meal I'd had in more than twenty-four hours.

The following day Mabel drove me to Holy Cross College in her small red Fiat. We spoke in the same dialect of Zhongshan, where her mother came from.

The car stopped outside a graceful three-storey sandstone building with a bell tower. A flight of steps led up to a double front door. There was no one in sight. I got out of the car with my Pan Am bag over my shoulder, my suitcase in one hand and the typewriter in the other, thanked Mabel and waved goodbye. I watched her car re-join the traffic and then promptly vanish down the gentle hill.

Suddenly I felt all alone for the first time since leaving Shiqi. Half-panicking, and not knowing what to expect, I began to mount the steps. In my fragile state, I started to wonder why I was there at all. There was no going back.

At the top of the steps, I opened the door and stepped into my future.

The foyer was large with high ceilings and offices on either side behind closed doors. At the end of the hall was a large stairway with a carved wooden balustrade, similar to the staircase at La Salle. This helped me relax a little.

I knocked on an office door and waited.

The door clicked open and a portly woman appeared.

'My name is Andrew Kwong,' I said. 'I am a boarder here.'

'Welcome, Andrew, we've been expecting you,' the lady said with a smile. 'I'm Mrs Pinch, school secretary. Welcome to Holy Cross.'

Mrs Pinch had short auburn hair and a kind face. I felt comfortable around her. She gave me an introduction to the college and very soon I began to feel at home. She showed me to my place in a dormitory. There were four rows of single beds, with five beds in each row, and all were neatly covered with gold bedspreads. A small table stood next to each bed. There were no screens or partitions; everything was open, even the four large windows. My bed was in a corner.

'You'll love it here, Andrew,' Mrs Pinch reassured me before disappearing downstairs.

She was right. Before the light went out that night in the large airy room, I had already made several friends. It was easy to feel at home, it seemed, in Australia.

CHAPTER 32

David Crowley was a tall and gentle boy with thick fair hair that made him look angelic when he sang as an altar boy at mass. We were in the same class and soon became good friends. When he realised I had nowhere to go at the end of my first term, he invited me to spend my holiday at his home in Coonabarabran in central western New South Wales.

The overnight journey was the first train trip of my life. Seeing those amazing long trains at Sydney's Central Station made me think of growing eucalyptus trees back in Shiqi, and hoping and dreaming that trains would come to our town.

We shared an eight-person cabin with several other passengers. It had two long benches facing each other, which seemed to be heated. Each time the train stopped at a station, the staff would open a trapdoor outside the window, pull out a large metal container from under the bench and exchange it for another much hotter one. I certainly welcomed the warmth that radiated from under my seat, as day turned to night and it got steadily colder. Even inside the cabin, the chilly autumn air bit at my face, hands and feet.

Some passengers snored on into the early morning, but I was already awake before the dawn glow seeped in through the rattling windows. Despite the occasional smell of burnt diesel, the air was cold yet fresh, pure as crystal, invigorating and sweet, and I breathed it in with great pleasure. Outside, a clear sky ushered in a beautiful day. There wasn't a cloud in sight and the moon hung high, perfectly round and glowing with gentle warmth. I thought about what Mama had always told us: how we had to wait patiently through hard times till the clouds dispersed and a bright new moon appeared.

Gradually the shadows of mountains gave way to true Australian outback: open plains and red earth aplenty, kangaroos and rabbits grazing on grasses. It was exactly as I had imagined it, and the vista uplifted me and a rhapsody of music rang in my ears. It was unforgettable. *What more do I want? How fortunate I am!* Now my heart was singing loudly and my mind was dancing to every unfolding scene as the train crawled across the landscape like a giant dragon making its own unhurried way.

The Crowleys lived in a modest home on the outskirts of Coonabarabran and had been there for a long time. In the small front foyer of their home a huge, ancient Bible sat on a tall rosewood stand, its yellow and worn but dignified pages open at the Gospel According to Matthew.

As well as his mum and dad, David had two brothers, Paul and Timothy, and a sister, Margaret. I can't remember what David's father did for a living, but he had an old utility truck. The first thing we did was pile into this truck and drive down the road to his friend's farm, where he bought a lamb. On our return, he slaughtered and dressed it, before hanging it. 'It'll be our dinner for the week,' he said.

At dinner Mr Crowley read, '"For God has not given us a spirit of fear and timidity, but of power, love and self-discipline." II Timothy 1:7.' He then gave thanks to God for our safe journey and welcomed me to his home and country.

'The eternal problem confronting us here is drought,' he said to me. 'So we have to be careful with our water. We don't take showers but share the bath, so please do not pull the plug after your bath tonight. Andrew, as our guest, you can take the first bath; then it'll be David's turn for the first bath tomorrow night, and so on.'

I'd been hoping for more than the three-minute showers we were allowed to have at Holy Cross College every day. But at least the weather was cooler and I didn't need to bathe daily. I imagined the colour of the bath water by the end of each day – it would be murky brown like the Wonder River in low tide.

Early the next morning after a simple breakfast, we all went out to help Mr Crowley with one of his jobs, delivering the local newspaper. Dust flew in every direction as cars went by. It was a brown town with brown vegetation all around, from cracked lawns to exhausted gum trees. People looked to the sky, searching for clouds that might bring them rain, their eyes showing hope, but were usually disappointed at the end of the day. Ever since my Coonabarabran holiday, I have always felt for and admired such brave and resilient country folks.

At the Friday night youth dance, I had my first lesson in barn dancing and loved it. Two girls, twins aged thirteen or maybe fourteen, were particularly interested in where I came from; they knew little about China, let alone colonies like Hong Kong and Macau. The night was too short and by nine o'clock the dance was over. The next morning an envelope addressed to me arrived. Inside was a photograph of one of the twins, Cheryl.

By the end of my Coonabarabran vacation, I felt I'd learnt a lot about Australia and about Australians, and I tried to emulate their pioneering spirit.

Before I left the Crowleys' house, I copied a verse from their Bible to take with me: "'For I know the plans for you," says the Lord. "They are plans for good and not for disaster, to give you a future and a hope."' A future and a hope, what more did I want?

CHAPTER 33

Every Friday at tea – which I now understood meant dinner – when Brother Benedict was in charge, he would walk around the dining hall with his long pointer, checking the boys' hair. A double tap on your shoulder meant it was time to visit the barber who dutifully came to the college every Friday afternoon. While we boys were at sport or mass, he would cut the brothers' hair, and then after school it was the boys' turn. Each haircut cost fifty cents – the cost of ten Wagon Wheel chocolate biscuits. Boys grumbled about losing their snack money for ten days, but we had to comply with the order or Brother Benedict would send us to the cowshed to take care of the cows. I'd already spent more time than I wanted to talking to the cows.

After paying my second-term tuition and boarding fees, I had only ten dollars, or twenty haircuts' worth, left in my Commonwealth Bank student account until Baba sent money for the third term. Even if I avoided going into town in order to save paying the five-cent bus fare, or managed to dodge double taps on my shoulder, the money was not going to go far. I knew how hard Baba and Ping were working to pay my school fees, and I couldn't bring myself to ask for pocket money.

By chance one afternoon I was in town with one of the boys who had offered to pay for my bus fare to accompany him to shop at David Jones, the department store. I borrowed seven dollars from him and bought a haircutting kit consisting of cutting and thinning scissors, a comb and a manual barber's hair trimmer. Then I offered to cut primary school boarders' hair for five cents and high school boys' hair for ten cents. Boys put up with the ugliest haircuts on earth to save their money for Wagon Wheels. As my skills increased, so did my fees. By the end of my schooling, I would be charging ten and twenty cents, respectively. Sometimes the day boys lined up for my haircuts. Eventually, the barber came only once a month. I decided not to offer my service to the brothers.

Although my side business at boarding school flourished, I never forgot what I really wanted in life: to be a doctor. The one thing I had carried with me from China was the idea that I should try to reduce the suffering of others. I wanted to see all people happy, and free of pain and misery, just as I wanted that deeply for Mama, Baba and the rest of my family. I couldn't stand watching people endure hunger, being ostracised or shamed in public, especially when it was at the hands of their own family, neighbours, friends, workmates or fellow students. Ever since I'd got into school in Hong Kong, I knew I had a chance of achieving my goal, but I also knew I would have to work extremely hard.

By the time I finished the Higher School Certificate, I'd decided I wanted to call Australia home one day. Even though the White Australia policy was still in place, it had been significantly modified by the Harold Holt government: now non-European visitors were allowed to apply for residency if they possessed qualifications that were in demand in Australia. Furthermore, I had witnessed firsthand in Coonabarabran and at Holy Cross how friendly and welcoming Australians could be. Plus people like Victor, Richard, Howard the sojourner and his Australian-born Chinese wife, Mabel Lee, had all shown me that it was possible for a foreigner to be successful in Australia. But first I had to become a person worthy of that privilege, and in my mind qualifying as a doctor seemed the best way to achieve that.

In the late 1960s and early 1970s, foreign student admissions to university courses were limited by a rather strict quota system. In the case of medicine, foreign students could make up only 5 per cent of the new faculty admissions at the University of Sydney, and 10 per cent at the University of New South Wales, the only two medical schools in the state at the time. Many foreign students, especially those from Asia worked very hard to get into medicine, either as their own goal, or to fulfil the wishes of their parents, as was the case with Victor, the part-time apprentice jockey. (When his parents came for his graduation some years later, they discovered he was graduating from accountancy instead. He'd managed to keep that from them until then.)

Needless to say competition was intense among overseas students for places in sought-after courses like medicine and engineering. At Holy Cross College, Asian students usually attempted challenging subjects like First Level Science and Mathematics in order to obtain higher scores. But they also had to pass the English exam.

In the last term holiday of Sixth Form, in 1970, one of my roommates Chalit, a Thai boy, returned to school with a big Holden car and a driver's licence. We were all excited for him and some were envious. From then on, from our large window facing the front lawn of the college, we could see the majestic Holden sedan standing on the far side of the turning circle in a space designated by the school especially for Chalit's car.

Chalit spent a lot of time hanging around his car, checking it and dusting it. The first thing he did when he woke in the morning was to rush to the window and make sure it was still there, as he also did before going to bed. As a Buddhist, Chalit recited chants daily before our pre-breakfast morning prayers at the school chapel; now he had his car to pray for as well. But he was not allowed to take the car out for a run without permission. On Saturdays he would offer to take half the soccer team to games so that he could practise driving the Big Mom, as he called it.

On the morning of the first exam, in October 1970, I couldn't eat the boiled eggs I usually enjoyed for breakfast. I was already petrified by the thought of flunking my First Level English paper. Even my favourite Shakespeare plays now all seemed to be muddled in my head. And passing this paper was vital for my future.

Six of us boarders got into Big Mom, heading for the same exam. But then Chalit's pale face began to sweat when he couldn't start the car. David said it was a cool morning and the engine was just cold. Chalit tried again and I started to perspire as each attempt to turn over the engine failed. Looking at my watch didn't help; the anguish building inside me was now worse than it had been when I'd stood on the platform preparing to swim across the Wonder River.

Mrs Miu's stern face began hovering over me. I closed my eyes and tried to picture Mama's face, hoping to draw strength from her, just as I had done when we had parted at the Shiqi bus station. *No, I must not fail,* I promised myself.

It was nearly nine o'clock, time for the paper to begin. Big Mom still wouldn't budge. My mouth was by now completely dry. Then, thank God, Brother Benedict appeared with two other members of staff and we all got out and did a push-start with only Chalit in the heavy car. It took off. Then there was another wait that felt like hours before Big Mom was warmed up enough, and returned to pick us up.

We arrived at the examination hall at North Ryde High School, late and trembling with distress. Fortunately, the kind examiner decided to allow us an extra half-hour to make up for our lost time.

For a long while I sat there in the large hall, just staring at the exam paper. My brain was numb. It took a lot of coaxing and reasoning with myself before my confidence came back to me. Then I dived into a question on *Hamlet*, which I knew so well, and from that point on it all flowed smoothly.

I was more relaxed in the subsequent exams, even in First Level Maths and Science. At the end of the exam period, to celebrate the completion of high school, a group of us boys chose to 'rumble' a couple of girls' schools nearby with flour bombs. Missing our graduation dinner was our punishment.

*

I was quietly pleased that school was finally over for me, even though we had now to endure the long wait for our exam results. What I needed to do in the meantime was find myself a job for the vacation, to alleviate the financial burden on Baba and Ping. During that time, I moved into a share house with another student, Ka-kit Lau, who came from Malaysia. He'd left Holy Cross and gone to live with his sister, who was studying at the University of New South Wales in Kensington. Through talking to other foreign students, I was delighted to learn that it was possible to work part-time while studying, though they acknowledged it was particularly tough if you were doing medicine.

Soon after, I found a job as a casual waiter at the Mandarin Club in downtown Sydney, in the Chinatown precinct. It seemed they had a big party booked for New Year's Eve 1970 and were short of waiters, so I was brought in to assist the bartenders. That night, almost intoxicated on the melodious tunes of the well-known band the Yin and Yang Duo, I began my first job as a waiter in a large up-market restaurant. I thought I looked rather smart with my white shirt, black trousers and black bow tie. As the guests partied into the evening, the drinks waiters were run off their feet. I tried to help and attempted to open a bottle of champagne for the first time in my life, to ensure partygoers had ample fizzy drinks within their reach. The cork popped off with a reassuring sound, prompting cheers from the happy revellers, but the straw-coloured liquid then gushed out so fast that many of them got soaked.

I was mortified and wished I could disappear into a hole in the ground. Fortunately, they just laughed more and said, 'No problem son. Happy New Year!' So friendly, and so Australian.

I went to see the head bartender to get another bottle of replacement champagne for the guests and found him adding extra empty bottles to the tally for each table.

'Don't worry,' he said, noticing my confused stare. 'They're too drunk to even remember how many bottles they drank. You'll get a share of it in your tip.'

This left me in a quandary. The pay was good at the club, and was a big help towards my goal of becoming self-sufficient. But I wasn't happy to be taking advantage of tipsy customers. The next day I went to see the owner of a small Chinese café, Sun Sung in Kensington, and settled for a waiter's job with lower pay, but a slightly higher rate for the weekend shift, plus a free meal before and after work.

I didn't need my First Level Maths to work out that even on a weekly income of $13.50 for one weekday and two weekend evenings' work, I'd be able to pay my rent and buy lunches for the week. I took the free after-work meal home and had it the following day for dinner. That left only one evening meal a week to be covered, and the solution to that was easy: I could just skip one meal a week; it wouldn't hurt much after my experience of the famine in Shiqi. Yes, I thought, it is doable!

So I happily went to work taking orders from customers at the Sun Sung Café. I was always given extra shifts during term vacations and felt fortunate that I was able to work towards my goal. I wrote to Baba and told him not to send me any money for my education unless I specifically requested it. I was concerned about him, as he had taken an extra teaching job at an evening school to try to support me, as well as Mama and the girls in Shiqi. Ping had decided to leave Hong Kong. After saving hard while working at Cathay Pacific Airlines, she had chosen to move to Hawaii to stay with Grandmother Young and pursue further education.

Nevertheless, Baba remained strong and never stopped encouraging me. 'Focus on your studies and aim high,' he said in each of his letters. 'The moon will shine again for us one day.'

*

Finally, the day in mid-January came when the successful HSC university entrance candidate list was to be published. A few friends and I followed our senior fellow students' advice and went to Martin Place at midnight to wait for the next day's *Sydney Morning Herald* to appear at the one and only all-night news stand. I jumped straight to the medical school announcements and there it was: my name on the University of New South Wales Medical School list! I read it several times to make sure it was true.

I remember watching the minutes tick by while waiting for the time when Baba would return from his evening class, as we were three hours ahead of Hong Kong. From a public phone at the GPO in Martin Place, an international call could be arranged via an operator, albeit for a fee equivalent to the pay for an evening's work.

'Baba,' I shouted, loud enough for him to hear over the hissing noises on the line. 'I have made it into medicine.'

'What? Ha! Medicine!' There followed a long pause, and I knew he was sobbing with joy. When he recovered, his first words were: 'Your Mama will be very proud of you.' Then, aware that I had to keep the call short, he finished by saying, 'I'm so happy for you ... so proud of you ... There will be challenges ahead ... but, remember, they'll only make you a better person. Work hard, my son. My love and thoughts are always with you.'

There was no international telephone connection to Shiqi, so I wrote to tell Mama the great news. I could just imagine how overjoyed she and my sisters would be, and I was more than certain that she would soon be sharing the good tidings with Sixth Aunt and Eighth Uncle, my cousins and friends and neighbours. My news would cheer them up. I could also imagine a positively glowing Mama in the third lounge room, giving thanks to the ancestors and other gods for this blessing.

*

In February that year, on the day when new medical students had to register at the university, I lined up with the other freshers. There were bright and cheerful faces all around me: boys and girls, just out of school, oozing energy and vigour. And beyond lay the handsome buildings and appealing lawns and gardens of the university campus. *This is my utopia*, I thought, while laughing to myself, *and all the hard work is worth it.*

'Hello, my name is Robert.' I turned round to find a young man thrusting his hand towards me. A pair of smiling eyes shone out from a youthful face rimmed by curly dark hair and a large beard.

'I'm Andrew,' I said, gripping his hand firmly. 'It's nice to meet you.'

Before long, and much to my delight, I found out that Robert Lewin and I were in the same class for tutorials and small group learning sessions. Over the next three pre-medical years we would attend lectures and laboratory work together and become the best of friends, so much so that I sometimes dodged waiting tables on Friday evenings so that I could go to the Lewin family home in Northbridge for dinner. There I was able to savour the sense of a secure home that I had so sorely missed. Moreover, the family's easy acceptance of me, a young Asian man, reinforced my desire to become a citizen of a society that already seemed to me forward-thinking, diversified and yet cohesive.

The Lewins were Jewish, and Dr Lewin, Robert's father, was a GP who practised in Leichhardt, in western Sydney. He worked long hours and was often late for the Friday Sabbath dinner. When he arrived home, Mrs Lewin would bring out the food and we men would each don a yarmulke to show humility and respect to God.

Dr Lewin said prayers in Hebrew to offer gratitude; sometimes Robert did also. I enjoyed listening to the language, even though I didn't understand it. It reminded me of my Shiqi dialect: melodious and gentle, if not entirely musical.

The long prayers usually intensified my hunger pains as I waited to tuck into the great variety of delicious food on the table. I would try to be patient, while recalling Third Aunt's lessons in table manners.

Dr Lewin always ended his prayers with: 'a time to bring goodwill and peace to all'. Then he would declare, 'Let's share the feast.'

Sharing, togetherness, kindness and peace: it was no different from what my family had been struggling to achieve and maintain, even while being punished for their 'counter-revolutionary' views. Now I was in such a fortunate position, I would do all in my power to attain a better future for my whole family. It was difficult not to be envious of Australian families, from Coonabarabran to Northbridge. But it steeled my determination to one day establish my own home and family in this new land I had discovered and chosen.

CHAPTER 34

During the long university summer holidays, many of my friends went on vacation to refresh themselves, but I worked full time as a nurse at Concord Repatriation Hospital, now Concord General Hospital. Combined with my restaurant job in the evenings, that enabled me to pay my university fees and even buy a twenty-year-old VW Beetle. It was my first car. I shared it with Peter Wong, a classmate from Holy Cross College, who was also studying medicine at the University of New South Wales.

Everything seemed to be going well and it was great that I could now drive myself to and from the hospital and the restaurant. Around this time, Peter and I moved into nearby rooms rented from the Szalay family, on Doncaster Avenue, Kensington. One evening when Peter was at work and I was studying at home in Kensington, there was a knock on the front door.

It was the police.

They informed me, the owner of the VW Beetle, that I had committed a hit-and-run traffic offence, injuring a twenty-four-thousand-dollar race horse. With that amount of money at the time, you could buy not one, but two two-bedroom apartments in the seaside suburb of Coogee. It nearly sent me into a convulsion, until I got Peter on the phone and he explained to the officers what had happened.

On his way to work, he had parked the car outside Kensington Post Office while he went to post a letter. When he came out, he saw that the VW was damaged, and covered in horseshoe imprints. A witness told him that a stablehand had been trying to walk his horse between the VW and another parked car, when the VW's sharp rear bumper snagged on the horse's leg and it went mad with pain and trampled the car. We had to obtain the assistance of the university's student legal service to make sure no charges were laid.

And that wasn't the end of the VW saga. We had the car repaired and were proud that it looked like new again, at least on the outside. But one afternoon Peter was driving us to work and, as we stopped to turn right, a large Valiant station-wagon smashed into the rear of our VW. The passenger seat collapsed and I turned to find the other car's front light a mere few inches away from my head. The other driver was rushing his wife to hospital for the imminent delivery of their first baby. Just imagine the chaos.

The second year of medicine, which began at the start of 1972, was extremely challenging, being the time when students had to demonstrate their mastery of two of the fundamental topics, anatomy and biochemistry. A large number of students flunked and had to repeat the year, but I couldn't afford to fail, so I kept my head down and worked hard.

On the evenings when I wasn't working to earn my keep, I stayed back after finishing the day's lectures, dissection classes and laboratory work to study at the UNSW Medical Library. On 21 February I was in the library's TV room watching the ABC news, as I often did for a break. The headline news that evening stirred up great emotions in me. As Beijing braced itself against the cold northern winds the US president's Air Force One jet touched down at the city's airport. On the screen the sun started to shine on the stubborn icicles on the eaves of the People's Palace in Tiananmen Square, and you could see the ice beginning to melt. Before President Nixon reached the bottom of the stairs from his plane, he was extending his hand in earnest towards China's Premier Zhou En-lai.

At that moment my eyes welled with tears as the implications of the event for world peace, and for my long-suffering family left behind in China, slowly dawned on me. As the two leaders grasped each other's hands, hope sprang again for Mama and my sisters. That historic handshake changed the world I lived in and the fate of my family.

Since my arrival in Australia, I had been closely monitoring any changes in the country's immigration policies. Gough Whitlam's first visit to China in 1971, when he was still leader of the opposition, had been a positive development, as was the Labor Party's promise to abandon the White Australia policy, which it would fulfil after forming a new government in 1972.

The thought that Mama might be allowed to leave Shiqi to come and live with me was now within the realms of possibility. But first I had to become financially able to support her, in case I got the opportunity to sponsor her. To do that, I myself had to meet the requirements for Australian residency: a tertiary degree and gainful employment. So, I kept reminding myself to be patient.

The medical course was tough. By the end of Med II, nearly half of our original class of 350 had failed and some students had dropped out altogether. I felt blessed that I'd managed to proceed to Med III. On hearing this news, Ying wrote to congratulate me, while at the same time reminding me to write home more often.

'Mama waits at the entrance to the street for your mail – the same way she used to wait for Grandmother's living allowance from Hong Kong,' she wrote. 'She worries about you and can't sleep when she doesn't hear anything. She only smiles when your news arrives, and then she is so happy that she can't sleep for a few more nights. But it brings a glow to her face. There are many sojourners returning to visit their families and we'd love to see you home one day in Shiqi. Things are changing and it is safe to come home for a visit now. Maybe when you've finished your study, but that's four more years to go. Such a long time to wait ... I'd also like you to meet my boyfriend, Hao-ming.' I was delighted for Ying but still worried about Mama.

Mama's regular mail carried her unfailing hopes and wishes, as well as her motherly concerns about what I was eating, whether I had warm clothes to wear, had enough rest and, now, was driving safely. They helped ease my homesickness and kept my spirit up.

Med IV was a phenomenal time for me, as it was the start of three fascinating clinical years at St Vincent's Hospital in Darlinghurst. The abolition of university tuition fees by the Whitlam government on 1 January 1974 took a great load off my shoulders. Now I could even afford a VW Fastback, a coupe-style car slightly larger than the Beetle. With it I was able to zip around between medical school lectures and hospital tutorials, as well as my weekend and evening jobs.

St Vinnie's, as we called it, was managed by the Sisters of Charity, a Catholic order of nuns, who devoted their lives to caring for the sick and destitute. The modest but elegant sandstone building then rose among old terraced houses, many of which were run down and in need of repair or rebuilding. Situated a short distance from Kings Cross, Sydney's red-light district, St Vincent's was, and still is, regarded as a beacon of hope and help for many unfortunate people.

By staying back in the evenings to hang around the Casualty Department, or ED in today's terms, we medical students gained a huge amount of experience and skills in areas such as resuscitation and acute medical care related to heart attacks and other organ failures; management of traumatic injuries, such as stab and gunshot wounds; treatment of drug overdoses; and, most interestingly to us wide-eyed male students, caring for practitioners of the oldest profession on earth, often when they had nowhere else to go. There at St Vinnie's we experienced firsthand the true miseries faced by many members of our society.

One day, I approached one of the nuns who worked in the Casualty Department and said, 'Sister Bernadette, none of your patients seem to feel pain when you give them an injection. Can you show me how you do it?'

Sister Bernadette, a dainty nun in a pale blue habit shifted from her statue-like pose in the corner of the casualty room. 'It's easy,' she said softly, and then she explained her methods to me. Soon I was offering to help do injections and blood tests, and had also picked up other practical skills, such as dressing and repairing wounds, plastering fractures and reducing dislocated joints, and I began to feel like I was useful to the Casualty Department.

The other exciting side of St Vinnie's was its recognised successes in medical research and innovation. I am proud to recall my modest role in the hospital's attempts to create an artificial pancreas, or the insulin pump, as it was also known, led by Dr Lesley Campbell. When the hospital offered to pay ninety-five dollars for six blood samples over three days to support the research, we students were all too happy to help. It took me only a split second to work out that fee was the equivalent of nineteen weeks' rent. Despite the fact that the kind-hearted Szalays did not raise my rent until I graduated and I could eat at the hospital's subsidised canteen, with the increasing demands of the senior years I had less time to work in the restaurant and meeting my payments for the house and the car was becoming challenging. Giving blood eased my financial strains, but the vein near my right elbow thrombosed and has never recovered. Still, I was pleased to learn recently that my humble contribution has finally borne fruit, after forty-four years or so, and insulin pumps are now widely used. Not as instant a result as sperm donation for ten dollars a time – an offer I politely declined.

Nothing, though, was more electrifying than to witness the pioneering work of a team of amazing cardiac surgeons at St Vinnie's, notably Dr Harry Windsor, Dr Mark Shanahan and Dr Victor Chang, who had recently returned from studying heart transplant techniques at the Mayo Clinic in the United States. It was inspiring to see the new hope they offered their patients, even though rejection of the new heart routinely took its toll. Through these pioneers' quiet and unassuming manners and their fascinating tutorials, we learnt dedication, humility and perseverance.

My world had now opened wide and I greedily immersed myself in the abundant opportunities for learning and development, feeling ever so fortunate to be witnessing cutting-edge innovations at firsthand. I couldn't get enough of it all. It left little time for other activities, except our weekly gathering of fellow students and other university friends for a game of soccer, and after that, a tasty Chinese meal at Coogee.

Every so often, an aerogramme would arrive from Mama. 'Oh, my son, it's been such a long time since I last heard from you and I hope you are fine and studying hard,' she would write, expressing her yearning for her son who was so far away and alone in a foreign country. In one letter around this time she told me about Weng's work on the flood-prone plain of the delta. She'd had to learn how to build a small hut to house herself, and how to develop untamed land for growing food. 'There was a good harvest this season and she was given a fifteen yuan bonus,' Mama wrote. 'She bought a big bag of lychees and we had a feast. But she always resents going back to the country after her monthly weekend off. How I worry about her: no education, sulking a lot and spending the weekend sleeping ...'

In a subsequent letter Mama told me how delighted she was when Ying was finally assigned a job at the new lightbulb factory in town by the side of the Wonder River, and she later took great pleasure in reporting that Ying was now engaged to Hao-ming – such a relief after the years of worry and unhappiness since she and Ho-bun had separated during their fateful attempt to escape. Mama also told me that Yiu-hoi had taught himself how to repair electric tools and radios. He had also taught himself to play violin beautifully, and had been offered a place in Shiqi's budding orchestra.

I was so immersed in my studies that time flew by. Soon I heard that Ying had married Hao-ming and, later, that they had had a son, Kuo-feng. The news made me very happy and I wondered if perhaps the tides were now changing for all of us.

While waiting for the Med VI marks – our final exam results – I again took on a relief nursing job at the Repatriation General Hospital, Concord, which diverted my attention from worrying about the outcome. The job also enabled me to save up in case

I'd failed the tough exams and had to repeat another year. I had my evening meals at the Prince of Wales Hospital canteen, close to the university, usually after a game of squash with friends. My social group came from many countries and studied many courses, and throughout the six-year medical program I enjoyed the great diversity of people at the university and liked to mix with them all. Other overseas students preferred to keep company with students of their own nationality, no doubt because it made them feel more at ease and secure in a foreign land.

One of the reasons I played squash was because, a few months earlier, I'd met a pretty young gweilo lady at the courts. Each time I played, she seemed to be there. She dazzled me with her warm smile and large blue eyes.

'Hi, my name is Andrew,' I said to her one day after gathering the courage to introduce myself. 'Enjoying the games?'

'I'm Sheree,' she said, gracing me with a big smile and holding out her hand to shake mine. *What a crystal-clear voice!*

We soon realised we were neighbours in Kensington and, just like that, we became good friends. So much so that after the last exam, when my classmates decided to have one last dinner together at a nearby restaurant, I decided to invite Sheree and was elated when she accepted.

It was a very happy evening at first. My classmates were stunned when I introduced my new friend, and I heard quiet murmurs ebb around the room. I knew how surprised they all were that the bookworm and hard worker in their class should be going out with such an attractive young lady. But I also suspected they were happy for me. One of my classmates handed out drinks to us and winked at me, then went away laughing with another guy.

I took a sip, maybe two, of Ben Ean Moselle, a very popular sweet wine at the time. Soon I had a banging headache, which I'd never suffered from before, and blurred vision. 'Sorry, Sheree, please talk to my friends,' I said, excusing myself, and I staggered away to lie down at the back of the restaurant for the rest of the evening while the party went on. Fortunately, later in the evening the headache eased and I was able to deliver Sheree safely home to her parents.

I was so embarrassed about being such a cheap drunk that I didn't even tell Mama and Baba about the amazing girl I'd met. But I did return to the squash courts soon after to apologise.

'Don't worry about it, Andrew. Let's have a game,' said Sheree, her happy disposition encouraging me to enter the court. I got the feeling she was interested in me – an overseas student all alone in this part of the world – and certainly we got along very well.

Over the next few weeks, we shared some memorable times together. She met more of my friends and I met her immediate family, who lived, together with their ageing grandmother in Day Avenue, just around the corner from my home at the Szalays' house. I visited several times for dinner and appreciated the warmth and the fact that the three generations lived under one roof. I wished it would be the same for my family one day.

On a Friday afternoon towards the end of November 1976, three days before the final exam results were due to come out, I invited Sheree to have dinner with me at the hospital canteen. As I mentioned, I was being careful with my finances in case I didn't pass the final exam and had to repeat a year. Sheree's curiosity about many things was one of her numerous qualities I was secretly tallying, as was her ready acceptance of hospital and university canteen foods.

When we looked at the menu, Sheree decided to try the oxtail soup on offer. It was not a regular item at the canteen and was a bit more expensive than the usual fare. But it looked rather delicious, was something I had previously yearned to try, and was certainly not part of Sheree's traditional Australian diet at home. I was just thrilled to share this new experience with her.

We had barely started our meal when Doug Lee, a junior medical student, stopped by. 'The results are out,' he announced, eyeing my companion with surprise and appreciation.

'No, Doug, Monday is the day,' I said, slightly baffled.

'Yes, they're out.'

'They can't be.' I sat up and looked at him.

'I saw them,' Doug said, without revealing any more details. I looked at my dinner date, who was half-puzzled and half-excited as well. I didn't want to interrupt our romantic meal, but my curiosity soon got the better of me. I jumped up and headed for the door, with Sheree following close by. We ran all the way to the Wallace Wurth Medical School building, ascended the front steps and halted in the foyer, out of breath. Only a few classmates were about.

'Yes! I passed! And so did Robert, and my other friends.' I turned to Sheree and sprang into the air. 'I've got my wings – now I can fly!'

Sheree hugged me so firmly I could feel her heart racing with mine, in chorus, in rhythm. Then she kissed me.

'Congratulations Andrew – Dr Andrew!'

My vision turned misty and she wiped away my tears.

'Let's go and ring your parents,' she said.

CHAPTER 35

I'd decided not to burden Sheree with the details of my past, but she had learnt that Baba lived in Hong Kong and Mama in Shiqi, and had gained some understanding of the issues that had torn our family apart. The decision I'd overheard my parents make in the quiet of the night back in Shiqi more than twenty years earlier – to send their son away for the benefit of the family – now echoed in my subconsciousness.

I must have seemed a little subdued in the days after I had told my father about my achievement in the graduation examination, for Sheree said to me on several occasions, 'You should go home and tell your parents and family in person about your success.' How I appreciated her compassion, empathy and, now, love.

Baba was more than eager for me to return to Hong Kong for a visit. During our phone calls, he kept telling me not to worry about the cost of the trip. 'As an intern, you'll begin to earn a proper wage,' he said. 'So, my son, do come home.'

In early December 1976, I set off for Hong Kong. The nine-and-half-hour trip on a jumbo jet (without a refuelling stop) was bliss, though this time I didn't sleep all the way, as I was so excited about so many things. For one, I was relieved that Mama and Baba might now start to feel that a heavy veil – the one that fell on us when Baba was sentenced – was being lifted. I longed to see Mama's smile that I had missed so much, and feel Baba's strong arms around me again. I hoped I might even have a chance to tell them about the beautiful and amazing woman I had fallen in love with.

At Kai Tak Airport, Baba was waiting for me. He couldn't take his eyes off me, and shed tears of joy and delight. He laughed heartily as he gave me a big, long hug. We went to his small rented room in Mong Kok, a busy suburb of Kowloon, then without delay he took me to thank his friends and relatives for their assistance and good wishes over the years, especially his cousin who had been my financial guarantor.

The next day, he took me back to the Diamond Hill Shanghai tailor who had made my first suit and ordered two more using the best materials available. Exuding the glow of a proud parent, Baba didn't even bother to bargain. The good tailor nearly cried, not for the extra money he'd make, but with gladness for me. 'What a pleasure it is,' he kept saying, 'to dress successful people from the shantytown.'

'Our children are all attending universities now,' said the delighted noodle-stall owners in Grand View Road as they served Baba and me a delicious lunch. 'And there are plenty of opportunities here in Hong Kong if you work hard,' they said with pride in their voices. I devoured my much-missed genuine Diamond Hill Spicy and Sour Noodles, which had since become more famous after a burgeoning number of influential people had discovered this gem of a shantytown.

'It's to do with the movie studio up the road from us,' Baba explained, referring to the hilltop establishment where Bruce Lee was now making his popular kung fu films, 'and other actors and singers who come from right here in Diamond Hill, like the Hui brothers. With their patronage, the area has become gentrified, and the restaurants on the main street now offer a variety of authentic northern-style cuisines we could only dream about in the past.' Baba very much enjoyed filling me in on all the happenings in the colony since my departure.

After lunch, Baba and I went to an exclusive department store in Hong Kong. As we entered, he announced to the sales assistants, 'Here's the young doctor. He needs two of your best ties.'

While I was in Hong Kong, I received letters from Mama and Ying. 'The whole of Shiqi is delighted by your achievement, my son. We are all very proud of you,' Mama wrote. Even Weng sent a short letter of congratulations: 'Well done my big brother, and how I've missed you.'

Baba noticed I was frowning and obviously missing Mama and my sisters. 'Things are a lot better back home, Ah-mun,' he said. 'Everyone says China is relaxing its grip on the expatriates like us, and some escapees have gone back to China and left again without any problems. Now that Mao is dead, Deng Xiaoping is in charge and things are rapidly changing, for the better. Perhaps you should go home and see your Mama.'

'But as for me,' he continued, staring at his Camel cigarette, 'I wouldn't go back to Shiqi, even if the way was lined with gold.' It was clear he couldn't erase the memories of his persecutors.

*

In the middle of the northern winter, in early January 1977, Baba accompanied me to Macau, and from there I proceeded to the Chinese border.

'I'll wait for you here, Ah-mun,' he said before we parted, but not until he reminded me once more, 'Don't stay at home for more than two nights, or you might give them an excuse to detain you. You can't trust them, even though Mao is dead.'

I was uneasy and fearful as I went through the border inspection under the scrutiny of the solemn Chinese border guards, yet I also felt a pang of familiarity and even fondness when I saw the large red flags adorned with five golden stars that fluttered in the warm sea breeze. Overriding all these sensations, however, was my growing excitement at the prospect of soon seeing my long-missed Mama, sisters, cousins and childhood friends. It lifted me high.

I'd brought a range of tempting food items, including tins of coffee grains and Eagle Brand condensed milk, as well as some new clothes for everyone in my family, fishing lines for my cousins, and a few toys for Ying's toddler son, Kuo-feng. And I hadn't forgotten the Camel cigarettes for Mama and Eighth Uncle – and perhaps also for the District Head if it might help oil the wheels for Mama's application to leave – or those arrowroot biscuits everyone adored. I'd even brought a camera with me, but the Chinese Customs officers noted it as a 'luxurious item', which meant it had to be taken out of China again or I'd face a severe penalty.

A large, modern, comfortable bus waited to take me and other passengers to Shiqi; its speed amazed me as we zipped through the countryside, which had changed little, and by noon I was stepping out of the bus into my waiting family's open arms in a new bus station at the same location on the west side of the town, albeit a lot larger.

It broke my heart to see how much Mama had aged, and seemed to have shrunk – I now rose head and shoulders above her, the exact opposite of fourteen years earlier. And standing by the side of her husband, Hao-ming, whom I met for the first time that day, Ying did not seem as tall as I remembered her being – in fact, Weng had overtaken her. Little Kuo-feng stared at the uncle he had never met before with a puzzled look.

Eighth Uncle was still the tallest member of the family, and he beamed at me. Yiu-hoi's eyes shone with joy that day too; he threw his strong arms around me and wouldn't let me go, and he was so choked that his speech was incomprehensible. I was delighted to see Sixth Aunt and Yiu-wei there too, wiping tears of happiness from their faces.

The Wonder River nearby winked in the winter sun as we walked back to Kwong Street, retracing the path I had taken through the narrow streets and alleyways when I'd left. We formed a large, loud party, now all wearing big glowing smiles and greeting friends and neighbours along the way, but at the same time eager to get to our destination and catch up with each other. The fifteen-minute journey was one of the most joyous walks of my life. Many a time I had to wipe my eyes.

A crowd of neighbours blocked the entrance to Kwong Street. Many children were there trying to get a glimpse of the modern sojourner – a young one, and now a doctor, from their very own street!

I saw the proud tears in Mama's eyes, and Ying and Weng cried too. They couldn't take their eyes off me.

'Welcome home, Big Brother,' Yiu-hoi finally managed to say. We embraced each other once more inside 1 Kwong Street and the warm lump in my throat broke, releasing years of choked-up tension.

His eyes still red, Yiu-hoi then sprang to his feet and grabbed his violin. Johann Strauss II's sweet 'Tales from the Vienna Woods' rang out, so comforting and so cheering, filling our ageing ancestral house with melody and warmth to welcome me back.

I'm home.

Mama, now wearing the biggest smile I had ever seen on her face, rushed around pouring lychee tea for all of us. My little sister, Weng, had grown up, and how her dimples flashed that day. I held her coarse but strong hands and sobbed.

Then we all burst out laughing as I dug in my bag, pulled out the tin of arrowroot biscuits and began to distribute them to the children crowding the entrance to our home – kids of all ages whom I'd never met before. They clapped, and some even showed off their Red Scarves to me.

'Oh Ah-mun, you've grown into a fine, handsome young man. You look so much like your father,' said Sixth Aunt, wearing her faded worker's tunic. 'I knew you'd do good one day ...' She too burst into tears, and laughter, as she thanked the gods and our ancestors. Her daughter Yiu-wei was also wiping her eyes.

'I totally agree. Hard work has paid off,' said Eighth Uncle, patting me on my shoulder. 'To be a good doctor is as important as being a good leader, and I'm sure our ancestors are proud of you.' He no longer seemed so tall, and was now a rather thin man with a permanent bend in his lower back. He had been beaten down by the tough times, and only his strong voice struck a note of defiance.

'Come, Ah-mun,' said Mama, 'let's give thanks to our forebears and the gods and angels that have guided you and protected you.'

She led me and the family into the third lounge room where the large rosewood table was adorned with three bowls of rice with chopsticks, and three small cups of tea. Being the most senior male in the house, Eighth Uncle took the lead and we showed our gratitude to our ancestors, gods and other deities. Mama had become old, but the joy that day rejuvenated her.

The old houses in our street hadn't changed much, but the former algae ponds were in ruins. Now that I was older, the levee wall looked much lower and I didn't need to climb onto it to see into the paddies and the lotus pond and fishponds.

'Look how those trees have grown,' Yiu-hoi said, pointing to the line of gums we had planted. 'Nearly twenty years old now, but there are still no trains here. And our kites get caught up in their branches.' Pondering this, he looked tired and older than his years. 'I'd like to go overseas one day like you, Big Brother,' he said. 'Things are improving here, but not fast enough. I've heard the authorities have allowed more people to leave town, but I'll be too old soon. You must help me, Big Brother.'

I put my arm around his shoulder and nodded. 'I'll try my best, Yiu-hoi. Learn English; it's your ticket to the world.'

He then told me that Earring had joined the PLA, and Ah-dong had gone to live in Macau around the time I'd left home.

'How's your baba?' Mama asked softly. 'I worry about him, and you and Ping too, every minute of the day.' She released a deep sigh, a familiar sound. I nudged close to her and put my arm around her shoulders. Her tiny frame trembled.

'Mama, I want you to come and live with me in Australia one day,' I said, hugging her firmly to calm her rush of emotions. 'We have a decent chance of success now that I'm a doctor, even though there's still a lot of training ahead of me. And with me earning a good salary, I'll be able to support you, Mama.'

She nodded and smiled.

'We'll live in Sydney,' I went on, getting excited. 'I'll take you to Centennial Park, and you'll love it, with its open spaces, ancient tall trees and amazing gardens. Oh, and there are beautiful beaches not far from there. And you know what? There's a Chinatown right in Sydney!'

'And we'll be the most blessed family in the whole of Shiqi,' Mama said, fixing her gaze on me, her eyes shining with life and excitement.

The two days went too fast for all of us. When I came to leave, I hugged my family goodbye one by one and promised to return one day, soon. Mama gave me a long embrace and reminded me once more to study and work hard to be a good doctor. The warm sun glowed in our hearts, kindled by a sense of new possibilities.

Baba was much relieved when I met him on the Macau side of the border. 'I'm so pleased you are happy now that you've seen Mama and the family. How's she coping? Poor dear.'

'Mama desperately wants to be with us one day,' I said. 'And I shall try applying for her to come to Australia when I go back.'

'Yes,' Baba nodded, then looked me in the eye and said, 'With hard work and perseverance my son, you'll get where you want to, one day.'

*

In mid-January 1977, soon after returning from Hong Kong, I began my internship at the Royal Prince Alfred Hospital in Sydney. I worked the so-called one in three: a thirty-six-hour shift every three days. That meant you started work at seven in the morning and stayed on to cover wards and Casualty at night, and didn't go home until whatever time you finished the following evening. It was challenging. 'But that's how you learn fast,' the seniors said to us. So we soldiered on. I felt quite a sense of responsibility with my photo ID over my white coat, my stethoscope around my neck, pens in one chest pocket and a small therapy guide in another.

I wrote to Mama as often as I could, keeping her hopes high, while I made inquiries with the immigration authorities as to how and when I could apply for her to come to Australia. Now that I was employed at one of Sydney's most prestigious hospitals, I had been approved for permanent residency.

'My dearest son,' Mama wrote on hearing about my new status. 'You can't imagine how relieved I am, even though it's taken fifteen years to get to where you are today from the time you left Shiqi. The thought of being with you soon keeps my spirit up. I can see things clearer now ... Take good care and don't forget to take adequate rest. An intern's job is a demanding one and I'll pray to the gods and our ancestors for you every day. How I wish I could be with you so that I could make sure you are well fed and resting properly.'

In another aerogramme Mama expressed the hope that the District Head might be merciful enough to let her come to my graduation ceremony. She was so hopeful, but it was not to be. The world was not changing as fast as I wished, much as Great-Grandfather Fu-chiu had found on his wedding day.

Baba decided not to come either, out of respect for Mama, he said. I couldn't help feeling somewhat deflated. But then, looking down from the podium on 8 February 1977, wearing my best suit and tie to receive my degrees in medicine and surgery, I was thrilled to see the happy faces of Ping and Grandmother Young; Uncle Chong Young, my mother's brother, and Aunt Bertha, who had come all the way from Hawaii for the ceremony; and Howard and Mabel Lee.

My joy would have been more complete if Mama, Baba, Ying and Weng had been there, but it was still one of the proudest days of my life.

*

Sheree often brought me dinner when I was working those unsociable night shifts; sometimes it was a yummy hot meat-and-three-veg dish cooked by Trich, her mother, covered with tinfoil, plus a sweet! This way we continued to see each other even when I was on prolonged weekend duties.

One evening I was so moved by Sheree's presence that I decided to test the depth of our love. 'Sheree, what would your parents say if we were to get married?'

'They'd be delighted. What would your parents say?' Sheree could hardly contain her excitement and she looked at me with those irresistible blue eyes, her face beaming.

I took her into my arms and said, 'They'd be thrilled too and so happy for us.'

This was soon confirmed when letters from both Mama and Baba arrived, conveying their best wishes. But others were not so sure our match would be a success.

'Andrew,' advised one of my Chinese friends on the eve of the wedding, 'you know that gweilo marriages don't last. I give you five years. It won't be like the marriages in our culture, which endure forever.'

I was shocked and found it hard to believe what he had said, so I dismissed it as a joke. Yet I knew that many of my fellow Asian students had been warned by their parents not to get involved with gweilos, and some were even told it was a condition of their ongoing financial support.

But Sheree and I were confident about our future, and determined to share a loving life, and a family, in Australia.

Much to my delight, Baba came to our wedding, and so did Ping, who had recently married Randall Kawamura, a specialist dentist, and moved to Washington DC. But once again, Mama was disappointed: the District Head wouldn't allow her to leave to attend our happy occasion. Ying suspected he did it to get back at Baba; the thorn still hurt in his side. The Camel cigarettes hadn't worked, nor had the many other presents. All we could do was write to Mama to console her, and send her photos of the wedding, as well as a big wedge of the wedding cake, smuggled to her by a friend of Baba's who was visiting Shiqi. Ying wrote to tell me that Mama had shed copious tears, but was also happy for us and held a dinner party at her home in Shiqi to bless our union.

PART IV

Moonrise

CHAPTER 36

It was three o'clock in the morning, New Year's Day 1978. I'd been called to the phone at the then Rachel Forster Hospital in Redfern, where I had been on duty since the day before. Oh, not another drunkard, I thought, in my drowsy state.

'Sheree's having contractions. I think she's in labour,' shouted her mother on the other end of the line. I woke up in an instant.

'I can't leave until seven. Call for an ambulance,' I said. My heart was racing and tears began to stream down my face as I experienced a huge range of emotions.

I rushed around the wards to announce my wonderful New Year's news. Patients cheered and handed me flowers from their vases. 'No florists are open now, so make sure you take these to your dear wife and baby,' they said.

At the Waverley Maternity Hospital I ran past the ward where Sheree was, and went straight to the nursery to see my baby, a little girl. I held the small bundle close then took her to the ward and placed her gently in Sheree's arms. Before long she took to the breast and suckled away. What a perfect picture of mother and child: so peaceful, so poignant. That's what the world should be, I thought: peace, love and compassion. It had made all the hard work worth it now that my own world had begun to change, to bear fruit. Through my misty eyes, I saw Sheree's tears of joy.

We named our daughter Serena Patricia. I could hardly wait to tell my family back home, so I went to Sheree's family home in Kensington, where they now had an international line, and called Baba. He was thrilled. The news soon travelled to Shiqi and within a week or so I received an aerogramme from Mama with her best wishes for the next generation of the family. Her disappointment and the torment caused by being separated from her family were obvious.

It was now several months since I had submitted an application for a visa for Mama to come to Australia. Aside from a short letter of acknowledgement, the information from the Immigration Department in Sydney was scanty. Nearly eighteen months went by, and we heard nothing from the department. When I inquired about the processing of Mama's application, the officer simply advised patience. To keep her spirits up, I wrote to Mama about all the little things Serena was doing.

Mama told us that the District Head had said on many occasions that she would never be allowed to go to Hong Kong to be with Baba – 'Over my dead body. Maybe when the sun rises from the west,' he often said – but apparently he had a more positive attitude towards Australia. 'Going to the New Gold Mountain is all right. Australia is now our friend.' Baba said it was because Australia could supply the minerals that China so desperately needed.

I arrived home one evening and stood there at the door, tired after prolonged weekend duties.

There was a subdued expression on Sheree's face.

'What's wrong? Is Serena all right?' I shook off my sleepiness and charged past her, heading to the baby's room. How relieved I was to find her sleeping peacefully in her cot, so tender, so sweet.

I returned to the kitchen, poured a glass of water and slumped into a chair. Sheree definitely wasn't her usual bright self.

She regarded me with sympathy. 'You look so tired,' she managed to say. 'And you have smears of blood on your glasses and shirt sleeves. It must have been a very busy weekend.'

Then she handed me a letter. 'It's from the Immigration Department.'

'Dear Mr Kwong,' I read,

We regret to inform you that your application for your mother
Wai-syn Kwong has not fulfilled the Australian Immigration
Rules on two counts:
    She has failed to pass the mandatory English test.
    You are the only one of her four children presently residing
in Australia, hence she does not meet the requirement of
having the majority of her children living in Australia ...

I couldn't carry on.

'What an insult,' Sheree said. 'After nearly two years of waiting
for the government's decision, that's all we get. At the interview
we told them your sisters weren't living in Australia and they said
that was okay as long as we could support your mother financially.
They didn't tell us about those rules, or that she'd have to do an
English test. Poor Mama: they gave her only five per cent in the
test – for attending. It's all so unfair.'

I was too upset to work out what our next step should be. I felt
sick thinking about how Mama would take the bad news.

'There must be a way,' Sheree said. 'Let's go and see our local
member of parliament.'

Our member of parliament was well known for his
approachability and was highly regarded in the Opposition party
at the time. After hearing our story, he said he was happy to assist
by appealing to the minister for immigration. So we decided to
wait and not give Mama the disappointing news yet.

'I pray it'll work,' Sheree said, trying to reassure me. 'Now that
I'm a mother I understand exactly how Mama would feel, and how
she'd love to be with us. Let's not give up. Not ever.'

*

Several more months passed. During that time we moved to the
Central Coast and in 1979 I set up as a general practitioner while

studying for a fellowship in the Royal Australian College of General Practitioners. We converted a run-down, flea-infested little cottage into a small medical practice, and I operated it seven days a week with Sheree's assistance, looking after a growing number of young families, many of whom had been drawn to the area by its cheap land and open spaces, not to mention its many glorious beaches.

Then one day a letter from our former local MP finally arrived, expressing his regret for not being able to secure a positive outcome for Mama's application.

'I thought the White Australia Policy had died years ago,' I grumbled to Sheree. The next day, I presented myself at the MP's office to seek further advice, and to explain to him the persecution and torment Mama was enduring.

After listening to my appeal for help, he looked up at me and said, 'Andrew, it's not going to be easy. We've accepted more refugees this year, and the family reunion quota has had to be cut. But how about this,' he said, nodding his head and tapping his fingers as he deliberated further. 'You leave it with me and I'll see what more I can do.'

I walked out of his office with a spring in my step. No wonder he was so popular with his constituents. It seemed there was still hope, and Sheree had been right not to trouble Mama with the bad news so soon.

Sheree listened patiently to my plan as she fed Serena, stroking the baby's chubby cheeks to encourage her to suckle. Then after tucking Serena into her cot, she said, 'I don't think that's a good idea. Imagine how awful it would be for Mama if she had to return to China after her visit. And if we try to keep her here illegally, it could be even worse if we're found out. We'd have a black mark on our records forever.'

I admired Sheree's clear thinking, but it didn't relieve the dread rising inside me. How was I going to tell Mama? How would she take it?

I eventually wrote to her, trying hard to explain all the options while keeping her hopes up. In reality, some of the alternatives had little chance of success: for example, the Hong Kong government had tightened up its border security and cracked down on people smugglers, and had adopted a policy of immediately repatriating all captured illegal immigrants.

After what seemed like a long time, an aerogramme arrived from Ying. 'Your news has devastated Mama,' she wrote. 'Poor Mama, after all these years of suffering persecution, enduring hardship, longing for the family to be reunited, and praying to the gods ...' Ying described the appalling situation Mama had fallen into: not eating, not sleeping, sighing all day and rocking herself back and forth as if in a spell. 'She cries a lot and won't talk to or see anyone, not even my young son or Aunt Wai-hung. She has become so thin that a breeze can blow her over. Please, Ah-mun, what can I do? Can you do anything to help? All these years Mama has been longing to leave Shiqi and Australia seemed like her only hope before now. I fear this is the last straw and it will break her. I don't like the blank look on her face, and the way she keeps looking at the old lychee tree.'

Hearing this and not being able to comfort Mama was hard to bear. Then one morning Sheree said to me, 'I think we should go to Shiqi and see your mama in July. She may come good if she could see us and the baby. Oh, how much I feel for her, my mother-in-law I still haven't met.'

Within a month, I had found a locum doctor to take over my medical practice and booked tickets to Shiqi for myself, Sheree, Serena and Sheree's by then ten-year-old brother, Adrian.

After stopping over in Hong Kong for two days to see Baba and meet friends and cousins, we travelled to Macau by ferry across the Lonely Sea, and then took a short taxi ride to the Macau–China border. Baba accompanied us, but, still fearful of being detained for his transgressions years earlier, he wouldn't proceed any further. The plan was for us to have a short stay in Shiqi, then take the train via Guangzhou back to Hong Kong; it ran all the way to Kowloon in the city centre, which would make the journey easier for the children.

'Don't forget to give my love to Mama and your sisters. I'll wait at the railway terminal for you,' Baba said. I could see how sorry he was not to be able to go home. And it was now only a three-hour trip on modern buses.

How things had changed in China since Deng Xiaoping had taken over and started opening up the country for business. The signs were immediately evident at the border: the guards and customs officers were much more relaxed than they had been three and a half years earlier. One officer even extended a hand to welcome us back to 'the Motherland', while another checked our passports and visas. He looked me up and down a few times more and nodded without much of an expression. Several female officers giggled as they practised their basic English on the children.

On the way to Shiqi I observed further signs of change. Some parts of the gravel and red-earth road had given way to widened, all-weather tarmac, while other sections were being straightened. It was already a lot smoother to travel on. The ruins of fortresses along the Wonder River, like tired warriors, continued to stand their ground, despite the many seasons of typhoons and tempests they had endured – a reminder of the resilience of the people of the Pearl River Delta facing foreign encroachment in bygone years. There were still rice fields aplenty, but a few tractors and other machines had replaced some of the teams of hard-working water buffalos. The July sun was merciless.

I prayed that Mama would cheer up on seeing me arrive with my gweilo wife and brother-in-law and half-gweilo baby. I also hoped the district officials would be civil enough to leave us alone.

As we reached the outskirts of the town, I began pointing things out to Sheree. 'See that straight row of grey brick houses, and the levee wall?' I said. 'That's Kwong Street, my old home. Not far behind it to your right is the town of Shiqi, with Pagoda Hill rising in the middle of it. And to the left, see the small hill with another pagoda on it? That's Old Crow Hill!'

Gum trees on both sides of the road rustled as the bus carrying us headed to the west side of town, joining the chorus of beeping, ringing vehicles: small cars and buses, and, more noticeably, a large army of cyclists on their way home for their lunchbreak. What a great leap from my day.

My heart beat faster and louder as the bus turned left onto the bridge over the Wonder River which Mama and I had crossed together on that chilly morning when Baba had been taken off to prison.

When we arrived at the bus station, a crowd of people surrounded the bus, craning their necks to see the passengers. I spotted Eighth Uncle with ease and then hands began to wave. 'Ah-mun is home. Ah-mun is home!'

I rushed forward to embrace Mama, trying to stop her emaciated, trembling body from shaking more. I unleashed tears of joy and sadness. Weng and Ying cried also, as did Sixth Aunt and others. In a big huddle we hugged, caring not what the world around us was doing or saying; it was our time together that mattered.

Then I turned to look for Sheree and the children. There she stood, surrounded by my family, smiling and nodding, with Serena cuddling close to her, peering at the strangers around her. Adrian already seemed to have made friends with a few kids. No English was required: we were one big family.

We crowded into a small bus the family had hired, which tooted all the way to our street while other vehicles and bicycles responded with honks and ringing bells as if rejoicing too for the return of a long-absent local.

I sat in the overcrowded bus with Sheree on one side and Mama on the other, my arms around them, feeling so proud. From time to time I turned to my two sisters and expressed my surprise at how the once sleepy outpost on the delta now seemed to be a booming town. It amazed me that Yiu-hoi and Ah-ki wore bell-bottom jeans, and had both grown their hair long like The Beatles. And Weng's big permed hairstyle was a standout: it matched her big smile. Clearly the Western way of life had begun to seep into the PRC.

Fewer people were wearing the worker's tunic; the familiar hues of blue and khaki were giving way to brighter colours. You could hear children laughing and singing nursery rhymes. There were scant propaganda posters in sight, just advertisements and public notices. No loudspeakers boomed out revolutionary slogans – they'd been gone for a few years now, I was told. Shops were open for business everywhere and filled with customers browsing and bargaining.

The District Head and his committee members had formed a special welcoming party for us at his office in town. We sat on cool rosewood chairs with marble inlays which reminded me of the chairs we'd once had in our Kwong Street home. The officials served us fine jasmine tea and the local sweet lychees I had sorely missed for many years. They were eager to explain the recent modernisation of the town, and their aspirations for its future. Even they seemed to have changed: there were no solemn speeches or revolutionary slogans, no vindictive attitudes towards their long-absent kinsmen – the District Head even extended an invitation for Baba to return, guaranteeing his safety.

'As for your Mama,' he advised in his now not-so-hoarse voice, while cradling the Camel cigarettes I'd brought, 'she's free to leave if there's a country that will accept her. China's policy has changed.'

Mama's eyes shone.

After the tea party, we were given a guided tour of a neighbourhood kindergarten, where perspiring but happy children sang and danced to make us feel welcome. The little school was housed in a big old residence, its peeling whitewash exposing the tired local grey bricks.

That evening, after Serena and Adrian finally settled and fell asleep in the town's best hotel, where we had a ceiling fan, tiled bath and flushing toilet, Sheree voiced her concern for those children who had sweltered and suffered while putting on their performance for us. We decided to pay for ten ceiling fans to be installed in the kindergarten.

'Every little thing will help,' Sheree said without hesitation. A few minutes later, she sang out from the bathroom, 'Oh no, there's no water coming from the tap.' I complained to reception and was told that water was only available at certain hours of the day, as it had to be regularly pumped to a tank on the roof to supply the guests' needs. First in, best dressed.

CHAPTER 37

When we arrived back in Australia, I rang Ping in Washington DC to discuss what we could do to help Mama. As soon as I started talking, Ping cut in and said breathlessly, 'The immigration laws have just changed! The relationship between America and China is being normalised. Retired parents, children and spouses from China are being re-classified as Priority One. That means Mama could be in America within months. I'm going to lodge an application straight away.' Suddenly our hopes were reignited.

We prayed that the District Head would keep his word to me and let Mama leave Shiqi, and that she wouldn't have to sit another English test. People in Australia had long complained that the English test was just a more subtle White Australia policy, a way of keeping non-Anglo people out. Whether that was true or not, it was enough to keep me worrying.

At last, after six months of bureaucratic procedures and nerve-wracking silences, Mama was given permission to leave Shiqi and move to America to live with Ping's family. We were all overjoyed. We felt blessed and grateful that our long-time goal of reuniting the family together now appeared to be achievable.

To reach the United States from mainland China in those days, you had to first go to Hong Kong to catch a plane. In early 1981, Mama set off from Shiqi for Hong Kong via Macau. I knew she felt torn about leaving my sisters behind, and I could also feel some of the joy and excitement she experienced as she crossed the border.

Waiting for her on the other side of the border was Baba.

For quite a while after Mama's arrival, I couldn't help wondering what they'd said to each other at that moment – the first time they had set eyes on each other since Baba's bold escape in 1962. A romantic at heart, Baba told me some time later how anxious he was as the day of Mama's arrival approached. He thought about their early days in Hong Kong, and back to the last night they had spent together in Shiqi before his flight, how they'd lain in silence in the dark room at home, no words necessary except for Mama's quiet sobs.

On the day, Baba made sure he was at the Shenzhen Bridge, which connected the colony to the mainland, well before Mama's train was due to arrive. He felt almost overwhelmed by nervousness and excitement at the prospect of being reunited with his selfless wife, who had sacrificed so much for the good of the family.

Passengers from China had to walk over the bridge to the British side and have their documents inspected before being allowed to catch the train into town. Baba recalled how thrilled he was as he watched Mama stand in line waiting for her turn to cross over to freedom and into his open arms. As they finally embraced for the first time in nineteen years, Baba was pained by how tiny and frail Mama felt. But as time stood still and they looked at each other through their tears, they rejoiced in being together again, this time, they hoped, forever.

One of the first places he took Mama when they arrived back in Kowloon was the King Fook Jewellery store where he replaced her lost gold wedding band and bought her a diamond ring. Then he accompanied Mama to the same exquisite department store he had taken me to, to equip her with modern city attire. He was so proud to introduce her to his many friends and relatives, and as they travelled the city, catching buses, trams and ferries, they were overjoyed to re-acquaint themselves with the place where they had first met and fallen in love.

Mama had planned to spend two weeks in Hong Kong before her departure for the United States, and the time flew by in Baba's company. Due to his work and financial commitments, Baba had to stay in Hong Kong, so Mama travelled alone on her first ever jet plane trip. She stopped over in Hawaii for an emotional reunion with Grandmother Young, the uncles and their families, then flew on to Washington DC, where she was met by Ping and Randall and their son, Brian.

On her arrival in DC, Mama immediately embarked on learning English and studying the US Constitution, to prepare for her application for American citizenship. After several attempts, she passed the naturalisation test and became a US citizen.

Mama and Baba wrote to each other and us regularly. They often expressed their concerns for the daughters they had left behind. The sisters' applications to emigrate to the United States had at least now been acknowledged by the US Immigration Department, so our hopes grew as time went by. In early 1982, Weng, who was still unmarried, was successfully sponsored by Ping to leave China and settle in Washington DC, where she later met and married David Lau and had a son, Alan.

In Hong Kong, Baba continued to study in the evenings to gain more postgraduate qualifications in teaching and administration, which helped him obtain a much better paid position as deputy headmaster of a large high school. He had to wait until he retired to be eligible to be sponsored to emigrate to the United States, which he finally did in the summer of 1983. Once settled in Washington, he volunteered to work in a Chinatown welfare association that cared for ageing sojourners and helped settle new arrivals. He and Mama lived with Ping and her family, as they did not have the means to live independently in a new country, but they loved being with the family again and were very happy together.

Baba and Mama visited Australia together for the first time at the end of 1983, and I was overjoyed to see my parents as a couple again. By that time, my medical practice on the Central Coast was thriving and Sheree and I had been blessed with two more children:

Harmony, then two and a half years old, and Andrew-James, or AJ, who was just over one. Baba and Mama were delighted by our two active toddlers and greatly enjoyed helping Sheree take care of them. Mama still had limited English, but she and Sheree had no trouble understanding each other. Both admitted with pride that it was because they were mothers, and mothers share a common language: love.

We managed to extend Baba and Mama's visitor visa by six more months so that we could savour our time together. It also allowed my parents to experience many of the joys of the Australian way of life: barbecues, picnics, beach-going. In Sydney's Chinatown, they even caught up with some old friends, sojourners from Shiqi.

One fine spring day we decided to take the ferry from Circular Quay to the seaside suburb of Manly. It was pleasantly warm and a gentle breeze caressed us all as we stood on the upper deck waiting to depart.

'This is the most beautiful harbour in the world,' Baba said to Mama, his arm draped over her shoulder.

The gigantic Harbour Bridge spanned the water before us. The water was calm. AJ and Harmony marvelled at the large ferry and its many passengers. Serena held Mama's hand and sang to her the new nursery rhymes she had learnt. Then the boat turned gently towards starboard and the whole of the Opera House came into view. Gleaming in the morning sun, it was elegant and majestic.

'Ah.' Baba let out a sigh of contentment and said, 'This is true paradise.'

Sheree and I looked at each other with big smiles on our faces and nodded. 'Well, we are in the Lucky Country,' she said.

*

Before my parents returned to the United States, Mama proudly showed off her American passport. She told us how she had lost count of the number of times her application to leave Shiqi had been rejected, and how she had clung to her little flicker of hope that one day we would be reunited, and that the bright moon would shine again for us all. Now that hope seemed like it might be realised. The glow on her face was contagious.

As Baba pointed out, the battle wasn't quite over yet. Ying and her family were still in Shiqi, awaiting approval of their applications to emigrate to the United States. But the end of our long journey towards reuniting our whole family was in sight.

After another agonising two-year wait Ping's sponsorship of Ying, her husband Hao-ming and their two boys was approved, and the family moved to the United States in 1985. Eager for a fresh start in a new country, Ying asked Sheree to choose English names for her boys. The firstborn became Jonathan and his young brother was named Luke. They both promptly settled into school in Maryland, near Washington DC.

We were all desperate to get together in America for a full family reunion, but now that everyone was safely out of China, I felt I had to get back to building my medical practice and spending more time with my young family. The reunion would have to wait.

Then, at the end of a visit to Australia with Mama in 1988, Baba said to me, 'Your kids are growing up fast. Ying and her family have settled well in DC, and so has Weng. It's time for us all to get together under one roof to celebrate.' It was still his ultimate, unfulfilled ambition: to see the whole family together again under one roof.

'You'd love the museums in DC, and there's so much to see and do there,' he added, trying to tempt me.

'What a great idea,' Sheree promptly agreed. 'The children will be old enough to endure the long flight. And how wonderful it'll be for them to meet their cousins.'

From then on, the anticipation of the occasion was overwhelming. Each passing day brought us closer to my whole family being together at last, to achieving what my parents and all of us had fought and worked so hard for all these years.

The June 1989 reunion was the first such gathering since 1957 – the year the family exodus began before Ping's departure from

Shiqi. How I delighted in Mama's smile and Baba's enthusiasm as every day they outlined our Washington sightseeing schedule, which took in sights like the Lincoln Memorial, Capitol Hill and Arlington National Cemetery. Most of the youngsters were at school during the day, but we would get together with them in the evenings and Mama was overjoyed to see her grandchildren play so well together.

For me, the most unforgettable moment was Baba's speech towards the end of the celebration dinner party. 'My dear family and friends, my children and grandchildren,' he began before thanking a long list of people, including the American government for accepting them. He paid special tribute to Mama's perseverance and endurance in their quest for freedom, and to the Kawamuras for their financial assistance, which repeatedly helped family members get out of Shiqi. We clapped and we cried, the children looking slightly puzzled at our heightened emotions. Mama leant on Baba, looking so proud.

'Ordinary people like us, throughout history, are often made to suffer by forces beyond their control,' he continued. Then he shifted his gaze towards his seven happy, healthy grandchildren, and said, 'The sea may be vast and treacherous, but we must steer our own boats. Hold on to hope and your life with both hands, always and forever.'

EPILOGUE

Our momentous 1989 gathering was tinged with a little sadness, as it coincided with the Tiananmen Square protest. Baba was glued to the non-stop media coverage, initially full of hope for the people of China. But his excitement and anticipation were crushed when the tanks rolled in and the massacre began. Then he looked the worst I had ever seen him: grey and dull, sighing continuously, and even shedding tears for those brave young people in the square. Fortunately, the joy of the family finally being together kept him buoyed.

After we returned to Australia, Baba continued his community work in downtown DC. But the following May we were all heartbroken when he was suddenly struck down by acute leukaemia and passed away.

Mama lived on in Maryland with the Kawamuras and continued visiting us in Australia nearly every year after Baba's passing, up to her eightieth birthday. Her English became good enough for her to deal with transits through airports, and she never missed a flight to and from DC. She went to eternal peace in her sleep in 2017, at the ripe old age of ninety-seven years, still holding the record as Shiqi's most persistent applicant for a departure visa, from 1960 to 1980.

Putting behind her all the pain of the denouncements and purges in Shiqi, Ying found work in the kitchen of the Hyatt Hotel in Washington and eventually became assistant banquet manager, organising and decorating every buffet lunch and function in the hotel until her retirement in 2018, when the hotel honoured her with a lavish party to which she was brought by limousine and then entered via a red carpet lined by the entire staff, from the general manager to the bell boys. Hao-ming still works at the same hotel as a sous-chef.

Weng changed her name to Anne. Her son, Alan, is currently completing an MBA at Cornell University after a stint as a US Marine Corps captain. To our great sadness, Weng passed away in 2009 after a brief battle with cancer.

Third Aunt migrated to New York in the mid-1960s to be with her husband. I went to see her during our 1989 visit to the United States. 'You've made it,' she told me as she fumbled with her beads, 'You've steered your boat well.' As I hugged her, I thanked her for all the prayers she'd said for me, and for teaching me good table manners.

Sixth Aunt passed away in Shiqi during the festivities of the annual dragon boat race in 2014, at the age of ninety-eight years. She is survived by my cousin Yiu-wei, who still lives in the family's ancestral home on Kwong Street.

After his imprisonment in the 1960s, Eighth Uncle was never employed as a teacher again. In 1996 he visited Australia when *The Phantom of the Opera* was in full swing. We went to the musical, where he repeatedly wiped his eyes and blew his nose. He later told us how, during the Japanese invasion of China in the 1940s, he had been tasked with leading more than one hundred children of army officers to safety in Guangzhou while dodging the pursuing enemy. When provisions dwindled, he and the children staged plays and operas for the locals in return for food and a place to rest their feet. He passed away in 2006 in Shiqi. Whenever *The Phantom of the Opera* soundtrack is played, I feel his presence.

I never forgot my promise during my 1977 and 1980 visits to Shiqi to try to help my cousin Yiu-hoi. On my return to Australia, I assisted him with his application to leave China and work as an electrician in Fiji, the only place that would accept him. In 1984, he came to Australia as a tourist. One evening he said to me on the phone, 'I don't want to leave Australia, Big Brother. This is my adopted home now. I have a driver's licence and I've found work around Sydney. Soon I'll have saved enough for a cheap car.'

He changed his name to Thomas and, making the most of his skills, soon established a sizeable clientele among the Chinese community in Sydney. He steadily improved his English and gained formal qualifications as an electronics technician from a college. While making many new friends, he also got to know the families of some sojourners from Shiqi. Thomas's residential status was eventually normalised and he became an Australian citizen when the Hawke Government granted an amnesty to Chinese nationals soon after the Tiananmen Square massacre. He is married with two bright Australian children, Anthony and Juliet, who are both successful in their own fields. Recently he retired from his electronics business to focus on music, and he now plays violin and cello with a Sydney orchestra and has even performed at Sydney Town Hall on several occasions.

Like Weng, my cousin Ah-ki, as the child of a disgraced family, was sent to live in the country for many years. He became a group leader of a People's Militia unit guarding part of the China–Macau waterfront during the time when many Chinese were attempting to flee to Macau. Once he told me how some of his comrades dropped their weapons and swam to Macau under the cover of night. Not willing to shoot at them, he walked the other way. He has retired now and lives in Shiqi with his wife, while going on regular trips to many beautiful parts of China. They have two grown-up children.

Ho-bun did not marry until many years after Ying did, and later migrated to Vancouver in Canada. He died several years ago. He and Ying never saw each other again following that fateful evening by the bank of the Nine Meanders River.

In a quest to find all the missing links in our family's story, I made a special trip in 2015 to Hong Kong to track down Ding-yan Lee, the Shiqi swimming instructor who escaped with Baba. Mr Lee had slotted into the Hong Kong metropolis with little effort and become a successful businessman. When I met him he had retired after suffering a stroke. He told me how Baba's persecutor stayed on in Macau to collect the fares promised by his fugitive passengers, but was later kidnapped by Chinese secret agents and smuggled back to Shiqi. He was taken to Pig Head Hill and executed for betraying China. Mr Lee wished he knew the whereabouts of the little child who had cried at that crucial moment on board the *Pearl River 173* during their quest for freedom. She would now be nearly sixty years old.

*

In 1995 a well-dressed businessman marched into my medical practice asking to see me. From his portly frame and jolly demeanour, I immediately knew it was my old friend Ah-dong. Laughing and chuckling as he always did, he explained that he was on a business trip to Australia and had made a great effort to locate me. I was so delighted that he hadn't sold himself for food for a hundred yuan, as he had threatened to do.

Ah-dong told me that he had also left Shiqi in 1962. His uncle was a senior comrade in town and, sensing the dire situation facing his people, he had issued Ah-dong with an exit visa, thereby releasing another young carp into the water. Ah-dong became a motor mechanic apprentice in Macau. During his whole apprenticeship, he lived in the workshop and slept in customers' cars. Later he became one of the best escalator mechanics in town, and when the gambling industry boomed he established his own escalator service and installation company. It's now one of the biggest firms in Macau.

Ah-dong was proud to inform me that before Macau was returned to the PRC he had sent his family to live in Toronto so that they would have a more secure future. 'I'm now an astronaut, ha, ha,' he said, his voice buoyant with confidence. 'Like many others in Hong Kong and Macau, I fly to faraway Canada to visit my family these days, at least twice a year. I'm glad they're safe there.' Ah-dong no longer stuttered; he glowed.

'I wish I'd had a good education like you,' he said in parting. 'I always knew you'd do good one day.' Then, before being driven away by his chauffeur, he added, 'Now that I've seen you again, I can die happy.'

Fortunately, he is still alive at the time of writing and we have since visited each other's homes and are in regular contact on social media.

*

In February 2012, Sheree and I paid a visit to Shiqi and Macau in the hope of finding some of my childhood friends like Big Eye, Hui, Earring and Ah-bil, initially to no avail. On the evening before leaving Shiqi, we took a walk in the old part of town, retracing familiar paths of fifty years earlier. I was hoping someone in the street might know my friends. I stopped at what had been the site of Come Happiness Bridge. The Nine Meanders River had been filled in and a park had replaced the bridge. It was now an unremarkable spot in the middle of a city of over two million people. Not far from there, I found Ah-bil's family home. It was old, falling into decay, and was no longer occupied. Disappointed, I then tried to reach Big Eye's house nearby. A high-rise apartment block stood on its site.

We backtracked to the good Mrs Lee's house, home to Flea, with whom I'd first left Shiqi and who now lives in Virginia, in the United States, not far from Ping. A café occupied the former front room. I took many photos to send to Flea. Until his recent retirement, he was an environmental scientist with a PhD from Stanford University, occupying a senior position with the US Environmental Protection Agency in Washington.

Heading south along Come Happiness Road, we reached Kwong Street, now not much wider than a laneway, in which only a few of the original ten houses still stood. Small remnants of the levee wall were still visible. They had become part of other, smaller buildings, obviously erected illegally, which made the street difficult to navigate. The paddy fields had long gone, the locals told us, together with the commune's vegetable gardens, lotus pond and fishponds, as had the lychee trees, and the gum trees we had helped plant. No one flew kites anymore, as the sky was now crisscrossed with electrical cables; instead, young children nearby were busy playing their handheld computer games, talking on their mobile phones or staring at me and my gweilo wife. Maybe they were wondering what kind of sojourner I was, but they probably didn't care that I hadn't brought any tasty biscuits for them. McDonald's and Kentucky Fried Chicken, their favourites now, were just around the corner.

Huge air-conditioned tour buses, trucks and cars ranging from popular Japanese economy models to prestige European limousines filled the streets. With its typical urban sounds, smells and pollution, Shiqi was now much like Hong Kong and any other big city. Not far from Kwong Street was a fast-train station, built in less than five years; from there, bullet trains depart for Guangzhou every thirty minutes. I was thrilled that trains had finally come to my town, as our teachers at the Dragon Mother's Temple School had promised they would, but it saddened me somewhat that the sleepers for the railway tracks had not been built with the trees we planted, but with steel made from Australian iron ore.

My old world had gone. A new China had sprouted.

Accompanied by Sheree, I left the street with a heavy heart, dragging myself in the direction of our hotel.

'Ah-mun?'

I turned to the call and recognised Ah-fat, who had once been a friend of Ah-ki and with whom I had been reacquainted during my recent visits to Shiqi. He had been made redundant at the age of fifty to make way for younger workers, and now worked as a bicycle courier.

I asked about Earring, Big Eye, Hui and Ah-bil. He simply pulled out his mobile phone and began dialling. His eyes brightened as he talked, addressing someone as 'Chairman'. It was Earring on the phone, and he said he would help find my other friends. My heart leapt.

We decided to meet in the foyer of our hotel at eight o'clock that night. Ah-bil arrived at seven, unable to wait any longer. Soon, fifteen or more men and women streamed in, including Earring, now the chairman of a city council department.

'You kicked gravel at us, then we never saw you again,' joked Ah-bil, while holding my hand tight, as if to say, 'I won't let you go this time without saying goodbye.'

I tried to explain. 'It was the circumstances—'

'I know,' said Earring, the chairman. 'But it's all different now.' He spoke with confidence, if not a tone of authority, and nodded while patting me on my shoulder. 'Welcome home.'

My friends then presented me with a copy of a photo that I couldn't recall being taken. They reminded me that it was a prize awarded to the class for being the most progressive and patriotic group that year when we were making steel. I was unable to identify myself in the picture until a classmate put his finger on a scrawny little boy in the back row whose sad eyes stared straight ahead. I was shocked.

When I was leaving my friends, they gave me Big Eye's phone number. He had migrated to the island city of Victoria, Canada. In October 2014, I made a special trip to visit him.

It was cold and raining on the afternoon I arrived, but I was glad, as the rain hid my tears – tears shed in joy but also for the time we lost, and had now found again. We talked for three days. He had just finalised the sale of his successful electronics business, and was now able to devote more time to working as a volunteer caring for the region's ageing population of Chinese sojourners. We are now in touch regularly.

*

Ever since that hot and humid day when I left Shiqi as a young boy, I have counted my blessings and held in my heart the many family members and friends who helped me to get to where I am today – a successful general practitioner caring for a large number of elderly and infirm people, a father of three adult children who are good citizens and, even more excitingly, grandfather to seven healthy and happy young Australians. Most importantly, I am husband to Sheree, the gweilo girl with whom I experienced my first oxtail soup. She shares with me a love that keeps on growing and giving, and has accompanied me through many of the endeavours I've recorded in the latter part of this book. It was not until I began to write about my early experiences as a young boy that she realised how effectively I had buried my challenging past. It was the resilience of youth, I tell her.

I often think of Mama's perseverance and patience as she waited so long for the dark clouds to disperse, and I thank my lucky stars – and the guardian angels, the door gods, the spirit of General Guan Gong and God – that she persisted and endured, and that, at last, a bright moon shines for us all.

ACKNOWLEDGEMENTS

It takes time to write a book. But it has taken me much longer than usual, as I wanted to make sure I wrote a good book. I am most thankful to Sharon Rundle, my original writing teacher, who so successfully drummed into my head the importance of 'show, don't tell', which was a vital principle for me when recreating scenes from the past. Sharon's continual encouragement over the protracted gestation of the manuscript is much appreciated.

I would like to acknowledge Professor Mabel Lee for her inspiration as a tireless, dedicated academic who has nurtured numerous scholars in studies of modern Chinese literature and culture. Most importantly to me, her well-measured, quiet advice helped bolster my determination to write a thorough, historically accurate account of the plight of an ordinary family during the early, desperate attempts of the PRC to raise the living standards of a long-oppressed people.

I am also most grateful to Susanne Gervay, an acclaimed author with whom I have shared space in two published anthologies of short stories – *Fear Factor: Terror Incognito* and *Alien Shores* – for believing in me and my story. More importantly, her regular cajoling helped me get over occasional impediments while I was trying to have my manuscript published.

It was an amazing privilege to have Carol Major as my writing consultant at Varuna, The National Writers' House, in the Blue Mountains of New South Wales. During several writing fellowships, her guidance, sensitivity and insights, and her thoughtful understanding of modern China, helped me bring my long-suppressed past back to life and, I hope, leap vividly from the pages.

I am also grateful to Stephen Measday and Peter Bishop at Varuna for their helpful input and encouragement during my several sojourns there, as well as to the dedicated staff, including the evergreen Vera Costello and consummate chef Sheila Atkinson, for providing sumptuous meals to complement the wonderful tranquillity and comfort there.

I would like to acknowledge the NSW Writers' Centre (now Writing NSW) for supporting budding authors over the years. My *One Bright Moon* manuscript wouldn't have been discovered without the centre's annual open-pitch program.

I am indebted to my publisher, Mary Rennie, for discovering my manuscript. The hard work carried out by the team at HarperCollins, from Hazel Lam, the amazing designer who took a tiny portrait that I felt captured an unwavering spirit and turned it into a haunting cover, to Georgia Williams and the rest of the publicity department and the proofreader, Pam Dunne, is much appreciated. My deep gratitude also goes to my editor at HarperCollins, Scott Forbes, for his assistance in the editing journey and for ensuring the relatively painless and safe delivery of my book. Thank you for the succinct, wonderful and highly professional advice you have given me.

As the old saying goes, it takes a village to raise a child. I am deeply indebted to my sisters, Ying, Ping (Fannie) and Weng (Anne, deceased), for their sacrifices and arduous work during our challenging childhood, which helped maintain the family's integrity. My gratitude also goes to the deceased members of the clan: Third Aunt, Sixth Aunt and Eighth Uncle. My cousin Yiu-hoi (Thomas) provided clarification of some past events while I was crafting the manuscript. A big thank you to the whole family for the nurturing that flows steadily from them, just like the eternal Pearl River.

Over the years, I have learnt a lot from my children, Serena, Harmony and Andrew-James. Their honest feedback and comments have been most helpful in maturing my manuscript. What's more, their love, sensitivity and support have been vital. Jacqueline Fisher Kwong, my daughter-in-law, herself an editor, also provided much advice as I toiled with my story.

During my search for my past, my wife, Sheree, has not left my side. With me, she has shared many tears as I exhumed those confronting times I had long buried successfully, determined not to let them interfere with my educational and professional pursuits.

A passionate book-lover herself, she has always been the number-one reader of my numerous rewrites and edits, and she provided countless valuable suggestions while taking care not to smother my voice. Her patience and support during my journey back in time are greatly appreciated. Throughout the decades we have shared, she remains the rock in my life. Sheree, I'll always love you.